Rapid SaaS Appl Development Using Salesforce

Build scalable SaaS applications
using the Salesforce platform

Tameem Bahri

www.bpbonline.com

First published: 2024

Published by BPB Online
WeWork
119 Marylebone Road
London NW1 5PU

UK | UAE | INDIA | SINGAPORE

ISBN 978-93-55519-009

www.bpbonline.com

Dedicated to

*My wife, **Lana**, who is my best friend and my greatest supporter.*

*My son, **Ameer**, the light of my life.*

*My daughter, **Lea**, who fills my heart with joy each and every day.*

Every teacher who ignites a spark in their students.

All those who pick up this book, thank you for giving my words a chance.

About the Author

Tameem Bahri is the Technology Leader for the CRM and CIAM platforms at A.P. Moller - Maersk and was formerly the European Chief Technology Officer for the Salesforce COE at Capgemini. He is an experienced technology specialist with a demonstrated history of working in the information technology and services industry with over 20 years of experience across Business Transformation, Digital Services, Innovation, Process design and redesign, Enterprise System Security, **Identity and Access Management (IAM)** Strategy and Enterprise Solution Architecture.

Tameem Bahri is a Salesforce **Certified Technical Architect (CTA)** and the author of other books concerning Salesforce architecture and solutions. Tameem is a public speaker who participated in multiple events, such as DreamForce, the Data Innovation Forum, and the Tunisia Digital Summit.

About the Reviewer

Subramani Kumarasamy is a Certified Salesforce Application Architect specializing in automating critical business processes within Salesforce. With expertise in end-to-end solutions, he has successfully managed diverse projects of varying complexities. With a passion for delivering technical excellence, he consistently goes above and beyond to provide automated solutions that drive business success. His dedication to building technical debt-free systems, expertise in license management, and mastery of the Salesforce core platform and integration make him a sought-after professional in the Salesforce ecosystem.

Subramani's passion for teaching led him to train numerous professionals globally, both freshers and experienced, in Salesforce. His ability to simplify complex concepts and provide hands-on training has earned him recognition in the Salesforce community.

Beyond his professional pursuits, Subramani enjoys indulging in his favorite television shows, such as Game of Thrones and Suits, during his leisure time. However, his true joy lies in spending quality moments with his family and friends, as he understands the importance of work-life balance and cherishes the relationships that matter most to him.

Acknowledgement

I want to express my deepest gratitude to my family for their unwavering support and encouragement throughout this book's writing.

I am also grateful to BPB Publications for their guidance and expertise in bringing this book to fruition. It was a long journey of revising this book, with valuable participation and collaboration of reviewers, technical experts, and editors.

I would also like to acknowledge the valuable contributions of my colleagues and co-workers during many years working in the tech industry, who have taught me so much and provided valuable feedback on my work.

Finally, I would like to thank all the readers who have taken an interest in my book and for their support in making it a reality. Your encouragement has been invaluable.

Preface

During the twenty-plus years of my career, I had the pleasure of working in the software development, consulting, and service industries. During my time in the software development industry, I had the pleasure of using different technologies to create and fine-tune different types of cutting-edge software, from desktop to web applications, from device drivers to mass IoT-powered distributed solutions, and from simple websites to SaaS applications using the Salesforce platform. I had excellent exposure to some of the finest professionals in software development and architecture, who taught me a lot.

In the past seven years or so, I had the pleasure of coaching multiple dozens of senior Salesforce architects. Many have developed into recognized **Salesforce Certified Technical Architects (CTAs)**. During that journey, I noticed differences between the activities followed by the Salesforce developers and architects and those adopted by their classic software development counterparts. The differences are mainly derived from the nature of the Salesforce platform and its incredible flexibility. Most of the missing concepts and activities are actually required to pass the CTA review board exam (one of the hardest and most thorough exams in the technology industry nowadays). The candidates I coached had to learn new concepts and generate specific artifacts to help them explain a solution end-to-end. Sometimes, the candidates had to unlearn some habits they had used for several years, which further prolonged the time required to prepare for the exam.

I also noticed that companies that fully embrace and adopt the Salesforce platform and extend it to cover different business needs often struggle with technical debts that slow the development pace of future requirements. Slowing down the development pace of Salesforce applications takes away one of the platform's key benefits: time-to-market. Addressing these technical debts is costly and time-consuming; therefore, avoiding them from the beginning would add immense value to the company.

Helping Salesforce professionals rapidly develop scalable, performant, and secure Salesforce applications while avoiding technical debt would benefit both the individuals and the companies they work for. This is precisely what this book aims at. This book teaches some essential Salesforce application development habits, activities, best practices, and concepts using a practical, example-led approach.

The Salesforce platform is an extremely powerful and flexible tool. It enabled millions of users to customize and build enterprise-scale applications used daily. The platform's flexibility means it is up to the implementer to use it right and make a scalable, expandable, performant, and secure application, or use it wrong and end up with a suboptimal application that is not aligned with today's agile and fast-paced businesses. Rapid SaaS Application Development using Salesforce shows how to design, document, build, validate, and release an application using a rapid prototyping approach without sacrificing the solution's quality or expandability.

This book is primarily meant for the following readers:

- **CRM enthusiasts** who are looking to learn more about the Salesforce platform and its rapid application development capabilities. For those readers, I recommend chapters 1, 3, 4, 5, and 10.

- **Salesforce citizen developers** who are looking to learn more about low-code/no-code development concepts while bridging the gap with full-code developers. For those readers, I recommend chapters 1 to 10.

- **Salesforce business analysts** who are keen to learn about techniques for excavating uncommunicated requirements and communicate them in a way that avoids misunderstanding by the developers and testers. For those readers, I recommend chapters 1, 3, 4, 5, 9, and 10.

- **Junior Salesforce professionals** who are open to learning some of the best practices in developing secure, scalable, and maintainable Salesforce applications rapidly. For those readers, I recommend chapters 1 to 10.

- **Senior Salesforce professionals** who are looking to refresh some of their past knowledge. For those readers, I recommend chapters 1, 3, 4, 5, 6, 9, and 10.

This book will teach you the structured rapid application development lifecycle for the Salesforce platform, which is derived from the solid software development lifecycle. This book will use real-life business scenarios to teach you foundational information and skills that you can use to develop enterprise-ready, AI-powered applications. I sincerely hope you enjoy this book and find it useful.Parte superior do formulárioParte inferior do formulário Tameem Bahri

Chapter 1: Introduction to the Salesforce Platform - This chapter provides general information about the Salesforce Platform and Salesforce SaaS Applications. The chapter explains the rationale behind creating SaaS applications on top of the Salesforce Platform. The chapter then explains the underlying infrastructure of the Salesforce Platform, which is essential to developing scalable enterprise-grade applications. The reader is then introduced to the Salesforce AppExchange, where applications can be listed in the Salesforce marketplace. The chapter will also briefly introduce the key Salesforce application building blocks and compare the different coding and configuration options supported by the platform. Finally, the reader is introduced to the concept of developing an application with off-platform capabilities offered by other platforms, including Salesforce Heroku.

Chapter 2: Deep Dive into Key Building Blocks and Tools - This chapter dives deeper into the Salesforce application building blocks and explains each in detail using simple examples. The reader will be introduced to Users, Licenses, Objects (standard and custom), Fields (standard and custom), Page Layouts, Sharing and Security models, App Builder, Report Builder, Flow Builder, and more.

Chapter 3: Develop a Sample Salesforce Application: PbP Phonebook - This chapter practically teaches how to build a simple Salesforce Application using point-and-click development tools. The reader will learn about analyzing and understanding requirements, defining process flows, creating prototypes, and building, rectifying, and deploying an application. The reader will then learn about the gaps and mistakes that could occur without a well-structured application development lifecycle.

Chapter 4: Learn the Salesforce Application Development Lifecycle - This chapter introduces the reader to the Salesforce application development lifecycle and compares it to its parent, the standard application development lifecycle, pointing out their differences and the rationale behind them. The reader is then introduced to a set of practices to follow while developing any Salesforce application.

Chapter 5: Understand the Supporting Tools and Artifacts - This chapter introduces a set of artifacts and tools that a Salesforce Application Developer can use to rapidly develop secure, scalable, extendable, flexible, and performant applications while avoiding creating technical debt. The chapter explains the importance of these artifacts and illustrates how they can be created using easy-to-follow examples.

Chapter 6: Create a Sample Application: Define and Refine the Requirements - This chapter practically puts all that the reader learned into action by introducing a real-world business challenge that the reader would solve using a Salesforce SaaS Application. The reader will first be introduced to the business challenge, then proceed to analyze the requirements and identify gaps. The reader will then create testable user stories that will form the basic requirements that will be solved in the two following chapters. The reader will also create high-level process flows and capability maps as part of the application requirement documentation.

Chapter 7: Create a Sample Application: Solve and Build the Application - Part 1 - The reader will start solving the business problem introduced in *Chapter 6, Create a Sample Application: Define and Refine the Requirements*, using the Rapid Salesforce Application Development Lifecycle tools and principles. The reader will solve the identified user stories one by one, creating and updating the relevant artifacts at each stage. The reader will be introduced to the process of identifying multiple solutions for a particular problem and selecting the most appropriate one, considering all the pros and cons.

Chapter 8: Create a Sample Application: Solve and Build the Application - Part 2 - The reader will continue solving the business problem introduced in *Chapter 6, Create a Sample Application: Define and Refine the Requirements,* and continue creating a solution based on the partial solution introduced in *Chapter 7, Create a Sample Application: Solve and Build the Application - Part 1.* The reader will continue using the Rapid Salesforce Application Development Lifecycle tools and principles. The reader will solve the identified user stories one by one, creating and updating the relevant artifacts at each stage. The reader will continue learning about the process of identifying multiple solutions for a particular problem and selecting the most appropriate one, considering all the pros and cons. The reader will also briefly learn about some scalability considerations for the Salesforce Platform.

Chapter 9: Create a Sample Application: Test and Deploy - The reader will deploy and test the application that was developed in *Chapter 7, Create a Sample Application: Solve and Build the Application - Part 1* and *Chapter 8, Create a Sample Application: Solve and Build the Application - Part 2.* The reader will learn about the different deployment tools and techniques and will be introduced to concepts such as CI (Continuous integration) and CD (Continuous Development). The reader will learn about the importance of testing the application and the test case format, types, and management. The reader will learn about tools for each test type and dive deeper into one of the major testing tools, the Apex test classes.

Chapter 10: Tips and Tricks and the Way Forward - This chapter introduces the reader to more advanced topics and will explain the value of release notes. The reader will learn how to create useful and impactful release notes and how to efficiently publish and share them with the right audience. The reader will also learn how to enrich an application backlog using ideas and feedback gathered from your customers directly. Finally, the reader will be introduced to further learning materials and resources to continue learning from.

Code Bundle and Coloured Images

Please follow the link to download the
Code Bundle and the *Coloured Images* of the book:

https://rebrand.ly/ca55e2

The code bundle for the book is also hosted on GitHub at
https://github.com/bpbpublications/Rapid-SaaS-Application-Development-Using-Salesforce
In case there's an update to the code, it will be updated on the existing GitHub repository.

We have code bundles from our rich catalogue of books and videos available at
https://github.com/bpbpublications. Check them out!

Errata

We take immense pride in our work at BPB Publications and follow best practices to ensure the accuracy of our content to provide with an indulging reading experience to our subscribers. Our readers are our mirrors, and we use their inputs to reflect and improve upon human errors, if any, that may have occurred during the publishing processes involved. To let us maintain the quality and help us reach out to any readers who might be having difficulties due to any unforeseen errors, please write to us at :

errata@bpbonline.com

Your support, suggestions and feedbacks are highly appreciated by the BPB Publications' Family.

Did you know that BPB offers eBook versions of every book published, with PDF and ePub files available? You can upgrade to the eBook version at www.bpbonline. com and as a print book customer, you are entitled to a discount on the eBook copy. Get in touch with us at :

business@bpbonline.com for more details.

At **www.bpbonline.com**, you can also read a collection of free technical articles, sign up for a range of free newsletters, and receive exclusive discounts and offers on BPB books and eBooks.

Piracy

If you come across any illegal copies of our works in any form on the internet, we would be grateful if you would provide us with the location address or website name. Please contact us at **business@bpbonline.com** with a link to the material.

If you are interested in becoming an author

If there is a topic that you have expertise in, and you are interested in either writing or contributing to a book, please visit **www.bpbonline.com**. We have worked with thousands of developers and tech professionals, just like you, to help them share their insights with the global tech community. You can make a general application, apply for a specific hot topic that we are recruiting an author for, or submit your own idea.

Reviews

Please leave a review. Once you have read and used this book, why not leave a review on the site that you purchased it from? Potential readers can then see and use your unbiased opinion to make purchase decisions. We at BPB can understand what you think about our products, and our authors can see your feedback on their book. Thank you!

For more information about BPB, please visit **www.bpbonline.com**.

Join our book's Discord space

Join the book's Discord Workspace for Latest updates, Offers, Tech happenings around the world, New Release and Sessions with the Authors:

https://discord.bpbonline.com

Table of Contents

CHAPTER 1

Introduction to the Salesforce Platform

Introduction

This book chapter will introduce you to the **Salesforce platform** (formerly known as **Force.com**) and the **Salesforce App Cloud**. Some still mis-interpret **Salesforce.com** as a **Customer Relationship Management (CRM)** system offered as a **multi-tenancy Software as a Service (SaaS)**. The massive success of Salesforce in the CRM industry might influence such misdefinition. In this chapter, you will learn about another powerful - yet less known - capability of the Salesforce platform as a **Rapid Application Development (RAD)** environment. But first, take a look at the following definitions.

In 1995, the term Customer Relationship Management was coined, then became popular from 1997 to 2000 thanks to the companies such as **IBM** and **Siebel**. At that time, CRM systems included tools that helped to standardize and manage business processes across sales and service. This term extended eventually to include marketing and digital commerce.

Multi-tenancy is a term used to describe a way to run software applications where a single instance of the software (in the Salesforce world, this is called an organization, or for short, org) runs on an infrastructure (such as a server) that is configured to serve multiple users and multiple instances of the software. In a multi-tenancy setup, the host ensures that the data of all tenants are not mixed up (Salesforce does that using a unique identifier for each org called the Org ID). However, tenants might share the same resources the infrastructure offers (such as memory and computing power).

Software as a service (SaaS) is a software delivery and licensing model (also known as on-demand software) where a vendor offers ready-to-use software via a subscription-based licensing model. The SaaS software can usually be configured to meet their end user's needs. The SaaS model simplifies the infrastructure challenges such as hosting, scaling, and maintaining software, as the vendor would be offering such services as part of the subscription fees. SaaS software is typically accessed via a web browser (also known as a thin client).

RAD describes a software development approach that promotes agile, fast-paced, and prototype-driven software engineering compared to traditional waterfall development processes, which are inherited from other conventional engineering models that are not necessarily fit for software.

Structure

This chapter covers the following topics:

- What is a Salesforce application
- Why develop a Salesforce application
- The Salesforce platform infrastructure
- Getting to know the Salesforce AppExchange
- Key building blocks and tools
- No-code vs. low-code vs. full-code
- Salesforce Objects, more than a database
- On-platform and off-platform

Objectives

By the end of this chapter, you will understand what a Salesforce application is and why the Salesforce platform is a very compelling RAD environment. You will better understand the underlying infrastructure of the Salesforce platform and learn about the application marketplace known as **AppExchange**. You will learn about the key building blocks available to developers to develop applications on the Salesforce platform rapidly. You will get terms such as no-code, low-code, and full-code demystified. You will then learn more about the underlying database of the **Salesforce platform**, which used to be known as database.com. You will also learn what type of applications and features are fit to be developed on the Salesforce platform and what type is better-fit off-platform.

What is a Salesforce application

Salesforce applications is an application program stored in the cloud on top of the Salesforce platform and delivered via a browser interface. It is a form of web application delivered as a SaaS using the pre-built capabilities of the Salesforce platform. Salesforce applications are built using many development tools ranging from point-and-click tools to fully customizable code. Point-and-click development can also be referred to as *declarative development* or *declarative configuration*.

The following diagram compares a simplified web application architecture to a simplified Salesforce application architecture:

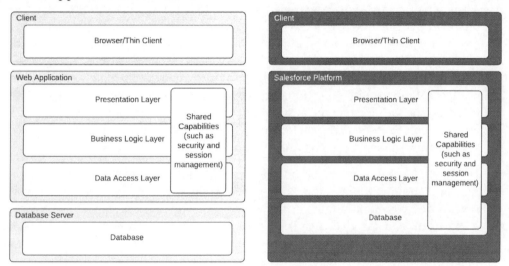

Figure 1.1: *Comparing web application architecture to Salesforce application architecture*

You might have noticed that the application in both cases is separated into multiple layers. This approach is called **Separation of Concern (SOC)**. In most cases, you will not need to bother yourself with creating SOC layers while developing Salesforce applications, mainly while using declarative development. Declarative development is faster, simpler, and usually more reliable than custom development. Moreover, it has a built-in SOC structure to some extent. You will learn about the declarative and non-declarative (coding) tools available in the Salesforce platform later in this chapter under the *Key building blocks and tools* section.

The Salesforce platform is part of a bigger organizational structure called the **Salesforce App Cloud**. Here are some of the main components of the Salesforce App Cloud:

- **Salesforce platform**: The heart and soul of the App Cloud and the underlying foundation for several other Salesforce clouds such as Service Cloud, Sales Cloud, and Experience Cloud. The Salesforce platform was formerly known as Force. com. The platform offers capabilities that enable administrators and developers to build secure, performant, and scalable web applications that are delivered using a SaaS model. The Salesforce platform is the primary technology covered in this book. You can think of the Salesforce platform as the classic LEGO blocks that you can use to build any LEGO model. In this analogy, products such as Sales Cloud and Service Cloud would be something like a pre-assembled LEGO Star Wars Millennium Falcon, where the classic building blocks are used to create a fully functional model that you can tweak or extend further. Salesforce also offers out-of-the-box **Artificial intelligence (AI)** products natively integrated with the Salesforce platform. These products are all branded under the **Salesforce Einstein** umbrella.

- **AppExchange**: The **AppExchange.com** website is a marketplace for the Salesforce platform's applications. AppExchange allows developers to publish their work to the marketplace, where it can be tried, installed, used, and reviewed by Salesforce customers. The AppExchange contains thousands of applications. It is a popular destination for Salesforce customers, enabling them to extend their Salesforce implementations with additional pre-built capabilities easily. The applications listed on the AppExchange can range in complexity from simple, single-purpose applications to very complex solutions such as fully-fledged ERPs. Publishing applications to the AppExchange is out of the scope of this book.

- **Heroku**: **Heroku.com** is a cloud platform that allows developers to build, host, run, and monitor their applications in a quick and simplified way. It supports several development languages and database technologies. Heroku is considered a **Platform as a Service (PaaS)**. The clear difference between PaaS and SaaS is that the former offers a set of tools that helps developers build, host, run, and monitor their applications. In contrast, the latter provides a ready-to-use pre-built application that is usually configurable/customizable. The Salesforce platform is much more customizable than a regular SaaS but more restricted and controlled than a classic PaaS. Configuring Heroku and developing applications on it is out of the scope of this book.

- **Salesforce Shield**: Offers services to protect and monitor the customer's data stored on the **Salesforce platform**. Salesforce Shield offers functionalities such as data encryption at rest which is a must for some businesses. Configuring and using Salesforce Shield is out of the scope of this book.

- **Salesforce DX**: This is a set of developer tools that enables building and managing **Salesforce platform** applications' development lifecycle in a controlled and efficient way. Salesforce DX allows developers to easily use **Source control management (SCM)** solutions such as Git (also known as version control solutions) to control code versions, collaboration, conflict resolution, auditing, code recovery, and release management. Configuring and using Salesforce DX is out of the scope of this book. All examples in this book will use simpler mechanisms to allow you to focus on the other essential aspects of the Salesforce platform application's lifecycle.

- **Salesforce identity**: Provides a set of trusted services to allow enterprises to manage their employees' and customers' identities. Configuring and using Salesforce identity is out of the scope of this book.

- **Salesforce Trailhead**: the **Trailhead.Salesforce.com** website is one of the leading online learning platforms available today. It contains a plethora of tutorials, exercises, and knowledge articles that teach a broad spectrum of topics to different audiences, such as administrators, developers, business analysts, UX designers, architects, and business owners from all levels of expertise. Salesforce Trailhead is a very handy tool for any Salesforce professional, and you are strongly encouraged to familiarize yourself with it. The Trailhead website will be referred to several times throughout this book.

Next, you will learn some benefits of developing apps on the Salesforce platform.

Why develop a Salesforce application

There are certain benefits of developing applications on the Salesforce platform (also known as Salesforce Applications). You will find some of these benefits for developers, entrepreneurs, and CRM platform owners:

Benefits for developers

As a developer, you enjoy the following benefits for developing Salesforce Applications:

- **More time to focus on core development:** As a developer, you would like to spend more time building core business functionalities and less time setting up the development environment and tools that you need. You would like to use all your brain power to solve business problems and challenges rather than worry about getting a set of libraries to work with each other. The Salesforce platform comes with a plethora of low-code/no-code development tools and a simplified coding environment to build more complex code. These tools help you focus on developing core business functionalities away from being bothered about nitty-gritty detail but also enables you to deliver these functionalities much faster. Low-code development platforms can speed up the development process by up to ten times. You can read the *Forrester* report at the following link **https://www. forrester.com/blogs/why-you-need-to-know-about-low-code-even-if-youre-not-responsible-for-software-delivery/**

- **Market value:** Salesforce developers have been in high demand for over a decade. High demand drives high wages and offers more chances to progress in careers.

Several Salesforce developers decided to go solo and offer their services on a contract basis or as **Freelancers**.

- **The server is always up and running:** Developers, system administrators, infrastructure engineers, and network engineers always dread that moment when the server is down. Nobody likes to deal with this critical moment. The Salesforce platform is offered as a SaaS, meaning someone else is taking care of the server's uptime for you. Salesforce has one of the most impressive uptime numbers for any SaaS. This is not only due to the solid infrastructure used but to the reliable and stable building blocks offered to extend the standard functionalities and build Salesforce Applications. When you develop your Salesforce Application, you can focus on its functionalities and the value it adds. Salesforce will ensure that you are not bothered by uptime concerns.

- **Someone else is marketing it for you:** So, you have built your application; what is next? You need to market it and sell it. You likely need a dedicated team to do so. This means additional upfront costs and, therefore, more potential risk. The **Salesforce AppExchange** ensures your product is listed on the very-popular marketplace for Salesforce customers. The AppExchange is the first place for architects and decision makers of Salesforce customers to look for quick and relatively cheap ways to extend their Salesforce implementations with additional functionalities. Furthermore, the AppExchange handles the tricky part of deploying your application to the customer's **Salesforce Org** and even facilitates a smooth way to provide upgrades. In exchange for these services, Salesforce takes a certain percentage of your application revenue. However, it is easy to justify that cost considering the added value.

- **More room to become a Rockstar:** Some developers have different skills and capabilities. Some might be better at understanding business problems and solving problems than writing hard-core code. However, survivor is the best developer in the land of pure coding. In the world of Salesforce, there is more room for others. The definition of the word developer differs in Salesforce compared to pure-coding environments. A Salesforce developer does not necessarily need to write code. You will see several examples throughout this book. Hard-core coders are still very much in demand and appreciated in the Salesforce world. However, non-coders or less-capable-coders also got a great career opportunity in the Salesforce world.

- **It is easy to learn:** This is not a secret. Salesforce is one of the easiest platforms to learn. Partially because it is easy to configure and develop using point-and-click tools, but primarily because of the fantastic and free-to-use learning website **Trailhead,** Salesforce made it easier for the public to experience and learn their platforms via structured, well-defined, and practical training materials offered via Trailhead. Learners can easily spin off a **Trailhead Playground (TP)** environment and practice configuring and developing functionalities on the **Salesforce platform**. No upfront cost, and no credit card is needed. All you need is a browser, an internet connection, and a desire to learn. You can also sign up for a free **Developer Edition (DE)** environment, allowing you to experience the **Salesforce platform** without using Trailhead. You can learn more about how to sign up for a DE at the following link: **https://developer. salesforce.com/docs/atlas.en-us.workbook_isv.meta/workbook_isv/isv1_1.htm** You can learn more about how to launch your first TP environment at the following link: **https://trailhead.salesforce.com/content/learn/modules/trailhead_ playground_management/create-a-trailhead-playground**

Now that you have learned about the benefits of developing Salesforce Applications for developers, explore what is in it for entrepreneurs.

Benefits for entrepreneurs

As a software industry entrepreneur, you enjoy the following benefits of investing in Salesforce Applications:

- **Access to a broad market:** The **Salesforce AppExchange** grants you access to a huge market segment. Salesforce is used and loved by many companies worldwide, including many from the Fortune 100 list. Architects and platform owners are looking to extend their Salesforce implementation with additional functionalities in these companies. The **AppExchange** is their first destination for such a task. Furthermore, **AppExchange** has a *review* functionality where application clients can review and rank it. Good reviews act as a self-marketing tool.

- **You can start with a smaller development team:** You do not need to invest in building a huge team of developers to start building your application. Due to the nature of the platform, you can begin without some rules, such as infrastructure engineers. Low-code development is also much faster than regular coding, so you can launch your application in a shorter time using fewer resources.

- **Despite the cost, you still have access to a decent talent pool:** The Salesforce market has been in severe talent shortage for years. This is intensified with the additional expansions that Salesforce is gaining across the market despite all efforts to train new talents. This high demand and short supply situation increased the hourly rate of Salesforce developers, particularly code developers. However, you can still achieve a lot with low-code development, where there is less of a talent shortage, you can train new developers efficiently via Trailhead, and you can benefit from the fact that Salesforce has adopted a lot of the open-source market standards in the past years. This shift towards open-source standards enables developers with other backgrounds (such as JavaScript developers) to easily cross-train on Salesforce technologies such as **Lightning Web Components**. You still need experienced Salesforce talents to design and develop complex applications, though.

- **Low maintenance cost:** Maintaining Salesforce applications usually are less of a burden. This extends to both normal bug-fixing and patching to emergency incidents. For example, on 24 November 2021, a vulnerability was identified and reported for a popular Java logging library, **Apache Log4j**. The vulnerability was later called **Log4Shell**. Apache assigned **Log4Shell** a **Common Vulnerability Scoring System (CVSS)** severity rating of 10, which is the highest possible score. The impact of this vulnerability was huge; it is estimated that 93% of cloud enterprise environments were exposed to it. Software companies were under immense pressure from their customers to patch their applications urgently. Salesforce itself used **Log4j** and therefore had to patch its code accordingly. However, most **Salesforce platform**-based software companies did not need to worry about this. Salesforce was patching its entire platform; applications built on the **Salesforce platform** will benefit from that automatically. This showed one of the key advantages of building on the **Salesforce platform**, you are standing on the shoulders of giants, and someone else is ensuring the platform meets the highest cybersecurity standards.

- **Ride the wave of innovation:** Salesforce is tirelessly releasing more functionalities to its customers via three yearly releases. These releases are given seasonal names and called the **Spring**, **Summer**, and **Winter** releases. When a particular functionality is released to the **Salesforce platform**, it becomes available for all its customers automatically and, mostly, without additional cost (although there are always some exceptions). For example, when the **Flow Builder** was launched in the Spring '19 release, it was made **Generally Available (GA)** to all Salesforce customers at no additional cost. Software owners of applications built on the **Salesforce platform** could use **Flow Builder** to develop highly sophisticated **Flows** and include them as part of their applications. You will see several examples of using Flows throughout this book.

Now that you have learned about the benefits of developing Salesforce Applications for entrepreneurs, explore what is in it for CRM platform owners.

Benefits for CRM platform owners

A Salesforce CRM platform owner works for a company that uses Salesforce as the core technology for its CRM and owns all responsibilities related to it, including extending Salesforce to meet business needs. A CRM platform owner can be the **Chief Executive Officer (CEO)** of the company, the **Chief Information Officer (CIO)**, the **Chief Technology Officer (CTO)**, or any Director/Manager who is assigned that responsibility. The CRM platform owner is responsible for creating and fulfilling the platform roadmap. The CRM platform owner typically leads all development and delivery activities on the platform; sometimes, this is co-leads by the CRM technology owner.

As a CRM platform owner or a CRM technology owner, you enjoy the following benefits of building or using Salesforce Applications:

- **Shorter time to market:** The **Salesforce AppExchange** grants you access to thousands of ready-to-use applications. Some of them have been tried and tested by several other customers and were highly rated. Finding the right application can help you quickly deliver the critical business functionality you are after. Most **AppExchange** applications come with an additional cost that could wrongfully put some people off. However, for the right use cases, a ready-made **AppExchange** application can save you months, if not years, of development, frustrations with bugs, the cost of building and running a high-quality development team, and practically re-inventing the wheel. For example, custom building a **Configure, Price, Quote (CPQ)** solution of a decent level of complexity could take a year or two from a team of 20-30 developers. Calculate the cost of that, add to it the overhead of managing such a team and the risk of ending up with the wrong product anyway, and you will find an excellent rationale to invest in a ready-made battle-tested solution.

- **You pay per user license, not per application:** If you decided to extend your own Salesforce implementation by building a **Salesforce platform** application and exposing it to the same set of users in your org, you would not be charged for additional license cost. You will not be charged for any computing power or additional memory. You might need to pay for extra required storage space or additional API calls (in case your application has heavy API usage). This sounds too good to be true! You can develop dozens of **Salesforce platform** applications that become available nearly for free to your existing Salesforce users. Business owners from other technologies might find this hard to believe. Still, Salesforce published several success stories from its key customers who saved millions using the **Salesforce platform** as their central **RAD environment**. There are some limitations that you need to be aware of, they are called the **Salesforce Governor Limits**, and they are introduced to mainly govern the usage of resources by the tenants sharing the same infrastructure (remember that Salesforce is a multi-tenancy environment). There are several types of governor limits that you need to keep an eye on while designing your Salesforce Application, such as **Apex Governor Limits**, **Inbound Email Limits**, **Salesforce REST API Requests limits**, **API Query Cursor Limits**, **Chatter REST API Limits**, **Metadata Limits**, **SOQL and SOSL Limits**, and several more. There is no easy way to learn about all these limits. However, they are all well documented on the Salesforce website. You can have a look at the documentation of one of these limits on the following link: **https://developer.salesforce.com/docs/atlas.en-us.salesforce_app_limits_ cheatsheet.meta/salesforce_app_limits_cheatsheet/salesforce_app_limits_ platform_apexgov.htm**

- **You can have citizen developers:** With the low-code/no-code development tools available on the **Salesforce platform**, almost every person can become a Salesforce developer. You can cross-skill your business users and create a citizen developer initiative where the business users make their own applications. The best results are usually achieved when you augment your team of citizen developers with some seasoned Salesforce developers and architects. This way, you ensure that the majority of the work is still delivered by your business users/developers but done while adhering to the Salesforce software development best practices. You will learn about several of these best practices throughout this book.

- **Extend the Salesforce clouds to meet your needs:** A common misunderstanding is that Salesforce is a CRM with limited configurability. As you learned earlier in this chapter, Salesforce has built some of its core clouds (such as the **Salesforce Sales Cloud** and **Salesforce Service Cloud**) on the **Salesforce platform**. Nothing stops you from extending these clouds with additional business-specific capabilities that extend and enrich the standard Salesforce clouds.

- **Modernize legacy applications in weeks, not years:** One of the main stoppers for enterprises to modernize their tech stack is the cost of change. This includes the cost of building the apps from the ground up, training and re-skilling the business users, and migrating all legacy data to the new tech stack. The RAD environment can cut down the cost of building the apps significantly. Salesforce applications are built using a modern **User Interface (UI)** and are based on smooth **User Experience (UX)** where many functionalities can be intuitive and easy to guess. That does not remove the need to train the users; it just makes it less costly and time-consuming. Finally, migrating data to cloud-based solutions such as Salesforce is usually straightforward due to the availability of several types of modern APIs, such as the **Salesforce Rest API**, the **Salesforce Composite API**, the **Salesforce Metadata API**, and many more.

- **Cut the cost of expensive integrations by building on the same platform:** The usual integration cost is estimated to be 25-75% of the overall cost of a distributed solution. This means up to 750k could be allocated to integration efforts for every 1 million spent. That is a huge cost to consider. Sometimes integration is oversimplified and considered a straightforward exposure or consumption of APIs. However, when calculating the total cost of integration, you need to consider the analysis efforts to determine source and destination data sources, the UX research done to identify and build a smooth transition across the multiple integrated systems, the business analysis efforts spent on understanding the exact requirement to consider the integrated system adequately connected, the architectural design efforts, the development efforts, the testing efforts, the exception handling actions, the continuous monitoring and maintenance of the integration interfaces, and finally the cyber security analysis, tools, licenses, implementation and validation efforts. On some occasions, there could be additional costs that you need to cater to, such as the cost of middleware, tools, data residency solutions, and computing power to handle any data transformation needs. The cost of integration should never be underestimated. Applications built on the **Salesforce platform** are natively integrated, yet they are still modular and can be managed by different teams (with the right organizational structures and design measures). This is a huge advantage that any platform owner should keep in mind and carefully consider.

Now that you have learned about the benefits of developing Salesforce Applications for CRM platform owners move on to learn more about the infrastructure of the Salesforce platform.

The Salesforce platform infrastructure

You learned earlier about **multi-tenancy** and that it means a single instance of the software runs on an environment configured to serve multiple users and multiple instances of the software simultaneously. The typical example used to describe this setup is the example of a building with multiple apartments. Each apartment is considered a private place where you can safely store your belongings and ensure no one can access them. This privacy is achieved via mechanisms such as walls and doors. Within the same buildings, multiple apartments share a set of building services such as water, power, elevators, and building maintenance. If you reflect this example on Salesforce, the building here represents the Salesforce platform, while each apartment represents a Salesforce Org rented and occupied by a tenant/customer. Data privacy is achieved via the unique **Org ID** of each Salesforce Org.

The apartments are not identical. They share many similarities but differ in size and functionalities. There are multiple types of apartments; similarly, there are various editions of Salesforce Orgs. There are six main editions of Salesforce Orgs:

Salesforce Edition	Designed for
Essentials	Small businesses that are looking for simple capabilities across sales or service.
Starter	Small businesses or first-time user that are looking for classic CRM capabilities across sales, service, and marketing.
Professional	Designed for small and medium businesses that require more sophisticated CRM capabilities such as customizations and integrations.
Enterprise	Designed to meet the demanding needs of large businesses. It includes all functionalities available in the professional org plus advanced customization abilities and access to the Salesforce APIs.
Unlimited	Designed for the most demanding and complex businesses. The unlimited edition can be extended to meet the needs of an entire enterprise. It contains all the functionalities available in the enterprise edition plus additional capabilities such as unlimited custom applications, more scale and customization flexibility, and increased storage limits.

Salesforce Edition	Designed for
Developer	Designed to allow developers and administrators to develop applications extending the standard Salesforce platform applications. The Developer Edition orgs are free and include many features available in the enterprise edition.

Table 1.1: *Salesforce editions*

Going back to the building and apartments example, imagine having several instances of the building, each residing on a plot in a specific region and having a different status at each given time (such as being under maintenance or fully operational). In the Salesforce world, a similar arrangement exists. A Salesforce instance is the installed version of a **Salesforce platform** on a server (or a group of servers, usually called a **Server Farm**) in a specific location. In each **Salesforce instance**, there could be multiple **Salesforce Orgs** (could be several hundreds of orgs).

Salesforce instances are given names that indicate their geographical and physical location, plus a serial number. For example, NA116 could be a name of a Salesforce instance in North America.

The following simplified diagram illustrates the relation between a Salesforce instance and the multiple types of Salesforce Orgs that might be contained inside it:

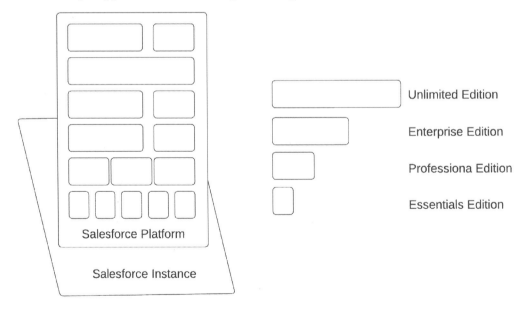

Figure 1.2: *Salesforce instances with multiple hosted Salesforce Orgs*

The following diagram illustrates the relationship between **Salesforce instances** and their geographical regions:

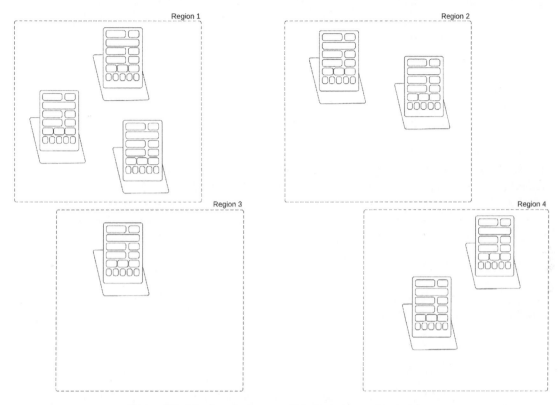

Figure 1.3: *Salesforce instances within their geographical regions*

The **Salesforce Trust** website provides up-to-date information about the health and status of every Salesforce instance around the globe. You can learn more about the **Salesforce Trust** website at the following link:

https://trust.salesforce.com/

Next, you will learn about the infrastructure powering the Salesforce instances.

Introducing Hyperforce

Salesforce was founded in 1999. At that time, the common infrastructure used to provide publicly accessible software service over the internet (which is what would be usually called SaaS) was to host the software over a server (or multiple servers, such as an application server and a database server). You would need to place the server(s) in a physically suitable location where airflow and temperature-controlling measurements are in place. You will need to hire network engineers to ensure your network is correctly connected to the internet, security engineers to help you keep the network and server(s) safe from cyber and non-cyber-attacks, and a team of infrastructure engineers to ensure your physical connections are scalable and performant.

Salesforce grew its infrastructure with time and employed an army of professionals to ensure their offered services were up to the highest standards. In the late second decade of the 21st century, Salesforce had hundreds of thousands of servers. They were organized globally in secure data centers, which offered many Salesforce instances for its customers. The geographic location of the data centers was crucial due to regulations in some countries and industries which required the data to reside in a specific region, such as the **European Union**.

The company continued to proliferate and was targeting new territories. However, opening a new data center is a challenging task, even for a tech giant such as Salesforce. At that time, there was a gradual shift in the market's mindset. Several enterprises started to accept hosting part or all of their software on the cloud, using services from the likes of **Amazon Web Services (AWS)**, **Microsoft Azure**, **Google Cloud Platform (GCP)**, **Rackspace Cloud**, and others in what has eventually been named the public cloud.

There were several benefits of switching to the public cloud services, including extending faster to regions where Salesforce did not have data centers. This meant that Salesforce could target customers in these regions who were hesitant to subscribe to its services due to their local data regulations.

To use the public clouds while maintaining the freedom to choose the right vendor, Salesforce invested in developing Hyperforce, a modern infrastructure that provides a level of abstraction from the underlying infrastructure. Hyperforce allows Salesforce to deploy its solutions rapidly and reliably anywhere in the world where there is a public cloud offering from its partners. **Hyperforce** brings more scalability, agility, security, and compliance to Salesforce. Data in Hyperforce is also more secure with encryption at rest and in transit.

Currently, not all Salesforce services are offered on top of Hyperforce. However, the **Salesforce platform**, the subject of this book, is now fully hosted on Hyperforce in multiple regions:

Figure 1.4: Hyperforce and the public cloud

Some of the key principles that Hyperforce is built on are:

- **Infrastructure-as-code**: Setup and configurations in Hyperforce are entirely based on artifacts stored in source control. Such infrastructure is referred to as **Immutable Infrastructure**.

- **Three-availability-zone design**: Salesforce used a **Two-availability-Zone** design before, where data would get replicated across the two sites/zones. With Hyperforce, the number of availability zones is increased to three, which should further improve Salesforce's availability record.

- **Focus on service health**: Rather than measuring the servers' health, **Hyperforce** aims at measuring and monitoring the aggregate measures of the service health to ensure a healthier service to its clients.

- **Zero trust:** This measure is the best practice for modern cyber security, where each service communication (internal or external) is treated with zero trust and requires strong identity, monitoring, and encryption in transit.

Now that you have learned about the infrastructure powering the **Salesforce platform** move on to learn more about the **AppExchange**.

Getting to know the Salesforce AppExchange

You have been briefly introduced to the **Salesforce AppExchange**, the leading **enterprise cloud marketplace**. **AppExchange** contains applications and components that are relevant to:

- **Existing Salesforce customers**: Apps and components from the **AppExchange** can be used to augment CRM with additional functionalities.

- **Any industry-specific users/customers**: The **AppExchange** includes battle-tested applications specific to some industries. These applications are relevant to both new and existing Salesforce customers.

- **Any users/customers**: The **AppExchange** contains horizontal applications relevant to specific departments within a company or the whole company. These applications are applicable to both new and existing Salesforce customers.

If you go to the **AppExchange** website, you will notice several available types of solutions. In the Salesforce ecosystem world, the term *solution* refers to any software that can be downloaded from **AppExchange**. This could be one of the following:

- **Applications solutions**: Applications solutions could contain one or more sub-applications within. This has been the most popular type of solution on **AppExchange** for a long time.

- **Lightning Bolt solutions**: Industry solution templates that are used to speed up the development of specific industries. Lightning Bolt solutions may contain one or more applications, lighting components, Salesforce flows, custom objects, and many more elements.

- **Flow solutions**: Configurable pre-built process flows based on Salesforce flows. This type of solution is popular for no-code process automation tasks.

- **Lightning Data solutions**: Pre-integrated data solutions that can enrich your Salesforce implementation with data-powered functionalities.

- **Lightning Components**: Reusable components that you can install and use to augment your solutions with additional functionalities. You can think of this type of solution as building blocks that can help you add extra functionalities.

Some of these solutions are paid, while others are free.

Many paid solutions can be tried out for free for a limited period. To get more familiar with installing solutions from the **AppExchange**, you will explore that next using a simple example.

Installing your first AppExchange solution

Start by signing up for a **Developer Edition** org at the following link:

https://developer.salesforce.com/signup

Fill in the required fields, such as First Name, Last Name, and Email. You can use the same email address to sign up for as many Developer Edition orgs as needed. One of the required fields is Username. The Username has to be:

- Unique across all Salesforce production orgs.

- In the format of an email address. For example, **JohnMiller@MyDomain.com.**

- It does not need to map to an actual email address. In other words, a username such as **JohnMiller@MyDomain.com** should be fine as long as it is unique across all Salesforce production orgs.

Make sure you read the Salesforce agreements' terms and conditions before accepting them, then click on the Sign me Up button to create a Developer org. The following screenshot shows an example of a filled Developer org signup application form:

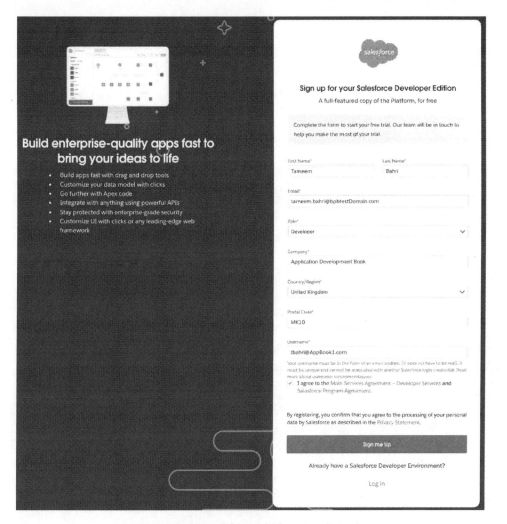

Figure 1.5: *Sign up for a Salesforce Developer Org*

You should receive a confirmation email with a link to verify your email address, activate your org, and set your password. Follow the link to set your password and login to your **Salesforce Developer org**. You will also be asked to provide a Security Question that will be used in the password recovery process if needed. You will need to provide your username and password the next time you attempt to login, so make sure you memorize them.

After setting your password and security question and submitting the form, you will be automatically logged into your **Developer org**. You will land on the Setup page.

Navigate to the **Account** tab and view one of the sample accounts created by default for each **Salesforce Developer Org**. For example, navigate to the account Burlington Textiles Corp of America. You should see a page similar to the following screenshot:

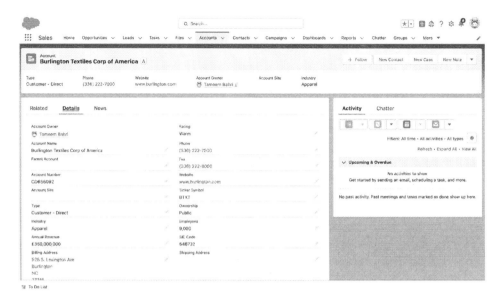

Figure 1.6: *A sample account page in a Salesforce Developer Org*

To install your first **AppExchange** solution, navigate to the **AppExchange** website at the following link: **https://appexchange.salesforce.com**

You will see a search bar at the top of the page. You can use it to search for a specific application or capability. Please search for the following application `Map My Records.` This application provides a **Lightning Component** that shows the location of an account on **Google Maps** based on the account's address. The search result should be similar to the following screenshot:

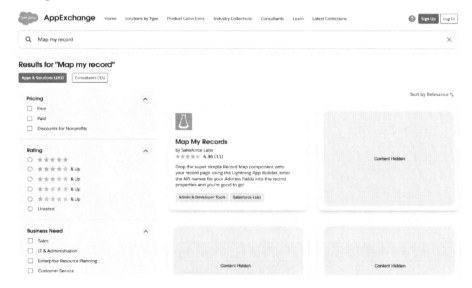

Figure 1.7: *AppExchange search result*

Click on the **Map My Records** link from the page to navigate to the solution details page. You will notice that this application is listed for free by **Salesforce Labs.** You will also see a button called **Get It Now**. This button allows you to install the solution on a target Salesforce Org. Click on it, and you will be redirected to a page that asks you to login to **Trailblazers.me**. The page should be similar to the following screenshot:

Figure 1.8: Screen shown upon trying to install an AppExchange solution

Click the **Log In** button, which will redirect you to another screen to confirm the logging method. This page will look similar to the following screenshot:

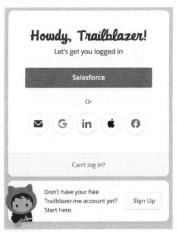

Figure 1.9: Screen to choose the login method

Click the **Salesforce** button to login using your identity in a Salesforce Org. You can use the login credentials you just created for your Salesforce Developer Org. You will be redirected to the standard Salesforce login page. The page will look similar to the following screenshot:

Figure 1.10: *The classic Salesforce Org login screen*

Enter the username and password you used to sign up for the Salesforce Developer Org. In the example shown in Figure 1.5, the username was **tbahri@appbook1.com**. After logging in, you will be redirected to a page that can help determine if you wish to install the **AppExchange** solution on a production org or a sandbox. You want to deploy the solution on the Developer Org you have just signed up for, which is a production org. Click the **Install in Production** button.

Note: Developer orgs do not have sandboxes, unlike other production org.

The page will look similar to the following screenshot:

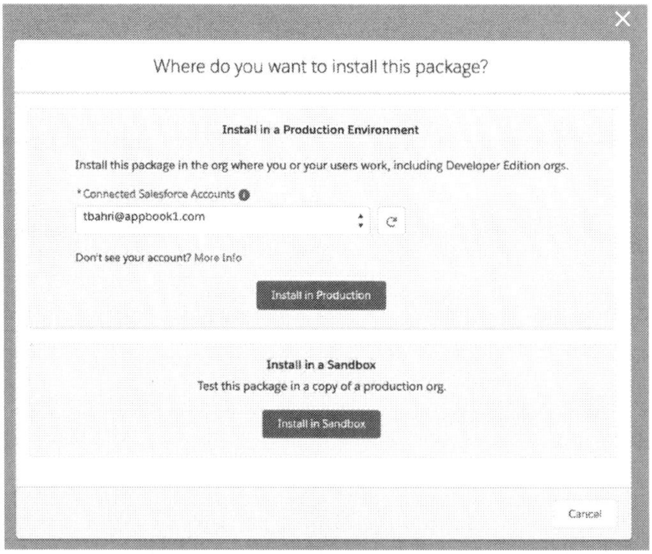

Where do you want to install this package?

Install in a Production Environment

Install this package in the org where you or your users work, including Developer Edition orgs.

* Connected Salesforce Accounts ⓘ

tbahri@appbook1.com

Don't see your account? More Info

Install in Production

Install in a Sandbox

Test this package in a copy of a production org.

Install in Sandbox

Cancel

Figure 1.11: *Choosing the org type to install the AppExchange solution*

Next, you will see a confirmation page. Read the Salesforce agreements' terms and conditions before accepting them. The page will look similar to the following screenshot:

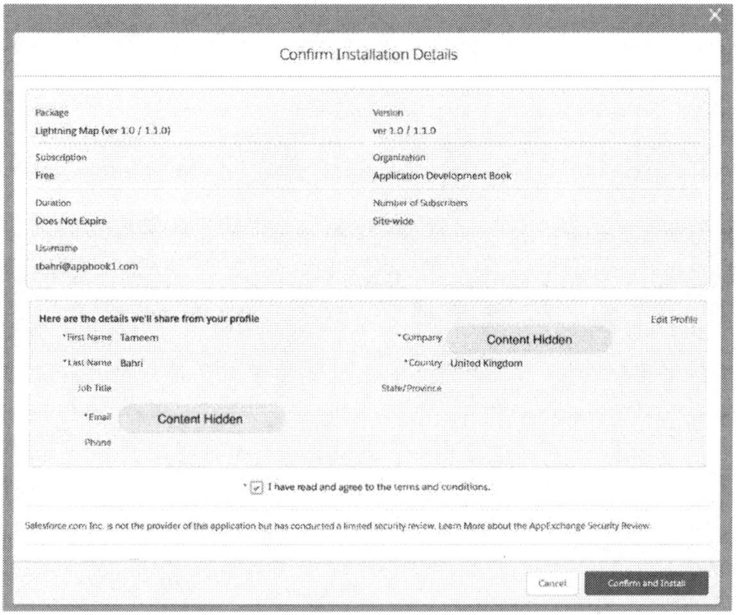

Figure 1.12: *Confirmation page before installing the AppExchange solution*

After clicking the Confirm and Install button, you will be redirected to the same Salesforce login page you have seen in Figure 1.10. The first time, you logged in to confirm your identity to **Trailblazers.me.** The second time, you need to login to the Salesforce Org, where the **AppExchange** solution will be installed. This step is required to ensure you have enough privileges for such action.

After logging in again, you will be redirected to a page that requests you to confirm who will get access to the **AppExchange** solution upon installation. This page will look similar to the following screenshot:

Figure 1.13: *Confirm the users who will get access to the AppExchange solution in the target org*

Choose to **Install for All Users,** then click the **Install** button. The installation process could take a few minutes. By the end of it, you will see a confirmation screen and receive a notification email to confirm the successful installation. To see the component in action, navigate to the account you viewed in *Figure 1.6*, the **Burlington Textiles Corp of America** account. Click on the **gear** icon at the top right of the page, then choose **Edit Page**. The page will look similar to the following screenshot:

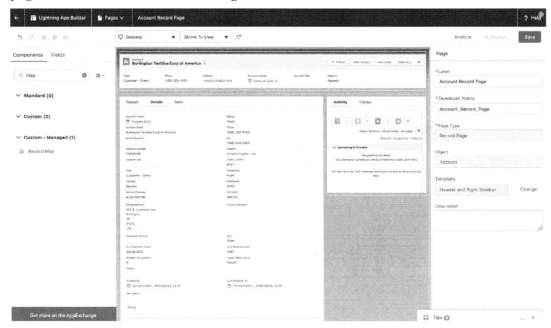

Figure 1.14: Edit the account record page in the Lightning App Builder

You are now using the **Lightning App Builder**, one of the powerful point-and-click development tools available in the Salesforce platform . You will learn more about the Lightning App Builder throughout this book. For now, search for the word **map** in the search box on the left side of the page. This search box will automatically filter the list of available Lightning Components based on the searched term. You will notice a custom component called **Record Map**. Drag and drop it in the middle part of the screen. The page will look similar to the following screenshot:

Figure 1.15: *The Account Record Page in the Lightning App Builder after dropping in the Lightning Component*

You might have noticed that you can drop the component on the Account Record Page at different locations. This is how simple it is to organize the elements in a **Lightning Page** using the **Lightning App Builder**. Next, you need to save the changes that you have made. Click on the **Save** button at the top right page corner. A screen will pop up to request if you want also to activate this page. The page will look similar to the following screenshot:

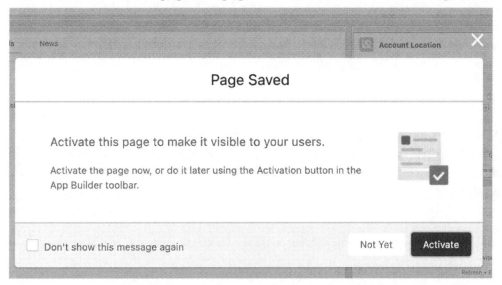

Figure 1.16: *Lightning Page activation confirmation screen*

Activating a page makes it visible to all relevant users. Click the **Activate** button. You will now see another pop up page that you can use to choose a different page to activate for other apps or users. This powerful capability lets you display the same record in multiple formats for different users depending on their profiles and permissions. The page will look similar to the following screenshot:

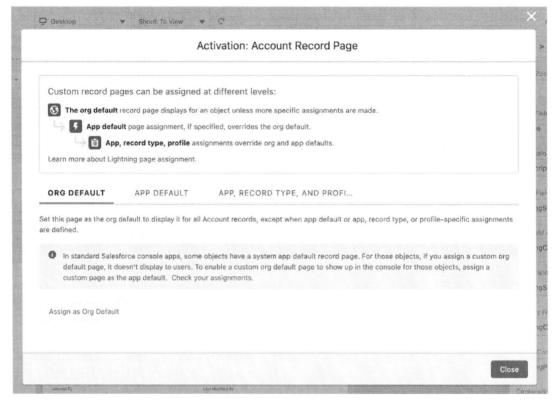

Figure 1.17: Activating the account record page

For the time being, click on the button **Assign as Org Default**. This will make this page the default for viewing accounts for all users and relevant apps. Next, you will be asked to choose the form factor, which can either be **Desktop**, **Phone**, or **Desktop and phone**. This will help you select the device types for which this page will be available. Choose **Desktop and phone** and click the **Next** button. The page will look similar to the following screenshot:

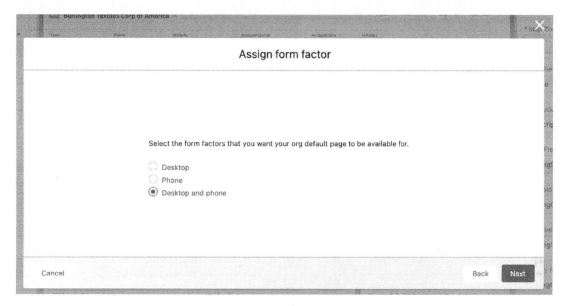

Figure 1.18: *Selecting the form factor*

You are nearly done. Next, you will see a confirmation page similar to the screenshot below:

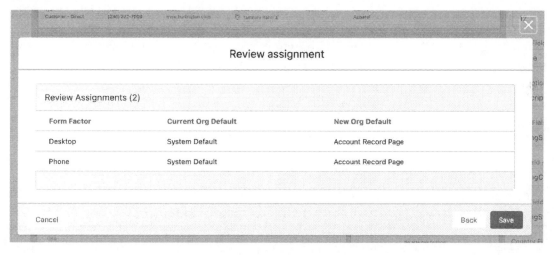

Figure 1.19: *Confirmation page*

Click the **Save** button. You are all done now. Close the Lightning App Builder by clicking the back-arrow icon at the top left page corner. Navigate again to the record page of the **Burlington Textiles Corp of America** account. The page will look similar to the following screenshot:

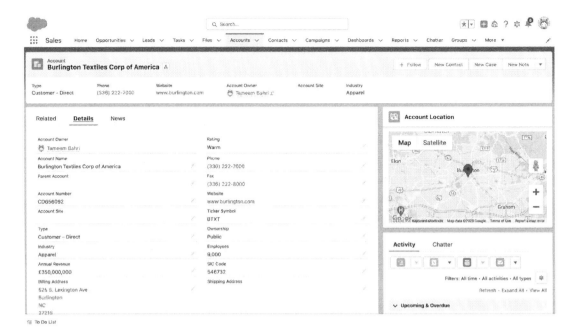

Figure 1.20: *A sample account page after embedding the Lightning Component*
from the AppExchange solution in it

The Lightning Component shows the location of the displayed account on a Google Map. You managed to do that in a few minutes without writing a single line of code. This is the power of low-code/no-code development that Salesforce and the **AppExchange** bring to you.

Now that you have seen the AppExchange in action. Take a brief look at the activities you must consider before publishing an application on AppExchange.

Activities to publish a solution on AppExchange

The scope of publishing your solution to AppExchange is beyond the scope of this book. However, the following will give you a high-level understanding of the usual steps:

1. **Plan your solution:** Define the scope of your solution by articulating what the expected value of this solution is. At this stage, listing all the features, the application covers might be challenging but aim to define as many as possible. The planning activity includes determining the type of the solution (application, lightning component, and so on) and if it will be listed as a free or paid solution.

2. **Join the Salesforce Partner Community:** You need to join the **Salesforce Partner Community** to become a **Salesforce AppExchange partner**. The **Salesforce Partner Community** is an excellent place to find resources, join webinars, learn best practices, and collaborate with other partners. This is also the place where you

can manage your solutions listing. You can join the **Salesforce Partner Community** via the following link **https://partners.salesforce.com/partnersignup**

3. **Develop/Build your solution:** You might already have a working solution or decide to start building it after joining the **Salesforce Partner Community**. Either way, you need a well-documented solution architecture, as you must provide such information upon submitting your solution for the security review. You will learn in this book the best practices for developing and documenting your Salesforce application comprehensively and efficiently.

4. **Document your solution:** In addition to the technical documentation, you must prepare more information, such as the pricing, go-to-market strategy, business plan, and key use cases.

5. **Sign the partnership agreement:** You officially become a **Salesforce Independent Software Vendor (ISV)** after signing the partnership agreement with **Salesforce AppExchange**. The **AppExchange** team will guide you through the required activities in this step.

6. **Submit your solution for security review:** You need to complete the compliance review and have the required documentation in place. Once that is completed, you can submit your solution for security review. Salesforce will review your solution and ensure it meets its strict security requirements, particularly customer data protection. The security review usually takes between four to six weeks. One thing to keep in mind is that there is a cost associated with this process. You can learn more about that cost from the following link:

   https://quip.com/lcZ8AH0kciFP#temp:C:HVTf075127f89e4451f8f6825d20

7. **Publish your AppExchange solution:** Once the security review is cleared, you can publish/list your solution on **AppExchange**. Make sure the content and design of your listing are clear and optimized, as this could directly impact your solution's success.

You have now learned about **AppExchange** and tried out one of its solutions. Next, you will learn more about the key building blocks and tools available to develop your Salesforce applications.

Key building blocks and tools

The **Salesforce platform** comes with a rich set of building blocks and tools you will be briefly introduced to next. You will learn more about a specific set of these building blocks and tools in Chapter 2, Deep dive into key building blocks and tools. These tools and building blocks can be categorized into three categories, **point-and-click building blocks**, **coding building blocks**, and **supportive development tools**. Move on to learn about each.

Point-and-click building blocks

The following list contains a key set of point-and-click building blocks that you can use to build Salesforce applications. This should be considered a partial list, as there are many others. Salesforce has invested heavily in developing and fine-tuning these tools in the past years:

- **Salesforce Objects and Fields**: The heart and soul of an application is its data model. A solid data model can set you on the path to developing a successful, world-class application. In contrast, a sub-optimal data model can become a technical debt in the longer term. In the Salesforce world, a database table is called an **Object**. However, tables and Salesforce Objects are different, as you will learn later in this chapter in the section Salesforce Objects, more than a database. Salesforce provides a set of standard objects that encapsulates certain business functionalities. Each object contains a list of Fields. Fields can be of one of many available types, such as Text, address, currency, ID, email, percent, phone, picklist, picklist (multi-select), lookup relationship, master-detail relationship, external lookup relationship, checkbox, data, date/time, geolocation, number, URL, auto number, formula, roll-up summary, text area (long), text area (rich), and time. You can extend the standard objects by introducing custom fields and creating custom objects that can include custom fields. Salesforce Objects and fields come with built-in functionality, making developing a data model on Salesforce much easier. It is worth mentioning that Salesforce owns the domain database.com, which used to exist as a standalone product before being merged with the **Salesforce platform**.

- **Formulas and validations**: Formula fields are one of the possible field types. However, it is called separately here to indicate its powerful ability as a building block. Formula fields are convenient as they offer on-the-fly calculation ability. Validations are an essential part of any application; they allow you to control the data quality in your solution and prevent certain behaviors. Salesforce validation rules are easy to configure and maintain. You will come across several examples of formula fields and validation rules throughout this book.

- **Approval processes**: The capability of submitting a record (or multiple records) for approval (by one or many approvers) is common across all business applications. Salesforce approval processes can be configured using point-and-click configuration screens.

- **Flow Builder and Salesforce flows**: This is by far the most potent point-and-click tool in the **Salesforce platform**. The **Flow Builder** is a development tool rather than a building block used to create **Salesforce flows**, one of the essential building blocks available on the platform. Salesforce flows allows developers to build complex automation using point-and-click configuration rather than code. **Salesforce flows** used to be called **Visual Flows** in the past. However, several iterations of investments and development by Salesforce took this tool to a whole new level. The **Salesforce Flow Builder** is a handy tool for an administrator (or a point-and-click developer). It bridges the gap between what can be done using simple point-and-click development tools and the full power of coding. You will learn more about this tool in Chapter 2, Deep dive into key building blocks and tools.

- **External Services**: Would it not be nice to be able to call an external web service and invoke a remote action or transmit data without the need to write code? This is precisely what Salesforce External Services does. External Services can be invoked from Salesforce flows or Apex code.

- **Platform Events**: Part of the **Salesforce Enterprise Messaging Platform**. **Platform Events** are messages that are published or subscribed to by your application. These messages contain data. **Platform Events** allows you to build an event-driven architecture and develop applications that can easily integrate with the rest of the enterprise's applications. You can publish and subscribe to platform events via different mechanisms, including **Salesforce flows** and **Apex** code.

- **Salesforce Einstein**: **Artificial Intelligence (AI)** is booming in all technology fields. However, not all companies can afford to hire a team of top AI scientists to help make their sales, service, and marketing processes smarter. **Salesforce Einstein** is an AI suite of products natively integrated into the **Salesforce platform** and mostly point-and-click configurable. The **Salesforce Einstein** suite of products is simply a SaaS version of AI that can help make your CRM smarter. **Salesforce Einstein** has several products within it, with a broad spectrum of capabilities. You come across some of these products in this book.

- **Salesforce Connect**: Salesforce Connect was introduced to allow administrators and developers to integrate with and consume data from remote systems in an easy and simplified way. Salesforce Connect can make the data stored in a remote server accessible and editable in Salesforce. Salesforce Connect displays the remote data using a Salesforce feature called **External Objects**, which shares many similarities with standard and custom objects.

Several other point-and-click building blocks are available and were not mentioned here for brevity, such as **MuleSoft Composer for Salesforce**, **Salesforce Business Rules Engine**, **Salesforce Omniscript**, **Salesforce Mobile Configurator**, **Salesforce Mobile Publisher**, and several others. Next, you will learn about coding building blocks in the **Salesforce platform**.

Coding building blocks

The **Salesforce platform** has several full-code building blocks that developers can use to create sophisticated logic. You will learn about some specific use cases where certain types of code are better written and executed outside the **Salesforce platform** later in this chapter under the section On-platform and off-platform. A well-designed and well-written code on the **Salesforce platform** can run performantly in most cases. Next, explore some of the coding building blocks available:

- **Apex**: **Apex** is a backend strongly-types, compiled programming language that shares roots and many of its syntax with **Java**. Apex is an **Object-Oriented Programming (OOP)** language that supports all OOP principles, such as inheritance and polymorphism. Apex is hosted, compiled, and executed on the Salesforce platform and can be used to create complex business logic and transactions. Apex code is usually organized using classes like other OOP languages such as Java and **C++**. Apex uses **Salesforce Object Query Language (SOQL)** to **create, read, update, and delete (CRUD)** information stored in **Salesforce Objects** (standard, custom, and external). SOQL is similar in syntax to the standard **Structure Query Language (SQL),** with some variations. **Apex** can also use **Salesforce Object Search Language (SOSL)** to search across multiple standard, custom, and external **Salesforce Objects**. **SOSL** shares some similarities with **Apache Lucene**.

- **Apex Triggers**: An **Apex Trigger** is a code extension triggered by a specific operation at the data level/record level. For example, a particular logic can be triggered upon creating a record of the standard Account object. Another logic can be triggered by the update of a record of a custom object, and so on. Apex Triggers are executed before or after the insert, update, and delete operations. Apex Triggers are written using Apex and are a powerful tool for creating data-level business logic. Many popular **Relational Database Management Systems (RDBMS)**, such as Oracle Database and Microsoft SQL Server, adopt the concept of database triggers.

- **Visualforce**: While Apex is a backend language, Visualforce is a front tag-based markup language that allows developers to build custom pages (called Visualforce pages) with rich UIs. Visualforce relies on code written in Apex to execute any backend logic (also known as server-side logic). Visualforce is hosted, compiled, and executed on the Salesforce platform. In the past few years, Visualforce fell out of favor for developers due to the rise of its sibling, Lightning Components.

- **Lightning Components**: Similar to Visualforce, Lightning Components can be used to create custom UIs. However, Lightning Components are designed to support component-based development where multiple reusable components can co-exist and communicate with each other (using a producer/consumer model) while being encapsulated within a container (which can be another component). Lightning Components are deployed as **Single-Page applications (SPAs)** that are usually more performant than **Visualforce**. Lightning Components evolved in the past few years, and a more modern framework that relies on web standards were introduced. It is called **Lightning Web Components (LWC)**, which can be built using **HTML** and **JavaScript**.

Several other coding building blocks, such as Ant Migration Tool, REST API, SOAP API, Metadata API, and several others, are available and not mentioned here for brevity. Next, you will learn about supportive development tools available for the **Salesforce platform**.

Supportive development tools

- **Developer Edition Environment**: You have already learned about the **Salesforce Developer Edition org**. They can be used for multiple purposes, such as learning a new feature, trying out a particular configuration, developing and testing code in a brand-new org (in isolation of other logic), or even developing a complete Salesforce application.

- **Sandboxes**: Similar to the concept used in many other programming languages, Salesforce offers **Sandbox** environments where the metadata (and, in some types of sandboxes, the data) is copied from your production org into a different environment. **Sandboxes** are used for various purposes, such as developing a new feature, modifying an existing feature, testing a functionality, training a set of users, and so on. **Sandboxes** are isolated from each other and from the production org they were spawned from. You can learn more about the different types of Salesforce **Sandboxes** from the following link: **https://help.salesforce.com/s/articleView?id=sf.create_test_instance.htm&type=5**

- **Scratch Orgs**: Shares many similarities with **Sandboxes** and is used for similar purposes (although, most of the time, it is used just for developing and modifying functionalities). **Scratch Orgs** are source-driven environments that are disposed of after completing the development and deployment of a particular feature. **Scratch Orgs** are designed to support **Continues Integration (CI)** and **Continuous Delivery/ Continuous Deployment (CD)** concepts in Salesforce.

- **Lightning App Builder**: You can use the **Lightning App Builder** to create custom Salesforce pages for your application. These pages can be viewed on the browser or the **Salesforce Mobile App**. The **App Manager** is a tool in the **Salesforce platform** that allows you to manage your different applications. The **App Manager** uses the **Lightning App Builder** to allow you to configure an application branding, navigation, and options and manage the Lightning Pages assigned to that application.

- **Developer Console**: Every programming language requires an **Integrated Development Environment (IDE)** to help the developers create, compile, debug, and test code. Salesforce has created the **Developer Console**, a cloud-based IDE fully integrated with the **Salesforce platform** , to help salesforce developers create the different coding building blocks, such as **Apex classes, Apex Triggers**, and **Lightning Components**. Salesforce has also introduced **Salesforce Code Builder** which should be the future of web-based development.

You can read more about **Salesforce Code Builder** from the following link: **https://developer.salesforce.com/blogs/2020/06/introducing-code-builder**

Several other supportive development tools available were not mentioned here for brevity, such as the **Visual Studio Code for Salesforce Development**, the **Salesforce CLI**, the **Salesforce Workbench**, the **Salesforce Lightning Inspector**, and several others.

Next, you will learn some key differences, pros, and cons of No-Code, low-code, and full-code development.

No-code versus low-code versus full-code

The agility and efficiency to rapidly deliver functionalities to the market are key success levers in today's digital ecosystem. The rise of agile delivery methodologies is just another attestation of this statement. The software industry's reaction to this witnessed an increase in no-code and low-code development tools. However, each development approach has strengths, weaknesses, and sweet applicability spots. Start exploring these three types of development tools.

No-code tools

No-code development tools are designed to allow non-technical individuals to create components, pages, and applications without writing any code. These tools usually come with drag-and-drop **what-you-see-is-what-you-get (WYSIWYG)** editors. Several hard-core development languages have had such visual editors for decades as part of their IDEs (such as **Borland Delphi** and **Microsoft Visual Studio**) which inspired the further development of such tools. **Salesforce Lightning App Builder** is an excellent example of a no-code **WYSIWYG** editor.

Here are some of the no-code development advantages:

- It promotes the citizen-developers concept, where enterprise employees build their applications without needing help from the IT department.

- As it promotes the citizen-developers concept, business is empowered and enabled to create the applications they need, which helps avoid engaging with costly third-party vendors.

- No-code tools are easy to learn and grasp. There is no need for lengthy training.

- Applications can be built very quickly and updated/maintained easily.

On the other hand, here are some of the no-code development disadvantages:

- No-code applications tend to be simple. Other forms of development would still be required for more sophisticated applications.

- Although reducing the dependency on the IT department is great, non-controlled citizen development programs can lead to a non-organized, poorly documented, and inefficient system landscape.

- No-code development may lead to a vendor lockdown if a single vendor is chosen.

Next, explore the concept of low-code development.

Low-code tools

Low-code development tools allow developers (familiar with one programming language or more) to create different types of applications with minimal hand-written code. Low-code development tools enable developers to develop applications faster using visual **WYSIWYG** editors that can be augmented with code if needed. **Salesforce Flow Builder** is a good example of a tool that combines concepts from the no-code and low-code development concepts. It allows creating of capable **Salesforce flows** without a single line of code and extending these Flows with **Apex** code if needed.

Here are some of the low-code development advantages:

- It can be used to create sophisticated applications by utilizing point-and-click development whenever possible and augmenting it with code when needed.

- Low-code applications can be built and maintained relatively quickly and easily.

- Low-code development tools can boost the speed and agility of your development team. Moreover, it increases the reliability of generated artifacts as the ready-made elements of the developed application are usually highly reliable.

- While enabling speedy development, low-code applications can also be governed using the same classic battle-tested methods used by the software industry.

- Simplifies the architecture of the built applications.

On the other hand, here are some of the no-code development disadvantages:

- Low-code developers require some level of coding skills.

- It depends on the IT department, although it is much less than what is needed in full-code development.

- Low-code development may lead to a vendor lockdown if a single vendor is chosen.

Next, explore the concept of full-code development.

Full-code tools

This type of development is simply called coding, the term full-code is hardly used, but it was used here to differentiate it from the other mentioned development methods easily. In this form of development, developers (familiar with one programming language or more) create highly customized and sophisticated applications. Developers can use ready-made open-source libraries to speed up the development activity. Salesforce **Apex**, **Lightning Components**, **Lightning Web Components**, and **Visualforce** are all considered full-coding tools.

Here are some of the full-code development advantages:

- It can be used to create highly customized and sophisticated applications. The sky is your limit.

- Well-architected solutions can be very performant.

- Complete control over the code, very minimal dependency on vendors.

- Full ownership of any developed artifact.

On the other hand, here are some of the no-code development disadvantages:

- High dependency on developers and the IT department.

- High development cost and time.

- Increases the dependency on developers, which are hard to recruit and retain. Particularly highly talented developers.

One of the significant advantages of the **Salesforce platform** is that it offers all three forms of development.

Next, you will learn about the fantastic underlying data layer that empowers your Salesforce applications, the **Salesforce Objects**.

Salesforce Objects: More than a database

You learned earlier that **Salesforce Objects** are analogous to RDBMS tables. Similarly, **Salesforce Fields** are analogous to table columns. The term record is used to describe a particular row in a database table; likewise, it describes an instance of a **Salesforce Object**.

Salesforce Objects have several differences compared to database tables, such as the fact that they have some capabilities and logic built into them; this applies to all types of Objects (Standard, Custom, and External). Tables are simply data storage elements, while Objects provide ready-to-use capabilities in addition to their ability to store data. For example, Objects are automatically accessible via the relevant **Salesforce APIs** (such as the **REST API**). Most Objects got their UI to manage and maintain them; this makes it easy to add, read, edit, and delete data stored within them, unlike database tables that usually require another tool to expose their data.

Salesforce Objects can be configured to be searchable and reportable immediately in the **Salesforce platform** and are compatible with other standard features such as **List Views**. Moreover, the **SOQL** language used with **Salesforce Objects** is much simpler and relationship-aware than traditional **SQL**. The visibility of Salesforce Objects can be controlled through highly sophisticated and customizable sharing and visibility modules in the **Salesforce platform**. This goes beyond **role-based access control (RBAC)** and into a highly advanced mode of **attribute-based access control (ABAC)** that enables controlling the visibility of each and every *record*, *field*, and *object* within the platform.

Salesforce Fields are more aware of their data types compared to standard database table columns. Due to that, Salesforce Fields has built-in data validation capabilities that can enhance your stored data quality. For example, you cannot input a character into a *number* field. This is available out of the box without introducing a single line of code or even configuration. Similarly, a date field will automatically render itself as a calendar when a user tries to input a value. This data-type-awareness capability dramatically reduces the time required to develop such data-quality validations.

There is another type of Salesforce Objects we have yet to mention, called **Big Objects**. **Big Objects** are used to store and retrieve millions of data, and they will not be covered in this book.

You can learn more about the different object types, field types, special field types, system fields, and more from the following link:

https://developer.salesforce.com/docs/atlas.en-us.object_reference.meta/object_reference/sforce_api_objects_concepts.htm

Next, you will learn about two common terminologies in the Salesforce ecosystem, on-platform and off-platform.

On-platform and off-Platform

The term on-platform refers to functionalities developed on the **Salesforce platform**. Applications developed entirely on the **Salesforce platform** are called **Native Applications/Native Apps**. In contrast, functionalities built outside the **Salesforce platform** (then eventually integrated with it) are considered off-platform.

Off-platform applications in the Salesforce ecosystem usually have built-in connectors that simplify integrating them with Salesforce. Some applications simplify this by hiding the configuration complexity behind a native application that integrates with the Off-platform solution; in these cases, the users feel that they are interacting with a native application while the fact is different. The following diagram illustrates the architectural difference between native applications and off-platform applications:

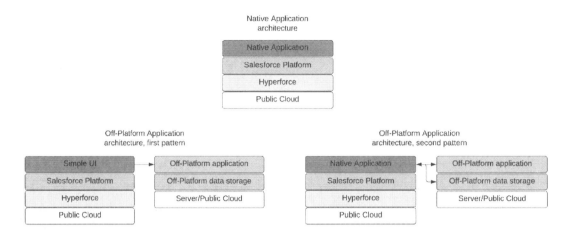

Figure 1.21: *Native apps vs. Off-platform apps*

Both Native Applications and Off-platform applications have their pros and cons. We will compare both across the following seven points: data security, data accuracy, development speed, required skills, capabilities and use cases, reliability, efficiency, and trust.

Comparison point	Native applications	Off-platform applications
Data security	Highly secured, as the data never leaves the Salesforce platform. This reduces the risks of data breaches via attacks on less-secure servers.	Data is usually transferred via the integration interfaces. Data security and compliance must be carefully assessed and managed.
Data accuracy	The data is always up to date and synced across the Salesforce Org, as there is no other system(s) to align with.	Data must be synced with an external system. In addition, there is a need for strict data quality measures across the integration interfaces.
Development speed	Developing applications on the Salesforce platform is estimated to be four times faster than classic development.	More time is needed for development.
Required skills	Salesforce-only skills are required.	Salesforce and non-Salesforce skills are required. The off-platform application will require a different skill set to develop and maintain. Moreover, there will likely be a need to manage the infrastructure (even if using a PaaS).

Comparison point	Native applications	Off-platform applications
Capabilities and use cases	Complex applications can be built natively on the Salesforce platform. However, remember that the Salesforce platform follows a shared tenancy model and has several governor limits to consider and adhere to. The imposed limits effectively restrict the type of applications that you can realistically develop natively. For example, applications that require an extensive amount of memory (such as processing hundreds of millions of records) or generate massive traffic over the network (such as communicating with thousands of remote endpoints) are not suitable for native development on the Salesforce platform.	It can be used to develop extremely complex and demanding applications. Including high performance applications, data-intensive, memory-intensive, or communication-intensive applications.
Reliability	If the Salesforce platform is running, then so is the application. There is no risk of a native app going down. The whole platform is fully managed by Salesforce.	The off-platform tech stack needs to be maintained. The availability and reliability of this tech stack impact the whole solution. APIs must be continually maintained even if both the external platform and Salesforce never go down. A communication glitch can create a data discrepancy across the two platforms which is costly to debug and fix.
Efficiency	All parts of the application are on the same platform, natively integrated, which means zero integration cost.	Integration cost should never be underestimated as it can get very complex and expensive to build and maintain.

Comparison point	Native applications	Off-platform applications
Trust	Native apps have no hidden maintenance or management fees. Moreover, they adhere to strict Salesforce security policies and regulations.	Data security and compliance must be carefully assessed and managed. Hidden fees could be applied and must be considered for the overall solution cost.

Table 1.2: Comparing Native applications to Off-Platform applications

Several well-known AppExchange applications are either built natively or off-platform. There is no right and wrong way. You must select the right architecture for your application based on its planned usage and functionalities.

Summary

You have learned much about the **Salesforce platform's** history, architecture, building blocks, and development tools. You also learned why it is important and rewarding to develop Salesforce applications. In the next chapter, you will dive deeper into some of the building blocks and development tools that you learned briefly about in this chapter. You will learn to configure and use these tools to develop secure, scalable, and reliable Salesforce applications.

Join our book's Discord space

Join the book's Discord Workspace for Latest updates, Offers, Tech happenings around the world, New Release and Sessions with the Authors:

https://discord.bpbonline.com

CHAPTER 2

Deep Dive into Key Building Blocks and Tools

Introduction

This chapter will teach you more about the key building blocks and tools you will mostly use during the rest of the book. Some of these building blocks require an entire book by itself to master; this chapter intends to get you introduced to these building blocks and tools to achieve a level of proficiency that allows you to practice the exercises and projects in this book and learn how to build real-world Salesforce applications.

If you are a seasoned Salesforce developer, you could skim through this chapter to refresh your memory. Less experienced Salesforce developers, administrators, and architects are strongly advised to practice every exercise in this chapter. In case you have not yet signed up for a free *Developer Edition* org, make sure you do so before starting this chapter using the following link:

https://developer.salesforce.com/signup

Structure

The chapter covers the following topics:

- Learn about Salesforce users and licenses
- Practice working with objects, fields, and page layouts

- Learn about the Salesforce sharing and security model

- Practice using the Salesforce App Builder

- Practice using the Salesforce Report Builder

- Get introduced to the Salesforce Flow Builder

- Get introduced to the Salesforce Apex and triggers

- Introduction to the Salesforce Lightning Components and the Lightning Design System

Objectives

By the end of this chapter, you will have enough knowledge and familiarity about the key Salesforce building blocks and tools that will be used throughout this book. You will gain hands-on experience by applying the exercises and understanding the best use cases for each building block. You will gain essential skills in this chapter that you will keep sharpening throughout the book and your professional life.

Learn about Salesforce users and licenses

You learned about the Salesforce platform in *Chapter 1, Introduction to the Salesforce Platform*, and got familiar with the SaaS software delivery and licensing model. The heart of the SaaS model is the **license**. A Salesforce license is a metadata building block that defines and controls the Salesforce features available to the users assigned to the license. The Salesforce license can be considered an agreement between the customer and Salesforce where certain services/features are delivered for an agreed price.

Each org typically has multiple licenses, even the free Developer Edition orgs. Some licenses can be combined and assigned to a given user (such as combining a user license with a permission set license). Here is a short definition of some of the main types of licenses in the Salesforce platform:

- **User license:** Only one user license can be assigned to the Salesforce platform users. The user license defines what features are available to this user. Here are some examples of Salesforce user licenses: Salesforce platform, Identity Only license, and Salesforce license.

- **Permission set license:** A type of license that can be assigned to supplement the functionalities available for a particular user. Multiple permission set licenses can be assigned to a single user. A permission set license should not be confused with permission sets which is another Salesforce feature used to control the assigned privileges to a particular user. Some examples of Salesforce permission set licenses are Field Service dispatcher, Analytics Cloud Builder, and Identity Connect.

- **Platform license:** A license that controls/enables certain functionalities to the whole org. There are several examples of such licenses in Heroku.

- **Settings license:** Any license (such as permission set license, user license, or platform license) that can be configured to control specific behaviors of the functionalities it enables.

A Salesforce administrator manages the allocation of Salesforce licenses and handles provisioning and de-provisioning of users. User provisioning is a process that refers to all activities required to create and activate a user, including assigning the correct type of licenses, profiles, and access permissions to the user. The de-provisioning process is about disabling an existing user from the target org.

It is worth mentioning that any additional purchased license will be enabled on production orgs only; you must refresh a sandbox to reflect any additional purchased license or use the functionality of matching production licenses.

Log in to your Developer Edition org to help you see an example of some available licenses in an org. If you are not on the setup page already, you can navigate to it by clicking on the gear icon at the top right of the page and then clicking on the **Setup** option from the drop-down menu item. The following screenshot shows where to click after logging in:

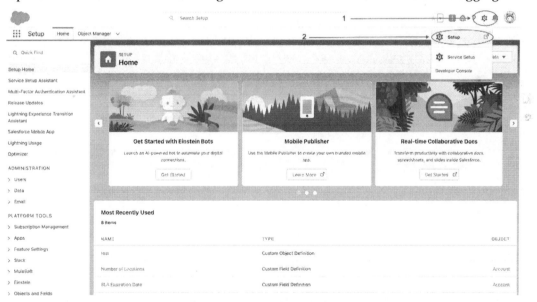

Figure 2.1: Navigating to the setup section

After navigating to the setup section of your Salesforce org, locate the search box at the left side of the page (this section is called the **setup menu**) and type the word **company** in it. The menu of configurable items in your org will get automatically filtered while you are typing; in fact, you might need not to type the whole company word before you can see the desired menu item that you want to navigate to, which is called **Company Information**, click on that menu item to view the company information page. The following screenshot helps explain this step:

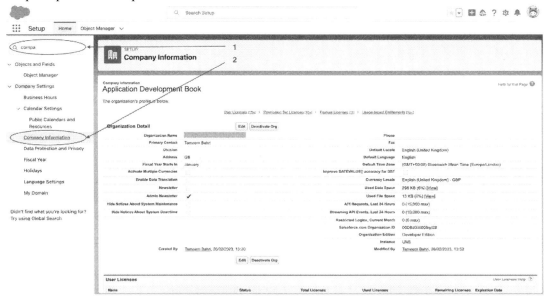

Figure 2.2: The company information screen

The company information page contains information about your org, such as the **Organization ID** (which is a unique identifier for this org), the primary contact, the default locale, and other information. Scroll down on this page to view the org's available user licenses and permission set licenses. Your screen could look similar to the following screenshot:

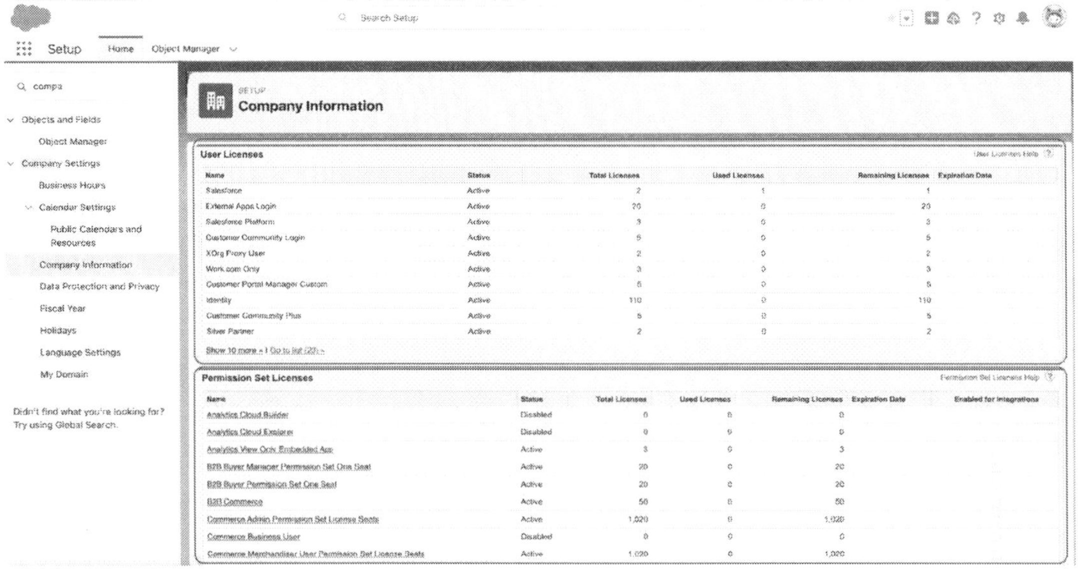

Figure 2.3: Example of the licenses available in a Salesforce org

You may have noticed that you have two **Salesforce licenses** in this org; one has already been used. All **Developer Edition** orgs come with two free **Salesforce licenses**; one will be assigned by default to this org's first/primary user.

To view the users defined in the org, you must navigate to the **Users** page. Search for the word **user** in the search box of the **Setup** menu, then click on the **Users** menu item to view the **Users** screen. The **Users** screen is where you can also provision and de-provision your salesforce org's users. The following screenshot helps explain this step:

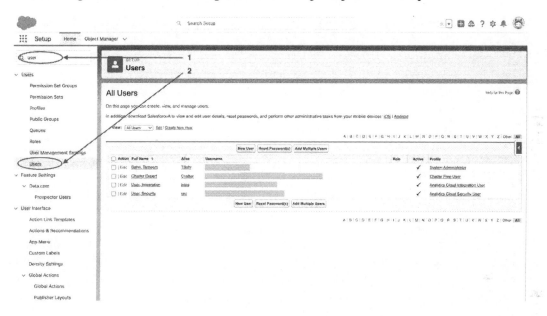

Figure 2.4: Navigating to the users page

On this page, you can see a list of the users in the org and whether they are active. Click the **New User** button to create a new user. You will now see a page that collects key information about the newly created user, including the **user license** to be assigned. Your screen will look similar to the following screenshot:

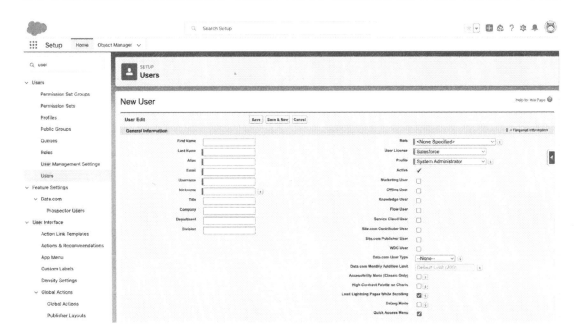

Figure 2.5: User creation page

Fill in the required fields and click the **Save** button; the newly created user will receive an email notification to set up a new password. Congratulations! You have created your first Salesforce user. Navigate back to the **Company Information** page and notice that the number of used **Salesforce licenses** is now two. Feel free to investigate these pages further and create more users or disable some existing users (make sure you do not disable your primary system administrator user).

Now that you have learned about Salesforce Users and licenses, move on to learn more about the Salesforce `objects`, `fields`, and `page layouts`.

Practice working with objects, fields, and page layouts

The Salesforce platform has a plethora of built-in standard objects, which vary by the Salesforce edition of the org. These objects provide different functionalities across the different Salesforce platform-based clouds (such as **Sales Cloud**, **Service Cloud**, **Financial Service Cloud**, **Experience Cloud**, **Health Cloud**, **automotive**, and others). Worth mentioning that Salesforce introduced clouds based on something other than the Salesforce platform in the past years, such as the Salesforce Marketing Cloud and Integration Cloud.

The platform-based clouds have access to standard objects such as the Account, Contact, Opportunity, Lead, Case, and others. The following link contains the official documentation of the Salesforce standard objects.

https://developer.salesforce.com/docs/atlas.en-us.object_reference.meta/object_reference/sforce_api_objects_list.htm

Remember that although these objects are meant for specific functionalities, you still have room to configure them to fit your business best. For example, an Account typically represents a customer business account (such as a company name). However, it can be modeled to represent a different entity for other businesses (for example, it can also be used to model a property in a property management implementation). Understanding all the relationships between the standard Salesforce objects is essential, as it will help you determine the correct usage of each object for your business.

On many occasions, you could find out that a specific functionality you would like to introduce is not covered by any standard Salesforce objects. For example, you might want to introduce a specific object to hold values related to your customers that are specific to your business. You learned in *Chapter 1, Introduction to the Salesforce Platform*, that you can introduce custom fields and objects to your Salesforce org. This book assumes that you have prior knowledge of creating, updating, and managing custom Salesforce objects and fields. You can also visit the following module on Trailhead to learn about custom object creation if needed.

https://trailhead.salesforce.com/content/learn/modules/create-a-custom-object-quick-look/create-a-custom-object

You can also learn about introducing the different types of custom fields from the following Trailhead project.

https://trailhead.salesforce.com/content/learn/projects/customize-a-salesforce-object

Each object (standard or custom) can have one or more page layouts. There are a few standard objects which do not have any page layout, but those are considered exceptions.

A page layout is a feature that allows you to control the appearance of records of a specific object in Salesforce. For example, it allows you to control the appearance of the records of the Account object. Page layouts allow you to control the location of the fields on the record page and can even be used to help you enhance the data quality of your org by making some of these fields mandatory. Using page layouts, you can also control the displayed related list, buttons, and links shown to the user.

To practice working with a page layout, login to your Developer Edition org, navigate to the **Setup** page and locate the **Object Manager** tab as shown in the following screenshot:

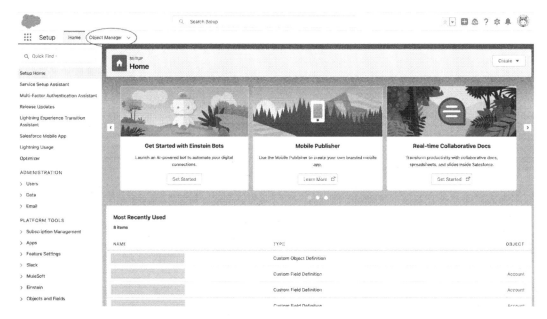

Figure 2.6: The Object Manager tab

Click on the **Object Manager** tab to open a page with standard and custom objects in your org. Click on the **Account** object. Then from the left side panel, click on **Page Layouts**. You will see a list of the available page layout of the Account object in your org, similar to the following screenshot:

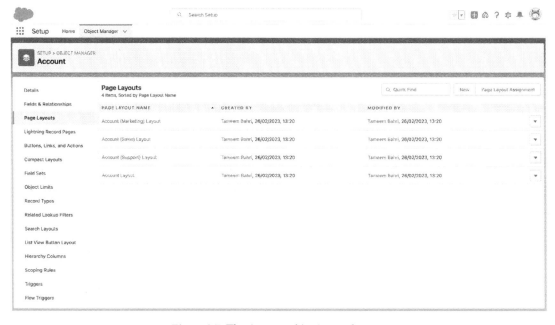

Figure 2.7: The Account object's page layouts

You can assign different layouts to your users based on their profiles. Click on one of the available layouts. For example, click on the **Account (Sales) Layout**. This layout is a standard layout available by default in the Developer Edition orgs. You will see the page layout editor page similar to the following screenshot where you can customize the layout:

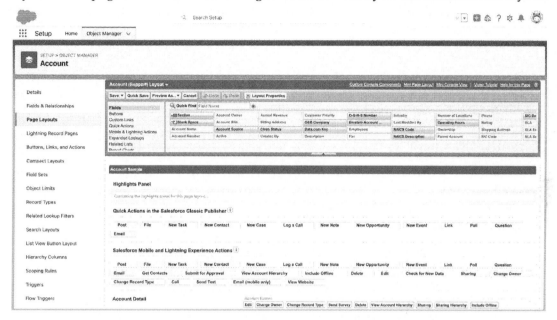

Figure 2.8: *The Page Layout Editor*

Try to drag some of the existing fields to different locations and try to add or remove fields to the layout (by dragging them from and to the panel at the top). Your changes will only become effective once you click the **Save** button. Get yourself familiar with page layouts and how they work.

You can learn more about customizing page layouts from the following link:

https://trailhead.salesforce.com/content/learn/modules/lex_customization/lex_ customization_page_layouts

Salesforce objects are more than just tables because they come with built-in functionalities such as page layouts and fields of different types. Page layouts, objects, and fields are simple yet powerful building blocks for the Salesforce developer. Next, you will learn how to control the visibility of your objects, fields, and records for the different user groups in your org.

Learn about the Salesforce sharing and security model

The Salesforce platform has a very powerful and sophisticated module to manage data access. The module itself can be looked at as multiple stacked layers of different features and functionalities, each providing further restrictions. Technically, you can think of the data access and sharing module as three distinct layers:

- The org layer
- The object-and-field layer
- The record-level layer

There is a rich set of configurable features at each layer. You will learn about some of them shortly, while others are considered more advanced than the planned scope of this book. For now, take a quick look at the following diagram that summarizes a key set of these features:

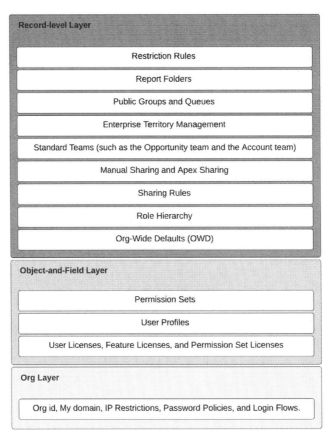

Figure 2.9: *The Salesforce platform data access layers and features*

Next, you will learn about the different layers of the Salesforce platform sharing module and get introduced to some of their features.

The org layer

You learned about the Org ID, one of the functionalities in this layer, in *Chapter 1, Introduction to the Salesforce Platform*. This layer contains the mechanisms that ensure your org's data is completely inaccessible by users of other orgs and vice versa (the Org ID). This layer also includes other mechanisms to ensure secure user access to your org, such as My Domain, IP Restrictions, and password policies.

- **My Domain**: This feature gives a unique URL for each Salesforce org. This is useful for both branding and security purposes. The unique URL for your org could be something like *https://yourcompanyname.my.salesforce.com*. You can learn more about the My Domain feature from the following link.

  https://help.salesforce.com/s/articleView?id=sf.domain_name_overview.htm

- **IP Restrictions**: This feature allows you to restrict user login to specific IP addresses only. This powerful security feature should be carefully used to avoid accidentally locking users (including yourself) out. You can read more about this feature from the following link:

  https://help.salesforce.com/s/articleView?id=000386441&type=1

- **Password policies**: This feature allows you to set complex password policies, requiring user passwords to include a specific number of characters and a mix of alphabetic characters and numbers. You can read more about this feature from the following link:

  https://help.salesforce.com/s/articleView?id=sf.admin_password.htm&type=5

Move on to learn about the object-and-field-level layer.

The object-and-field layer

At the object and field level, you can configure which objects are accessible to which users and if they can read, create, edit, and delete records of this object. You can also configure which fields within each object will be visible and editable to the user; this feature is usually called **Field-Level Security (FLS)**. Kindly note that these data access and visibility rules will be applied to all records of the target object. You can read more about the FLS feature from the following link:

https://developer.salesforce.com/docs/atlas.en-us.securityImplGuide.meta/securityImplGuide/admin_fls.htm

The object-and-field-level mechanisms are commonly used across digital systems. However, the record-level takes the Salesforce data access module to the next level.

The record-level layer

The record-level layer includes functionalities that allow you to control access and visibility of every record of the target object. The different sharing module layers work in sequence, which means that if a user does not have access to an object (for example, the Lead object), then the user will not have access to any records of the Lead object regardless of the configurations you have on the record-level layer.

All records of independent custom objects (objects not linked to another object via a master-detail relationship) and most standard objects in the Salesforce platform have an *owner* field. This field contains a look-up to the user owning the target record. The owner of a record has full access to it subject to their object and field level permissions. A record owner can edit a record only if they have the object and field level permissions that enable them to do so.

The record-level layer includes features that allow you to control data access to records other than their owners, such as the following key configurable features:

- **Org-Wide Defaults (OWDs)**: This feature defines the default access levels for the object's records. The OWD of an independent object (such as the Lead object) could be private, public read-only, or public read-write. This defines the default user access to the Lead objects. The impact of other functionalities, such as Role Hierarchies, Sharing Rules, and several others, can alter the default level access. You can read more about this feature from the following link: **https://help.salesforce.com/s/articleView?id=sf.admin_sharing.htm&type=5**

- **Role hierarchies**: This feature allows you to control data access in your org based on a specific hierarchy. Users in a higher hierarchy can access data owned by (or under particular conditions, shared with) users directly below them. You can learn more about this feature and practice creating a role hierarchy from the following link: **https://trailhead.salesforce.com/content/learn/modules/data_security/data_security_roles**

- **Sharing rules**: This feature enables you to configure rules (based on who owns a record or based on values in certain record fields that meet specific criteria) to share a record with one or more users in your org (could be a public group or a role). While the OWD defines the default access level, sharing rules enable you to extend the user access to specific users beyond the OWD. For example, if a Lead object is private, all records of the Lead object will only be visible to their owners (and users above them in the role hierarchy). You can introduce a sharing rule that shares Leads of specific criteria (for example, from a particular source) with a specific user group. This is an example of a criteria-based sharing rule. You can learn more about this feature and practice creating sharing rules from the following link: **https://trailhead.salesforce.com/content/learn/modules/data_security/data_security_sharing_rules**

The structure of your data model also impacts record access and visibility. For example, the *Master-Detail* relationship allows the records of the child object to inherit the data visibility status of their master record.

Next, you will learn about a convenient Salesforce platform tool, the **Salesforce App Builder**.

Practice using the Salesforce App Builder

The **App Builder** (also known as the **Lightning App Builder** or the **Salesforce App Builder**) is a handy point-and-click development tool in the Salesforce platform. You can use it to create custom applications (which may contain one or more pages) for both web and mobile (via the **Salesforce Mobile App**). You do not need coding skills to develop applications using the Salesforce App Builder.

The App Builder can also be used to manage the application's branding and options. Moreover, the App Builder allows you to edit an app and change the pages (Also known as **Lightning pages**) assigned to it. You have seen Lightning pages before while viewing records of the different Salesforce objects. Lightning pages include regions and contain different types of components. Some of these components (such as the Record Details and Related List components) can derive their contents from the page layouts that you learned earlier about in this chapter.

The Lightning pages are adaptive by nature and can render differently based on the device used to view them. You can choose from specific predefined page templates, and you can also develop a custom template. The following screenshot can help illustrate some standard templates:

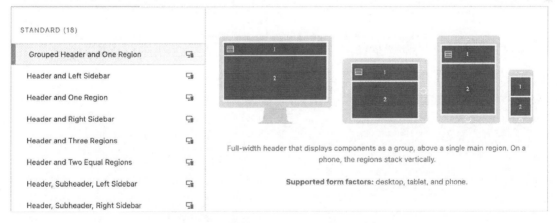

Figure 2.10: Lightning pages standard templates

The App Builder can help you develop the following:

- **Applications with a single page**: These applications consist of a single page with multiple sections that can interact with each other and can be reloaded simultaneously without needing to submit the whole page back to the server and move to another page.

- **Applications with multiple pages**: These applications usually focus on delivering a specific set of functionalities to a targeted user group, such as a procurement app where users can create, submit, and track procurement requests.

- **Object record pages (also known as Record Pages)**: You can create customized object record pages that fit your business needs.

- **Home pages**: Customized to include the most used components for your users.

- **Apps with dashboards**: The apps can help visualize and track some information.

- **Embedded service pages**: This type of page is out of the scope of this book.

- **Customized extensions for Salesforce Voice**: This type of page is out of the scope of this book.

You have already experienced editing an Object record page in *Chapter 1, Introduction to the Salesforce Platform,* under the title *Installing Your First AppExchange Solution.* You will practice creating an application with multiple pages in this chapter. But you need to get familiar with the App Builder's interface first.

The App Builder's interface

The following screenshot helps clarify the App Builder's user interface:

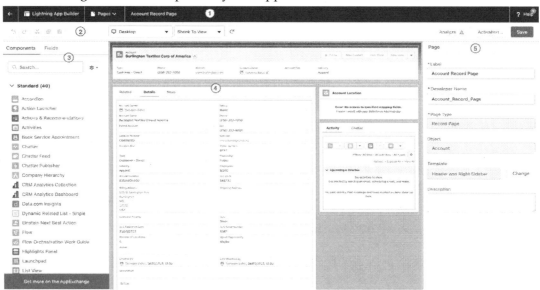

***Figure 2.11**: The Lightning App Builder User Interface*

Here is a brief description of each of the marked areas:

1. **The header:** The header contains information such as a label of the page you are working on and quick access to a list of pages. The back-arrow icon at the left end of the header section allows you to return to the Setup menu without saving any of the introduced changes. When editing an app, this section will include a tab for the application settings. The page list will also display active pages associated with this app.

2. **The toolbar:** Similar to toolbars that you can see in other applications, the App Builder's toolbar contains some shortcut functionalities such as Cut, Copy, and Paste. The toolbar also includes a drop-down menu that allows you to view the page in different rendering formats (for example, Desktop or Phone).

3. **The Lightning Components pane:** This page contains all Lightning Components that can be used with your Lightning page. This includes both standard and custom components. You can drag and drop components from this pane to the Lightning page Canvas.

4. **The Lightning page canvas:** The main area used to design and build your Lightning page.

5. **The Properties pane:** This context-sensitive pane displays different content based on the item selected in the Lightning page Canvas. It can also show the overall page properties if no component is selected. This page allows you to configure the design-time properties of your page and page components.

Now that you are familiar with the App Builder's UI, it is time to practice using it.

Practice creating a multiple pages application

Start by navigating to the setup page, then search for the word **app manager**. Click on the **App Manager** item from the menu to display the App Manager's main page; click on the **New Lightning App** button, as illustrated in the following screenshot:

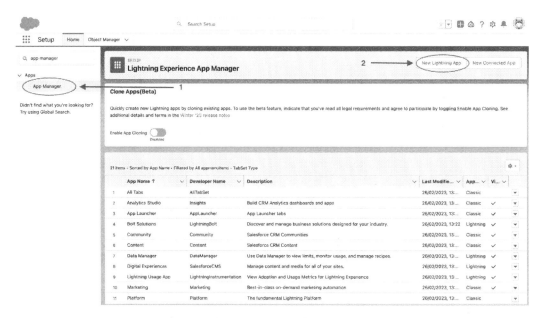

Figure 2.12: Creating a new Lightning application

A new popup will be displayed to input details about your application, such as the **application** and **developer names**. The **Developer Name** is a unique name for this application that can be accessed by code, while the **App Name** is simply a label displayed to the end users. Enter values as shown in the following screenshot:

Figure 2.13: Filling in details for the new Lightning application

Click on the **Next** button at the bottom right corner of the popup page. A new page will appear to set up the **app options**, accept the default values, and move to the next page by clicking again on the **Next** button. The next page allows you to configure *utility items* to your application. The **utility items** help add shortcuts to the bottom side of the page (the utility bar); there is no need to add **utility items** for this application. Click **next** to move to the next page, which allows you to select the **navigation items** of your app; these are simply tabs that will be visible for the application users (assuming they have the proper permissions to access these tabs). Add the **Accounts** and **Contacts** tabs to your application, as shown in the following screenshot:

Figure 2.14: Selecting the Navigation Items of the Lightning application

Click **Next** to move to the following page, which allows you to set up the profiles that will have access to this application. Find and select the **System Administrator** profile; you can add multiple profiles if you wish. The screen will look similar to the following screenshot:

Figure 2.15: *Assigning profiles to the Lightning application*

Click **Save & Finish** to save the application. Congratulations, you have created your first multi-page Lightning App. Your app has two pages, the **Account** and **Contact** pages. To view your application, click on the App Launcher icon at the top left corner of the page, then search for your application's name, similar to what is shown in the following screenshot:

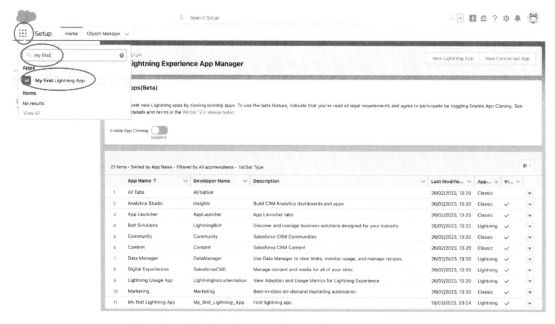

Figure 2.16: *Finding the new application from the App Launcher*

You will be redirected to the application when you click on your new app's link. Please note that only users with profiles assigned to this application can find it in the **App Launcher** and access it. Your newly created application could look like the following screenshot:

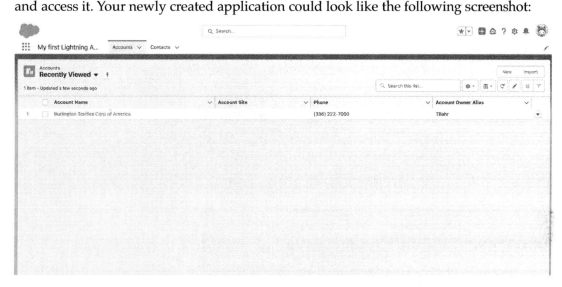

Figure 2.17: The newly created multi-page application

The view you see on your screen could be slightly different depending on the accounts that you recently viewed.

You can learn more about the App Builder from the following link:

https://trailhead.salesforce.com/content/learn/modules/lightning_app_builder

Intro:

Now that you are familiar with the **Lightning App Builder** move on to learn about the **Report Builder**.

Practice using the Salesforce Report Builder

The **Report Builder** is a tool to create reports and dashboards in your Salesforce org. Dashboards are based on reports, and the reports themselves retrieve their data from standard and custom objects in your org based on the structure of the used report types. There are standard report types that you can choose to create for each custom object. Several standard objects have ready-to-use report types as well. You can also create Custom report types.

A *Report Type* consists of a primary object and none, one or more dependent/related objects. The **Contacts & Accounts** standard report type is an example of a *report type* with two objects; The *Contact* here is the primary object, and the *Account* is the related object.

To create a report, click on the **App Launcher**, then search for the **reports** application. Your screen could look similar to the following:

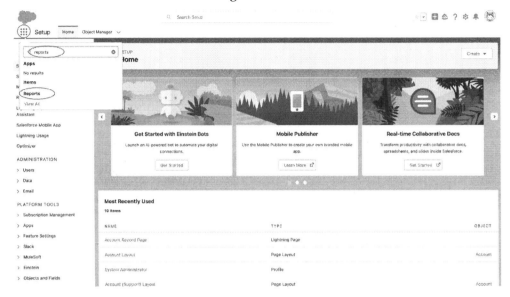

Figure 2.18: *Accessing the Reports application from the App Launcher*

To start creating a new report, click on the **New Report** button. Select the **Report Type** for this report; choose any from the list. For example, select **Opportunities**, then click the **Start Report** button. The screen you see now is the main UI for the **Report Builder**. It will look similar to the following screenshot:

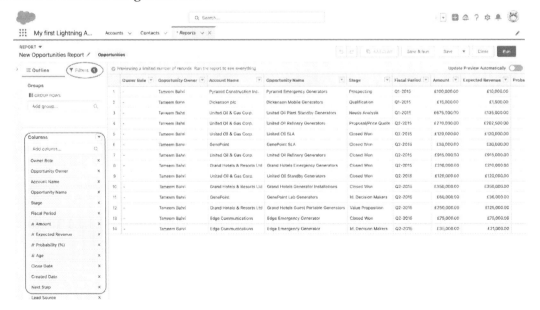

Figure 2.19: *The Report Builder's UI*

You can drag and drop additional columns/fields from the left pane to the report in the middle of the screen. You can also add **Filters** to control the retrieved data (for example, you can add a filter to retrieve only the Opportunities that have their closure data in the current financial quarter). Once you are satisfied with your report, you can save it. You can also run it without saving it to check how it would look exactly.

You can learn more about the **Report Builder** and `Custom report types` from the following link:

https://trailhead.salesforce.com/content/learn/modules/reports_dashboards/reports_ dashboards_getting_started

Next, you will learn about **Salesforce flows** and the **Salesforce Flow Builder**.

Get introduced to the Salesforce Flow Builder

The **Salesforce Flow Builder** is a powerful point-and-click tool for developing different types of flows. The full details of the **Flow Builder** can easily fill a book; we will cover its basics only in this book for brevity.

Flows are built using a combination of **elements**, **connectors**, and **resources**. Have a quick look at the definition of each.

- **Elements:** Each element is an *action*, such as reading from a Salesforce object or creating records. An *action* can also be collecting input from the user or displaying certain information.

- **Connectors:** A connector is a path the flow can follow during execution (run time).

- **Resources:** A resource can hold a value that can be referenced in other parts of the flow.

At this stage, it is probably good to look at a ready-made flow and use it to explain the key components of the **Flow Build's** UI and the standard elements of the flow.

From the setup page, search for the word **flow**, and click on the **Flows** menu item; this will display a page with all flows in your org. Click on the one called **Book Appointment from Invitation**. The screen could look like the following:

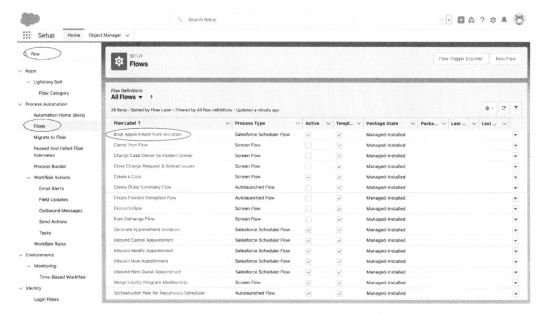

Figure 2.20: *Accessing the list of flows in your org*

Another page will be displayed; this is the main UI for the Flow Builder. It will look like the following screenshot:

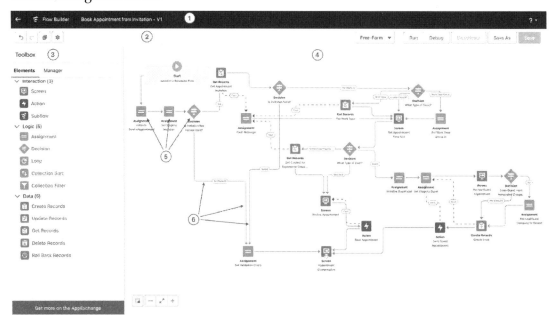

Figure 2.21: *A sample flow in the flow builder*

Here is a description of each numbered point in *figure 2.21:*

1. **The header:** The header contains the label of the flow you are working on. The back-arrow icon at the left end of the header section allows you to return to the Setup menu without saving any of the introduced changes.

2. **The toolbar:** Also known as the *button bar*. The **Flow Builder's** toolbar contains shortcut functionalities such as **Run, Debug, Undo**, and **Redo**.

3. **The Toolbox:** The toolbox is a dual-purpose pane. It contains the **Elements** tab, which can be used to add elements to the canvas, and the Manager tab, which can view a list with details of elements and resources. You can drag and drop elements from the toolbox to the Canvas.

4. **The Canvas:** This is the main area where you will create your flow.

5. **Elements:** These are the main building blocks for a Salesforce flow. Elements are where you configure specific logic, behaviors, UI components, and more.

6. **Connectors:** The connectors are used to link elements together, and they show the path the *Flow's* logic would follow in run time.

If you double-click on an element, an editor will be displayed. Here you can see the **resources** within an **element** and their values. Double-click on the **Create Lead** element from the opened flow, and you will see an editor similar to the following screenshot:

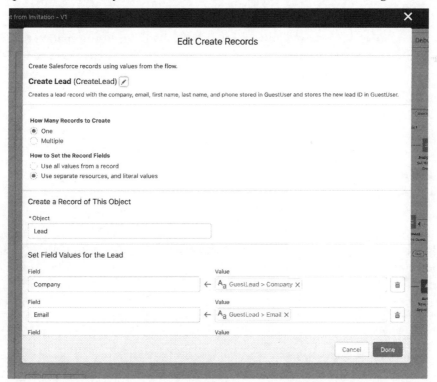

Figure 2.22: An editor displaying the resources of an element

A resource can be a **Variable, Constant, Formula, Text Template, Choice,** or **Collection Choice** Set. You will come across resources later in this chapter and in other examples where you will build **Flows**. You can learn more about resources from the following link:

https://help.salesforce.com/s/articleView?id=sf.flow_ref_resources.htm&type=5

Now that you are familiar with the **Flow Builder's** UI move on to learn about the different types of **Flows**.

The flow types

There are several types of *Flows*; each is designed for a specific set of use cases. We will focus on six core types. The names of these types could slightly change from one Salesforce release to the other. Remember that the Flow Builder is one of the tools that Salesforce has invested heavily in for the past few years. The following table contains a list of six core *Flow* types and their best suitable usage:

Flow type	Description	Best used for
Screen Flow	A flow with a UI that requires user interaction. This flow type includes screens, steps, choices, or dynamic choices.	Create a step-by-step wizard-like screen to interact with the user and gather or display information.
Autolaunched Flow with a Schedule Trigger	A flow without a UI that runs based on a scheduled time and frequency.	Create automation that runs based on a specific schedule (could be recurring).
Autolaunched Flow with No Flow Trigger	A flow without a UI that runs when invoked by other flows, Apex, REST API, and more.	Create sub-processes that can be used as building blocks or flows that run in the background.
Autolaunched Flow with a Record Trigger	A flow without a UI that runs when a record is created, updated, or deleted.	Create an automation that runs based on changes in your data (such as a change in a value of a certain record).
Platform Event Triggered Flow/ Platform Event Process	A flow without a UI that runs when a Platform Event message is received.	Create automations that runs based on received Platform Events. This is very useful when designing event-based solutions.

Flow type	Description	Best used for
Orchestrator	An orchestration contains a series of stages, each containing one or more steps. Steps can either be Interactive steps or Background steps. Orchestrations are out of this book's scope.	Create highly advanced Flows.

Table 2.1: The core types of flows

You can learn more about the Flow types and their characteristics and limitations from the following link:

https://help.salesforce.com/s/articleView?id=sf.flow_concepts_type.htm&type=5

Now that you are familiar with the *flow's* core types move on to practice creating a flow.

Practice creating a flow

Assume that you are building a small *Screen Flow* to help your call center easily create cases while speaking with the customers on the phone. There is already some very efficient out-of-the-box functionality at Salesforce that do such tasks but assume for a moment that such functionalities do not exist so that you can start with this small task to help you learn how to use the Flow Builder.

Ask yourself, what could be the steps to create a *Case*? The customer would likely call to request something or raise a concern or complaint.

You would probably:

- Start by getting some information about the customer, such as their name, phone, and email address.

- Then you would capture more details about the case, such as its type and description.

- Finally, you would create the case and the customer's contact, then display a confirmation to the user (the call center agent in this scenario).

In a real-life scenario, you may request more details, and there could be multiple other customer verification steps before that. But the above scope will be enough to start learning about the **Flow Builder**.

Go to the **Setup** page and search for the word **flows** from the search box. Click on the **Flows** menu, then click on the **New Flow** button. Choose **Screen Flow** from the popup screen. You will now see a screen similar to the following:

Figure 2.23: Building a flow, the first step

Your canvas is almost empty at this stage. You only have the **Start** and **End** elements. Click on the plus sign and choose **screen**; this will add a screen element to your flow. A popup will be displayed where you can set some values for this screen, such as the **label** and **API Name**. The label is the text that the users would see as the name of this screen in runtime, while the API Name is the actual unique name of the component that can be referenced in code or by other Flow elements.

You can already see a placeholder for the flow label at the upper part of the form, as shown in the following screenshot:

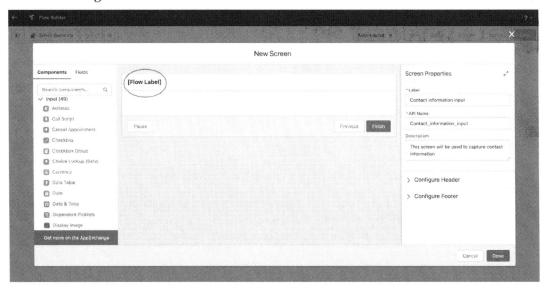

Figure 2.24: Building a flow, the second step

Note that there is a section on the right side of the popup (the screen properties) where you can configure some parameters for the header and footer of the screen. Have a look at the values there, but leave the default values. Enter a screen label and name; these are mandatory fields. As a best practice, enter a description that can help you remember the purpose of this page in the future. The description can also help explain the purpose of the screen to other developers and admins.

You now need to add a few components to the screen. On the left side, you will see a list of components categorized into *input* and *display*. In this screen, you want to capture the customer's contact name, phone, and email address. Add two *text* components (for the first and last name), one *phone* component, and one *email* component. Selecting the suitable component will help validate the input data without writing any code. For example, you could have used a *text* component to capture the email address. In that case, however, you need to write logic to validate whether the input is in the email format. Why would you reinvent the wheel? There is already a pre-built component that does that job and more.

Set the property values for each component (by clicking on the component, then set the value in the properties section). You can use the following values:

Component	Property	Value
First text component	Label	First Name
	API Name	First_Name_Input
	Required	Yes
Second text component	Label	Last Name
	API Name	**Last_Name_Input**
	Required	Yes
Phone component	API Name	**Phone_Input**
	Label	Phone
	Required	**{!$GlobalConstant.True}**
	Leave the remaining properties empty.	
Email component	API Name	Email_Input
	Label	Email
	Disabled	**{!$GlobalConstant.False}**
	Placeholder text	**emailaddress@domain.com**
	Read Only	**{!$GlobalConstant.False}**
	Required	**{!$GlobalConstant.True}**
	Leave the remaining properties empty.	

Table 2.2: Component values of the screen flow, the first screen

Values such as **{!$GlobalConstant.True}** refers to a global constant value within the context of the *Flow*. There are several global constants available, and the values of constants do not change throughout the runtime period of the *Flow*. There are also several global variables. The global variables can change their values during the runtime of the *Flow*.

Your Flow screen could now look like the following:

Figure 2.25: Building a flow, the third step

Click **Done**, then click **Save** to save your work. Choose a label and API name for the *Flow*, such as **Create a Case** and **Create_a_Case**, respectively. If you want to see your Flow in action, click the *Run* button from the toolbar. Your screen flow already has some working functionalities, such as a way to indicate mandatory fields. But it still lacks the capability to create a Contact and a Case; nothing will happen at this stage if you click the **Finish** button.

You can add the fields to capture the Case details (type and description) to this screen or do that in another. Separating this into two screens has multiple benefits, including providing a simpler UI for the user that is not cluttered with too many fields.

From the **canvas**, click on the plus icon again, then choose **screen** to add another screen. Set the label and API name of the screen to something meaningful such as **Case Information Input** and **Case_Information_Input**, respectively. Add a **picklist** component and a **text** component to the screen. Picklist components are very useful when you want to provide the user with a pre-defined set of values to choose from.

Set the properties of these components as per the following table:

Component	Property	Value
Picklist component	Label	Case Type
	API Name	**Case_Type_Input**
	Required	Yes
	Data Type	Text
	Let Users Select Multiple Options	No
	Choice	Click the plus icon to create a new choice resource. From the popup menu, choose **Picklist Choice Set**. Set the API name to Case_Type, the object value to **Case**, the Data type value to **Picklist**, and the field value to Type. Similar to *Figure 2.26*. This will help you create a resource while setting up the value of the picklist component.
	Leave the remaining properties empty.	
Text component	API Name	**Case_Description_Input**
	Label	Case Description
	Required	No
	Leave the remaining properties empty.	

Table 2.3: Component values of the screen flow, second screen

Here is a screenshot from the popup page you used while creating the **Picklist Choice** resource:

Figure 2.26: Creating a picklist choice resource

Save and run your flow. You will notice that the **finish** button on the first screen got renamed automatically during runtime to **next**. If you fill in the required value of the first screen and click **next**, you will see the second screen. You created a multi-step wizard in a few minutes! Your Flow still does not create any records, however. This will be the next step.

From the canvas, click on the plus icon and add a **Create Records** element. You will find it under the *data* category.

You need to add two of these elements. One to create the **Contact** record and one to create the **Case** record. Note that the **contact Id** generated from the first element needs to be passed to the second as you need to link the newly created **Case** to the created **Contact**.

Set the properties of these elements as per the following table.

Element	Property	Value
First create record component	Label	Create Contact
	API Name	**Create_Contact**
	How many records to create	One

Element	Property	Value
	How to set the record fields	Use separate resources, and literal values
	Object	Contact
	Set field Values for the Contact. field FirstName	`{!First_Name_Input}`
	Set field Values for the Contact. field LastName	`{!Last_Name_Input}`
	Set field Values for the Contact. field Phone	`{!Phone_Input.value}`
	Set field Values for the Contact. field Email	`{!Email_Input.value}`
Second create record component	Label	**Create Case**
	API Name	`Create_Case`
	How Many Records to Create	One
	How to Set the Record fields	Use separate resources, and literal values
	Object	Case
	Set field Values for the Contact. field **Type**	`{!Case_Type_Input}`
	Set field Values for the Contact. field **Description**	`{!Case_Description_ Input}`
	Set field Values for the Contact. field **ContactId**	`{!Create_Contact}` This is where we are passing the contact id of the first element to this element as an input.

Table 2.4: Component values of the two record creation elements

Your canvas could look now similar to the following screenshot:

Figure 2.27: Flow canvas after adding the two record creation elements

We now need to add one more screen to display the case creation confirmation message to the user. Add another screen at the end of your Flow, set the values of its properties as you did to the previous screens, and add a Display Text component. Set the API name to something relevant and add a descriptive message to its body, such as **Congratulations! Case created.** Your canvas could look now similar to the following screenshot:

Figure 2.28: Flow canvas after adding the confirmation screen element

Save and run your Flow. Fill in the required fields until the last screen. Check your Contact and Case objects; the new records should be there. Your first screen flow should look like the following in runtime:

Create a Case

* First Name
Tameem

* Last Name
Bahri

* Phone
123456

* Email
TameemTest@somedomain.com

Next

Figure 2.29: Your Flow in runtime, the first screen

Your second screen flow should look like the following in runtime:

Create a Case

* Case Type
Electronic

Case Description
A problem with a bought device.

Previous   Next

Figure 2.30: Your Flow in runtime, the second screen

Finally, your third screen flow should look like the following in runtime:

Create a Case

Case created!

Previous   Finish

Figure 2.31: Your Flow in runtime, the third screen

You may be wondering how to deploy this Flow. How to make it accessible to the users outside the Flow Builder. You will come across that in the chapters to come. For now, you managed to build a simple Flow that adds value to the business in a few minutes. The requirements for this Flow were significantly simplified. In a real-life scenario, you might consider checking for existing similar contact and case records before creating duplicates. You would likely need to display the case number at the end of the *Flow* to inform the user of the case number. Plus, some other functionalities. In your Developer Edition org, you can find an example of such advanced Flow, it is also called Create a Case, but it is part of a managed package installed by default on all Developer Edition orgs. Here is how it looks:

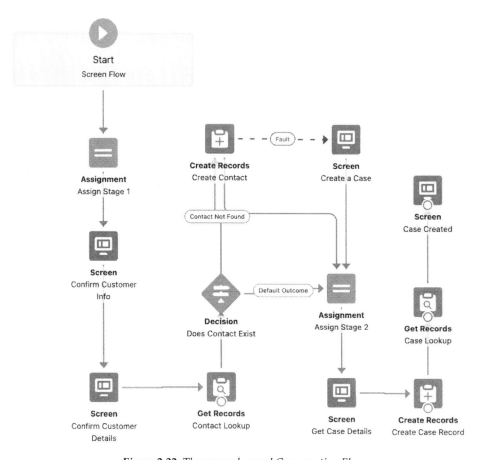

Figure 2.32: The more advanced Case creation Flow

Look at it, and explore how the different elements pass variables to each other and interact. You will come across other Flow examples in the chapters to come.

Next, you will be introduced to **Apex**, the programming language supported by the Salesforce platform.

Get introduced to the Salesforce Apex and triggers

Apex is a modern, object-oriented programming language fully hosted on the **Salesforce platform**. This means that it is compiled and executed in the cloud. Salesforce even provides an **IDE** to write Apex code in the cloud called the **Developer Console**. Apex is easier to write and test than similar programming languages (such as **Java**, which is the root of Apex) due to the nature of the **Salesforce platform**. For example, writing a code that queries and updates a set of Salesforce records is more straightforward in **Apex**

because you do not need to worry about hosting your code, connecting to a data source, or executing logic through a data access layer.

Similar to other object-oriented languages, your code is encapsulated inside a **Class**. An instance of a Class is called an **Object**. You can also write **Apex** code directly in **Triggers** (although the best practice is to invoke a class from within a Trigger instead). A **Trigger** is a code snippet that gets executed upon certain data-level transactions. These transactions are:

- Before inserting a record
- Before updating a record
- Before deleting a record
- After inserting a record
- After updating a record
- After deleting a record
- After undeleting a record

This book will not cover the details of Apex programming as it can easily fill a book by itself. Several available books are available to teach Apex programming, including sections about trigger patterns and best practices. However, to get a brief idea about Apex, classes, and triggers. You will build a class that does a similar job to the Flow you created in the previous section.

As a reminder, you managed to build a Flow that does the following:

You would probably:

- Gather some information about the customer, such as their name, phone, and email address.
- Capture more details about the case, such as its type and description.
- Create the case and the customer's contact.

Apex does not have a UI to interact directly with the user; you will need to build a UI using **Visualforce** or **Lightning Components** that invokes actions from the Apex class. The Apex class you will develop will hardcode the input values to simplify things.

Start by opening the **Developer Console** in your **Salesforce Developer Edition** org. You can find the link by clicking the **gear** icon at the top right of the page, as shown in the following screenshot:

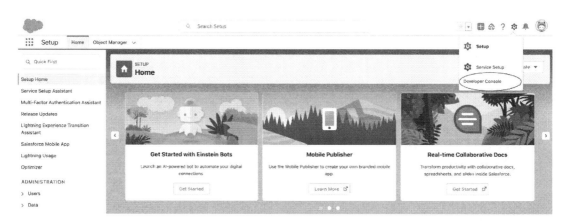

***Figure 2.33:** Opening the Developer Console*

This will open the Developer Console in a new browser's window / tab. Choose **File | New | Apex Class** from the menu. A popup will request the class name; name it **MyFirstClass**. Please copy the following code and paste it into the body of your class:

```
public class MyFirstClass {
    public void createCaseAndContact(){
        Contact oNewContact = createContact('Tom', 'Smith', 'TSmith@
somedomain.com', '+447900000000');
        Insert oNewContact;
        Case oNewCase = createCase('Electronic', 'Created via Apex',
oNewContact.Id);
        Insert oNewCase;
    }


    private Contact createContact(String pFirstName, String pLastName,
String pEmail, String pPhone){
        Contact oNewContact = new Contact();
        oNewContact.FirstName = pFirstName;
        oNewContact.LastName = pLastName;
        oNewContact.Email = pEmail;
        oNewContact.Phone = pPhone;


        Return oNewContact;
    }
```

```
    private Case createCase(String pCasteType, String pCaseDescription, ID
pContactID){

        Case oNewCase = new Case();

        oNewCase.Type = pCasteType;

        oNewCase.Description = pCaseDescription;

        oNewCase.ContactID = pContactID;


        Return oNewCase;

    }

}
```

Within this class, there are three methods **create CaseAndContact, createContact,** and **createCase**. A **method** is a programmed function with specific inputs (called **parameters**, a method could have none or more parameters), does a particular task, and returns an output (some methods do not return any output).

Running/executing the **method createCaseAndContact** will invoke the two other methods. **createContact** will create and populate a **Contact** record (represented within Apex as an object of the class **Contact** as all Salesforce objects are considered classes in **Apex**) and return it to the calling method (**createCaseAndContact** in this case). **createCase** will create and populate a **Case** record/object and return it to the calling method. **createCaseAndContact** will receive the output of both methods and then insert both records into their respective Salesforce objects.

You will also notice hardcoded values in the class, such as **Tom, Smith, TSmith@ somedomain.com**. This is different from how you would write your classes in real life. Instead, you would use parameters passed from the UI (built using VisualForce, Lightning Components) or a related API. However, that level of **Apex** complexity is beyond the scope of this book.

To run this code, click the **debug** menu and choose the **Open Execute Anonymous Window** menu item. Copy and paste the following code to the popup.

```
MyFirstClass oMyFirstClass = new MyFirstClass();

oMyFirstClass.createCaseAndContact();
```

Your screen could look like the following:

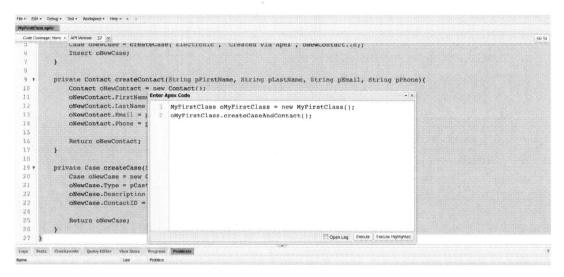

Figure 2.34: Anonymous Apex window within the Developer Console

Click the **Execute** button, then navigate to the **Cases** tab in your org (you can do that by searching the word **Cases** from the **App Launcher** search bar). You should be able to locate a newly created Case with the same set of data hardcoded in the Apex Class.

What next? You can have a look at a simple Trigger. From the **Developer Console,** click on **File | New | Apex Trigger**. Name the trigger **CaseTrigger**, and set the associated **sObject** to **Case,** similar to the following screenshot:

Figure 2.35: Creating a Trigger for the Case object

Please copy the following code and paste it into the body of your trigger.

```
trigger CaseTrigger on Case (before insert) {
        if (Trigger.isInsert) {
          if (Trigger.isBefore) {
              for(Case iCase : Trigger.new) {
                  iCase.Description = 'This statement has been added by a
trigger. '+ iCase.Description;
              }
```

```
        }
    }
}
```

This trigger adds the hardcoded statement This statement has been added by a trigger to the beginning of the value stored in the **Description** field of the created **Case** record. Run the code of your **MyFirstClass** again, then check the newly created **case;** you will notice the added statement in the **description** field.

Apex code and Apex Triggers are powerful building blocks for the Salesforce platform. They are heavily used by Salesforce customers who want to add sophisticated customizations to their orgs that cannot be done using the Flow Builder and other point-and-click development tools.

Next, you will have a brief intro to **Lightning Components** and the **Salesforce Lightning Design System (SLDS)**.

Introduction to the Salesforce Lightning Components and the Lightning Design System

You learned in *Chapter 1, Introduction to the Salesforce Platform*, that **Lightning Components** are one of the building blocks in Salesforce that allows you to create fully custom UI elements and pages. Lightning Components can be designed to communicate with each other and can be nested within each other. Before the existence of Lightning Components, Salesforce developers used Visualforce pages to achieve the same. Lightning Components are usually more performant than Visualforce pages and designed to support a modern event-driven architecture where an event raised by one component can be received and reacted on by another.

Lightning Components have a clear edge over Visualforce when designing UI-heavy screens, such as screens with dozens of input fields where a change in one immediately impacts the others.

Lightning Components can be built using two different programming models, **Aura Components** (the earliest version of Lightning Components) and **Lightning Web Components (LWC)**, which are designed to allow developers familiar with other JavaScript-based languages and modern HTML to develop Lightning Components in Salesforce easily. LWC and Aura Components can coexist on the same page. Lightning Components can be used in the App Builder regardless of whether they are LWC or Aura based.

Developing a custom Lightning Component or Visualforce page can be time intensive, and the efforts required are more or less aligned with other modern programming languages. Developing a Lightning Component or Visualforce page requires coding skills. Such components are usually required for complex applications with sophisticated fancy UIs, and learning how to develop/code them is a great career advantage for Salesforce developers.

Rapid application development, on the other hand, is all about building, testing, adjusting, and rolling out applications quickly. Therefore, learning how to develop Lightning Components and Visualforce pages is out of the scope of this book. You can learn more about developing Aura Components from the following link:

https://developer.salesforce.com/docs/atlas.en-us.lightning.meta/lightning/intro_framework.htm

You can learn how to develop **Lightning Web Components (LWC)** from the following link:

https://lwc.dev

You can also learn about **Visualforce** (which is still used by many Salesforce customers) from the following link:

https://developer.salesforce.com/docs/atlas.en-us.pages.meta/pages/pages_intro.htm

Salesforce also created ready-to-use HTML and CSS UI elements that the developers can easily use while developing Lightning Components and Visualforce pages. These UI elements are part of the **Salesforce Lightning Design System (SLDS)** framework, which allows the developers to focus on developing the core logic of their components and worry less about how they look. The SLDS is open-source and can be used by other non-Salesforce technologies. It can be compared to other common UI frameworks, such as **Bootstrap**.

You can learn more about SLDS and see some live examples at the following link:

https://www.lightningdesignsystem.com

The combination of SLDS and Lightning Components or Visualforce pages allows Salesforce developers to build sophisticated, responsive, pixel-perfect UIs for their applications.

Summary

This chapter taught you a lot about the primary Salesforce building blocks and development tools. You started by understanding how Salesforce licenses work and get assigned to users. You learned how easy and quick it is to create type-aware fields and custom objects that can extend the rich standard data model offered by Salesforce. You also learned how to control the UI displaying records of these objects by editing page layouts. You then explored the very capable sharing and visibility module in Salesforce, which can help you control which objects, fields, and records are accessible to each user. Later on, you started practicing with the App Builder and Report Builder; and then you got introduced to the very capable point-and-click development tool Flow Builder. You finally got introduced to more coding building blocks such as Apex, Triggers, Lightning Components, and Visualforce pages.

You are now set to practice developing your first Salesforce application. Buckle up and move to the next chapter.

Join our book's Discord space

Join the book's Discord Workspace for Latest updates, Offers, Tech happenings around the world, New Release and Sessions with the Authors:

https://discord.bpbonline.com

CHAPTER 3

Develop a Sample Salesforce Application: PbP Phonebook

Introduction

This chapter will introduce you to the **Rapid Application Development (RAD)** methodology and lifecycle for Salesforce applications. Worth mentioning that a considerable part of this methodology is interoperable and can be used with other RAD tools. You will gain a more detailed understanding of the RAD methodology and application lifecycle in *Chapter 4, Learn the Salesforce Application Development Lifecycle*, where all your how and why questions will be answered.

In this chapter, you will see a practical example in action first. This will help you link back the theoretical information you will learn in *Chapter 4, Learn the Salesforce Application Development Lifecycle*, and *Chapter 5, Understand the Supporting Tools and Artefacts*, to a practical experience. You will further solidify that practical experience in *Chapter 7, Create a Sample Application: Solve and Build the Application - Part 1, Chapter 8, Create a Sample Application: Solve and Build the Application - Part 2, Chapter 9, Create a Sample Application: Test and deploy the application*, and *Chapter 10 Tips and Tricks, and the Way Forward* while designing, building, and deploying a more sophisticated Salesforce application.

The primary concept of RAD is to develop and deploy applications fast, which helps realize the application's **return on investment (ROI)** quickly. However, doing so without following the suitable methodology, governance, and documentation could lead to developing a very hard-to-maintain group of siloed applications that lack a vision—significantly impacting the value gained from RAD in the first place. The selected example application in this chapter is intentionally simple to show that even the most straightforward applications can go wrong without using the proper software development methodology.

You will need a Salesforce Developer Edition org to practice the exercises in this chapter. You can use the same org you used in the previous chapter or sign up for a new one using the following link:

https://developer.salesforce.com/signup

Let us have a look next at the structure of this chapter.

Structure

The chapter covers the following topics:

- Introducing the high-level requirements

- Read between the lines and extract more requirements

- Define the high-level process flow

- Design the data model

- Design a low-fidelity prototype

- Build, validate, and rectify the application

- Deploy the application

- Identified gaps and the lessons learned

Objectives

By the end of this chapter, you will gain practical experience with RAD methodology for Salesforce applications. This will set you up for the following chapters that will further explain the methodology and the application lifecycle. You will gain hands-on experience to which you can relate the theoretical information, making it easier to turn the acquired knowledge and expertise into a second nature that you can apply consistently in your professional life.

Introducing the high-level requirements

Project and application requirements are gathered in multiple ways and are usually managed by **Business Analysts (BAs)** and **Product Owners (POs)**. Several methods and techniques exist to gather, document, and share these requirements. This book is not going to cover this activity in detail. It will assume the requirements have already been gathered by previous activity. Investing in a strong team of BAs and POs is an excellent plan to ensure a healthy pipeline of prioritized requirements for your application.

This chapter uses the following assumed hypothetical scenario to create the high-level requirements.

The CRM department of **PbP World Traders (PWT)** would like to create an application to manage their customer contacts. PWT is a global digital retailer that sells various goods via multiple channels. PWT uses Salesforce to manage its sales pipeline. All their customers are stored as **Accounts** (for enterprise customers) or **Person Accounts** (for individuals). Each enterprise customer can have one or more Contacts defined in the system representing the key individuals within that enterprise.

Due to the nature of PWT's business, it is of utmost importance to have up-to-date contact details for all the individuals they negotiate business deals with, including individual and enterprise customers.

In the past, PWT struggled to introduce a standardized process for updating these contact details. This time, PWT is looking to develop a specialized application to help them solve this challenge.

Your BAs conducted several interviews with PWT and gathered the following requirements.

- The contacts could have one or more phone numbers that they can be reached at. PWT would like to store all these numbers and identify which is used on WhatsApp.

- PWT would like to introduce a bi-annual contact refreshment exercise where third-party contact center agents are expected to attempt calling the contact and ensure that PWT is retaining their latest contact details (phone numbers)

- A *task* record of contacting each contact is expected to be created in Salesforce and assigned to a third-party agent. Once the call is made, the task should be marked as completed.

- When an agent calls a customer, the agent is expected to ask a predefined set of questions. PWT could change these questions from time to time.

These four requirements are all that you received from the BA team. You might have noticed that they are written in different ways. The first two are written as high-level desires of PWT, the third is written as a *solution* rather than a *requirement*, and the fourth is expressed as a process. This should not happen ideally, but it is precisely what you should expect in the real world due to multiple factors. Endless reasons could make it challenging to extract requirements from users, including personal reasons such as the natural resistance to change. Moreover, in reality, the level of skills and experience amongst the BAs will vary; this is common across all other roles in the software industry and, to a reasonable extent, every other industry.

Those who have worked in the software development industry for years can tell that you do not necessarily need a team of superstars to build a good application, but a team with a good mix of talents who can cover for each other and eventually play together as a high performant team. In other words, requirements of such poor quality should still be expected in the real world. As a software designer and developer, you should be prepared to help close the gap by asking questions, challenging requirements, and ensuring you understand the *big picture* (how the application works end to end).

Next, you will learn to scrutinize and challenge requirements, read between the lines, enhance existing requirements, and reveal hidden and non-communicated requirements.

Read between the lines and extract more requirements

Professionals use multiple techniques to extract an adequate level of detail for requirements, such as breaking the requirements into smaller parts and probing them further, **User Experience (UX)** research, and the utilization of a comparable product.

A **comparable product** is, by definition, another product with similar characteristics to the one that is compared and delivers similar functionality. Software products are no exception. You can try to learn from comparable products in the same industry/vertical. However, the best practice is to avoid limiting your ideas and think of the product functionalities holistically, then find a comparable product or more that you can learn from.

Try to break down the shared requirements and probe with more questions. Start with the first requirement.

- The contacts could have one or more phone numbers that they can be reached at. PWT would like to store all these numbers and identify which is used on WhatsApp

This requirement can be broken down into the following requirements, and each can be probed with a question.

- *The contacts could have one or more phone numbers that they can be reached at.* You can ask, what is the maximum number of phone numbers that can be stored against a single contact? You can easily assume that the number is infinite, but that is far from reality and would add unnecessary complexity to your proposed solution. You can also ask who would be reaching out to these numbers and how? Phone calls can be made in multiple ways, including **Voice Over IP (VoIP)** technologies such as **Skype**. Do not just rely on assumptions.

- *PWT would like to store all these numbers and identify which is used on WhatsApp.* You can ask how many WhatsApp numbers PWT would like to keep for each contact.

After the probing question, you can end up with a more detailed requirement, such as the following.

- **Requirement 1**: The contacts could have at least one and up to five different phone numbers that a sales, service, and third-party agent can reach via the standard enterprise telephony solution.

- **Requirement 2**: Each contact can have a maximum of one phone number associated with WhatsApp.

This looks more solid. A requirement number was added to help refer back to a requirement later in this chapter. In *Chapter 4, Learn the Salesforce Application Development Lifecycle* , you will learn about *user stories*, which provide an effective way to format requirements that minimizes the chances of misunderstanding and gives a greater view of the requirement's overall impact on the solution.

Try to break down the second shared requirements and probe with more questions.

- *PWT would like to introduce a bi-annual contact refreshment exercise where third-party contact center agents are expected to attempt calling the contact and ensure that PWT retains their latest contact details (phone numbers).* This requirement is clear enough as the primary purpose of it is to give you a better understanding of the processing timeframe and the involved actors (the third-party contact center agents in this case).

No need to change or elaborate on the requirement; add a requirement number to it, such as.

- **Requirement 3**: PWT would like to introduce a bi-annual contact refreshment exercise where third-party contact center agents are expected to attempt calling the contact and ensure that PWT retains their latest contact details (phone numbers).

Moving on to the next requirement.

- *A task record of contacting each contact is expected to be created in Salesforce and assigned to a third-party agent.* This requirement is written as a solution (by suggesting using the Task object). You should look for the details behind this proposed solution and ask what the expected fields/data to be captured in this record are. Such information could lead to selecting a different object or even using a custom object. You can also ask about the mechanism of assigning such tasks to third-party agents; is that expected to be based on spreading the load equally on the agents, or are there other considerations you need to be aware of?

- *Once the call is made, the task should be marked as completed.* The obvious question is what would happen if the call was unsuccessful, such as when a contact does not pick up or the number appears invalid. A different action should be taken based on the outcome of the call attempt that has been missed in this requirement. This question leads to another, how many times should the agent attempt to reach out to a contact? What should be the cool-down period between the reaching-out attempts?

After the probing question, you can end up with more detailed requirements, such as the following.

- **Requirement 4**: A record that represents a task of contacting each contact is expected to be auto-created in Salesforce with the following details (a subject of the task which indicates that this is a bi-annual contact refreshment exercise, a due date of two weeks from the current date, a status field that includes the values *Assigned*, *Completed*, and *Deferred*). The generated records should be assigned to the available agents equally. Each record should be linked to the contact and the user to whom the task is assigned.

- **Requirement 5:** If the call was successful, the agent is expected to update the status to *Completed*, and if the call was unsuccessful, the agent is expected to update the status to *Deferred*. A follow-up activity should be created automatically for Deferred call attempts. The follow-up activity would contain the same values as the original activity but with the word *Follow up* appended to the subject and a *due date* after one week. The follow-up activity should be assigned to the same user who handled the original activity unless that user is not active anymore. In that case, it should be assigned to a random agent.

- **Requirement 6**: After five failed reach-out attempts, the system should stop auto-creating follow-up activities and mark the Contact *unreachable*.

- **Requirement 7**: Upon successful reach-out attempts, the contact should be marked as *up to date* with a timestamp that indicates the last data refreshment date.

You could extract even more requirements by continuing probing. This is a good example of why a good developer should ask questions and challenge the given requirements rather than implement them without question. This is also a good example that can explain why the focus of the requirement should be within the *what* and *why* spaces and never extend to the *how* space.

Moving on to the next and final requirement.

- *When an agent calls a customer, the agent is expected to ask a predefined set of questions.* You can ask how many questions are expected to be asked on average; this information could impact the way you design the UI of the solution.

- *PWT could change these questions from time to time.* You can ask how often this would happen. And would such change occur during the contact refreshment process? The latter question could open the door for a much more complicated challenge where two copies of the questionnaire are expected to be live simultaneously.

After the probing question, you can end up with the following requirements.

- **Requirement 8**: When an agent calls a customer, the agent is expected to ask a predefined set of questions. Historically, PWT used five questions on average.

- **Requirement 9**: PWT could change these questions multiple times during the year. However, only one active version of these questions can be available for use. PWT can only publish a new set of questions when no ongoing contact refreshment activity is taking place.

You can start developing your solution now that you have detailed requirements. Right? Absolutely not. Developing applications on Salesforce is quick and easy. However, this does not mean you can start developing without a proper design first. Next, you will create high-level process flows and low-fidelity prototypes to help verify the proposed solution before you start developing it.

Define the high-level process flow

Documenting a high-level process flow can take multiple shapes and forms. However, the best results are achieved when using a standard diagramming language. Standard diagrams evolved through multiple years by professionals who cumulatively enhanced and matured these diagrams into a common architectural language. A language known and understood by many professionals, a common tongue to help people exchange ideas regardless of boundaries and time. One of the most mature business process diagramming languages is the **Business Process Modeling Notation (BPMN)**. BPMN is an open standard to document business process workflows in an intuitive graphical manner, making it easier to read and understand by technical and non-technical stakeholders such as BAs, developers, architects, and even end users.

You can learn more about BPMN from the following link:

https://www.bpmn.org

You can also practice creating some BPMN diagrams using tools such as **Lucidchart**. You can learn more about that from the following link:

https://www.lucidchart.com/pages/bpmn

BPMN can be used to design and document business processes, not requirements. However, BPMN can represent how these requirements would fit together to deliver a specific functionality within the company. The business process representing the expanded list of requirements could look like the following:

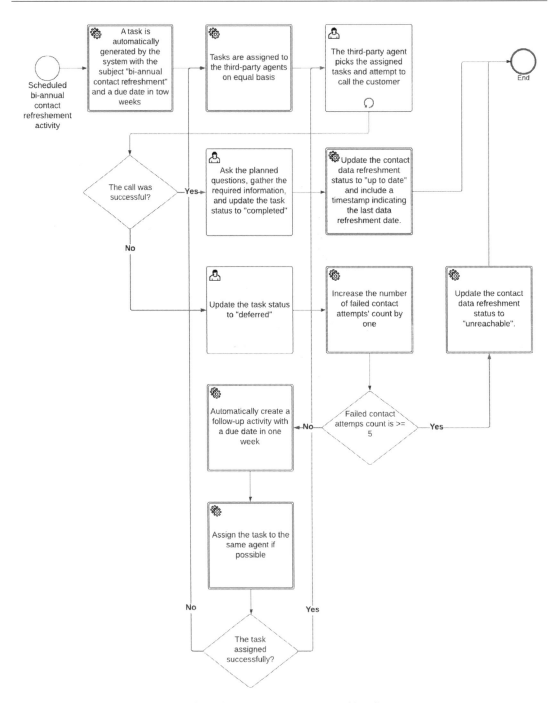

Figure 3.1*: The task creation, assignment, and handling process*

The diagram could be further elaborated to reflect more details. However, it is a best practice to determine the targeted scope and level of details upfront to avoid adding too many details that will add no value. You can create multiple versions of the same diagram for different stakeholders based on their roles and the level of detail they are after.

Another best practice is to fit the BPMN diagrams on one page, regardless of the page size. And use a horizontal flow whenever possible (the width of the printed book will restrict the diagrams in this book).

You can also create another BPMN diagram to document the process of creating a new set of questionnaires.

The BPMN will explain in a glance what needs multiple pages to explain in words. Maintaining and keeping the diagram up to date is also easier, considering its summarized nature.

BPMN diagrams are usually created and maintained by BAs. However, depending on their level of detail, architects and developers might also participate in creating and maintaining it.

Next, you need to design a data model for your application.

Design the data model

The design of the underlying data model for a particular solution is highly crucial and could determine if an application is successful or not. A sub-optimal data model can introduce significant technical debt to the solution and impact its chances for success. A sub-optimal data model could also affect the user/customer experience, a defining factor in any application's success or failure.

The best way to design (and simultaneously document) a data model is to create a data model diagram (sometimes referred to as **Entity Relationship Diagram or ERD**).

There are multiple ERD notations in use today. This book will use the crow's foot database notation. You can learn more about this notation from the following link:

https://support.microsoft.com/en-us/office/create-a-diagram-with-crow-s-foot-database-notation-1ec22af9-3bd3-4354-b2b5-ed5752af6769

You can practice creating an ERD diagram for free using tools such as Lucidcharts. You can learn more from the following link:

https://www.lucidchart.com/pages/templates/erd-crows-foot

Creating a data model diagram is part of the application solutioning stage. At the solutioning stage, you need to think about how to solve the shared requirements considering any limitations and the overall desired end-to-end solution. Solutioning is a lengthy process that requires a good understanding of the platform, a solid technical acumen of what can and cannot be done, and much imagination to think about how everything would fit together.

You will learn more about solution creation in the chapters to come using practical examples. You will also learn how to shape, communicate, validate, and document your design decisions. However, for the time being, this will be skipped for simplicity.

One of the critical design decisions for the PWT application could be regarding using the standard Task object (to represent the contact refreshment task assigned to the third-party agent) or replacing it with a custom object.

Assume that the proposed solution for this application is the following:

- The standard **Task** object represents the contact refreshment task assigned to the third-party agent.

- A set of custom fields will be introduced to the **Contact** object to hold the additional required phone numbers.

- Two new custom objects will be introduced to represent the questions used during the call with the customer and the gathered answers.

The data model diagram for this solution will look like the following:

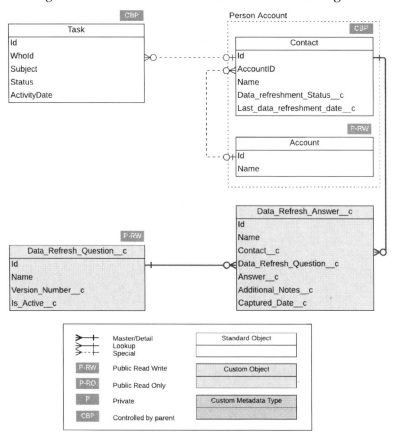

Figure 3.2: *The data model diagram*

You can notice the following in the preceding figure, *Figure 3.2.*

- Not all object fields are listed. Data model diagrams can have multiple levels of detail. The level you see in *Figure 3.2* is the logical-level which shows the key fields for each object. The logical-level data model diagram usually is good enough to design, document, and communicate the general structure of your data, which is what we are after at this stage. The physical-level data model diagram will help you thoroughly document your data model.

- You will notice that all objects have an *ID* and *Name* fields. These two fields are standard in Salesforce for all objects (standard and custom), with few exceptions.

- Adding labels that describe the OWD settings for a given object to your data model diagram is a good practice. For example, in *Figure 3.2*, you can see that some objects have an OWD **Controlled by Parent (CBR)**. The OWD of objects related to a master object via a master/detail relationship is always CBR. The **Data_Refresh_ Answer__c** object is an example. You can optionally add a CBR symbol for child/ detail objects such as **Data_Refresh_Answer__c**.

- When an object is linked to two master objects, it is referred to as a *junction object*, such as the case with the **Data_Refresh_Answer__c** object, which is linked to both the Contact and the **Data_Refresh_Question__c** objects via master/detail relationships. The junction object inherits the OWD of its *primary master*, which is the first object that a master/detail relationship has been established with.

  While the data model diagrams used in Salesforce are standard and similar to what is used in any other technology, combining OWD settings with the data model diagram is specific to Salesforce and helps you understand at a glance the basics of the sharing model you are planning to use.

- The *Person Account* is a special type of the standard *Account* object. A *Person Account* record is technically a combination of one *Account* record and one *Contact* record. It represents individual customers (rather than enterprise customers, such as companies and so).

- You will notice that the **Data_Refresh_Answer__c** object is linked to the Contact only. You would typically want to relate it to the Contact and the Task to reflect the correct relationship between these objects. Each **Data_Refresh_Answer__c** record is ideally associated with one *Task* record. However, you cannot create lookup relationships to the *Task* object in Salesforce; this is one of the limitations of this object. It is essential to create a data model diagram for your Salesforce application (similar to any software application that uses a database) as it helps you and your team to identify such gaps and address them (for example, in this case, you might decide to compromise and use the standard Task object despite the limitation. Alternatively, you could introduce a custom object instead of the standard Task object).

Now that you have a planned data model design, the UX designers can work with the architects to design a low-fidelity prototype for the application.

Design a low-fidelity prototype

The prototype can cover the whole solution or the most critical parts of it. Building the prototype must be very fast and agile, or otherwise, it will lose its purpose and value. Several tools in the market can help you sketch out a set of UIs for your prototypes, such as **Figma**, **Adobe XD**, **Marvel**, **Justinmind**, and **Lucidcharts**. The diagrams in this book are created using the latter. Some tools can make a still image wireframe, while others can create an interactive set of wireframes that form a testable prototype. Remember that scratching a UI on paper or a whiteboard is a good starting point, too. Use the technique and tool that suits you best and ensures that the prototype is created fast and of adequate quality.

The UX designers would typically create the prototype. However, depending on the size of the team, developers and BAs might also take part in this. The developed prototype must respect the design language used in Salesforce. Ideally, the UI elements should be part of the **Salesforce Lightning Design System (SLDS)**. A slight deviation is usually acceptable, but the primary design language and elements must be respected; otherwise, the created UIs could provide a sub-optimal experience to the user. Many of the UI prototyping tools allow you to create custom UI elements. You can use such a feature to build your own library of SLDS-compatible UI elements.

The UX designers usually focus on screens with user interaction, such as the screen the third-party agent would see upon picking a specific task. This screen's wireframe/ prototype could look as the following:

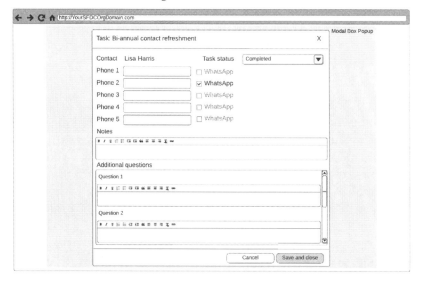

***Figure 3.3**: The wireframe of the screen used to handle a data refreshment task by third-party agents*

In this screen wireframe, you can notice the following.

- The UI elements used are not fully compliant with SLDS. However, there are no alien UI components used. The developer should easily know which UI element should be used on this screen.

- It might take several iterations to build an optimized UI. This is precisely why the prototyping stage is essential because it offers you a quick and cost-efficient way to try things out with the users before you start a more time-consuming coding exercise. This concept is true even if you use point-and-click tools, such as Salesforce Flow Builder, to develop your screens. Scratching a set of wireframes should always be quicker; if not, you need to review the process used to create these wireframes/prototypes, as it might include some areas to improve.

- It is a best practice to use a UI layout that aligns the critical fields on the UI with the shape of the letter F. This will ensure that the critical fields will intuitively catch the user's attention. In *Figure 3.3*, the most important fields are the task title, contact name (read-only), task status (specific pre-defined values from a dropdown list), phone numbers (editable in case the user needs to update them), and the additional notes field. The additional questions and answers list are assumed to be less critical at this stage, yet they still fall under the F-letter shape, more or less, as shown in the following image:

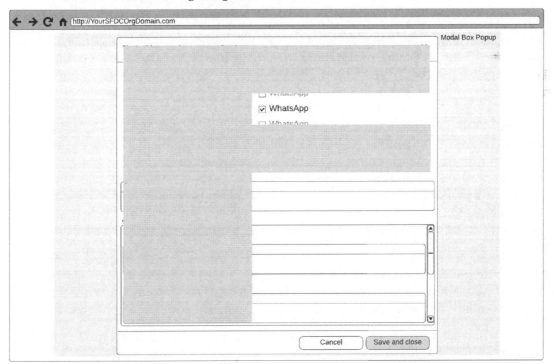

Figure 3.4: *The key UI elements should be aligned in an F-letter shape*

The prototype must be validated and tested with the end users and adjusted based on their feedback. It should also be tested against other comparable products in the market (if available). This will help inspire the designer to create an intuitive UI aligned with the typical behaviors the user expects. For example, many applications and web applications that use a data input popup screen will offer two buttons at the bottom right corner of the page. One of these buttons would save the data and close the popup, while the other would cancel any data changes and close the popup. Your custom-built screen should align with these expectations. Even simple experiences, such as the location of these buttons, could make a difference to the end user.

Users have always preferred applications with intuitive UIs. This is particularly tangible in customer-facing applications, where the end-user would simply switch from an application with a non-friendly UI to another with a more intuitive and friendlier UI. The impact of poor UI on agent-facing applications (applications designed to be used internally by agents/employees of an enterprise) is different, as these users rarely get a chance to switch to another application. The impact of poor UI on agent-facing applications is usually measured by less agent productivity.

Now that you have a low-fidelity prototype, you can start building your application.

Build, validate, and rectify the application

It is time to start building your solution and interactively validate it with the right stakeholders to gather feedback and rectify the application accordingly. In a RAD environment, this happens in iterations called **Sprints**. The RAD concepts find their home very well in the **Agile Delivery Methodology**. This should not be surprising, as the software industry first spawned the agile methodology. The fundamental concept of agile delivery is to allow closer collaboration between the tech team building software and other stakeholders. The best way to achieve this level of collaboration is by bringing the stakeholders closer to the development process and including them in the testing and validation activity, which happens frequently and iteratively as part of the delivery sprints. In comparison, testing and validation would occur after development in a classic Waterfall Delivery Methodology, leaving less room to adjust the software. You will learn more about the **Agile Delivery Methodology** and its relationship with Salesforce application development in *Chapter 4, Learn the Salesforce Application Development Lifecycle*.

You have already defined and documented the high-level process for this application (there could be several processes in more complex applications). You designed the logical-level data model and created a prototype. These three artifacts are part of the design of the overall solution. You now need to create a detailed solution for each identified user story.

The following diagram illustrates the relationship between your artifacts and the detailed solution you will create next:

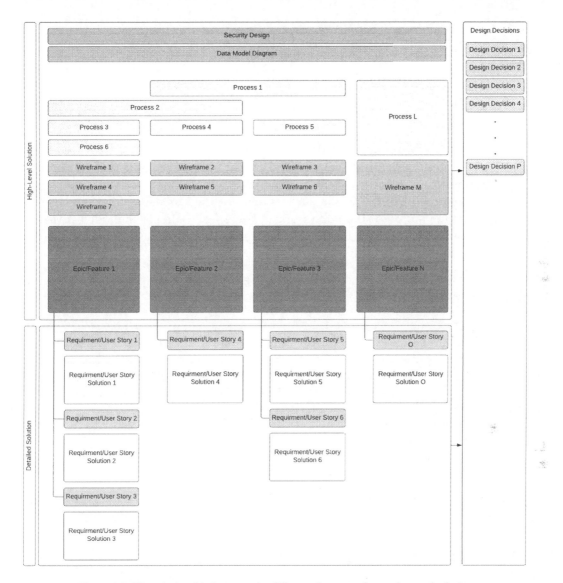

Figure 3.5: The relationship between the different elements of an end-to-end solution

You can notice the following from the previous diagram.

- Each epic/feature must have at least one requirement/user story. There is no upper limit to the number of requirements/user stories associated with a single epic/feature; however, it is best to keep the number manageable and relevant.

- Each requirement/user story must have one and only one associated solution. The solution can have multiple bullet points/steps and should reflect the latest confirmed/approved solution per the design decisions. Not all requirement/user story solutions must have a related design decision. However, for those who have, the link between the solution and the design decision must be established and kept up to date.

- Each epic/feature can have zero or more wireframes and could be covered by zero or more BPMN process diagrams. Some epics/features might not have an associated UI, and others could be too simple to create a BPMN. Epics/features could be related to one or more design decisions.

- There should be one and only one data model diagram associated with the solution. The diagram itself could be separated into sub-diagrams. Still, they all should be inherited from a single-parent diagram that you can easily relate to and get an end-to-end view of the whole data model. The data model can get very complex and include hundreds if not thousands of objects; reading such models on a single diagram is challenging. Splitting a data model diagram makes it easier to read as long as the integrity of the whole diagram is maintained.

- The security design could include several elements such as profile design, licenses used, user roles, and so on.

- The data model diagram and the security design are living artifacts. They are not expected to be created once and used throughout the project. They both should evolve and get more precise with time. The number of changes to each of them is expected to become much less with time, but they should never be considered a one-time activity set in stone, nor will they be perfect at the beginning.

- The design decisions repository is an essential element in your solution design. It must be maintained and linked with the right artifact of your solution. The design decisions can include details such as the multiple investigated possible solutions, the rationale behind selecting one of them, who made that decision, and when.

At this stage, you can proceed with creating a solution for each requirement shared by PWT.

Solving the requirements and creating design decisions

The following table references each of the PWTs shared (and then elaborated/extracted) nine requirements with the possible solution(s) for each. The list of possible solutions is a simplified representation of a design decision. You will see more detailed examples of design decisions in *Chapter 7, Create a Sample Application - Solve and Build the Application - Part One*, and *Chapter 8, Create a Sample Application - Solve and Build the Application - Part Two*. Remember that all requirements will require a solution. However, not all of them require a design decision. Design decisions should only be used when comparing two or more possible solutions and weighing their pros and cons to determine the right solution considering all known limitations, risks, and dependencies. Refer to the following table:

Requirement reference	Potential solution(s)
Requirement 1	This requirement can be solved in multiple ways, including the following. • Option 1: Introduce a set of custom fields (of type Phone) into the Contact object. This approach is feasible considering that we already know that the maximum number of phone numbers to store is five. • Option 2: Introduce a new custom object with a field (of type Phone) and link this object to the Contact object. This will allow for storing an unlimited number of phone numbers. This solution is also feasible; however, it adds an additional layer of complexity to the contact page UI. This is unnecessary as we have a confirmed requirement that the maximum number of phone numbers to store is five. Conclusion: Option 1 is to be used.
Requirement 2	This requirement has a direct dependency on *Requirement 1*. • Option 1: If Option 1 from Requirement 1 was chosen, another custom field (of type Phone) could be introduced to store the WhatsApp number. • Option 2: If Option 1 from Requirement 1 was chosen, a checkbox field could be introduced to the custom object. A custom logic will be required to ensure that only one check box can be checked per contact. Conclusion: As option 1 was chosen for *Requirement 1*, option 1 will also be used for this requirement.
Requirement 3	This requirement can be solved in multiple ways, including the following. • Option 1: You can set up recurring tasks in Salesforce. However, there are multiple limitations associated with this approach, and it has a dependency on selecting the standard Task object to represent a refreshment exercise. • Option 2: You can create an *autolaunched flow with a schedule trigger* or a scheduled *batch Apex class* to ensure the tasks are created bi-annually. The pros of this approach are that you get complete control of the behavior of task creation, and the standard functionality's limits do not bind you. A flow is easier to configure but has less flexibility than *Apex*. This requirement is not very complex and could be achieved via a *flow*. Conclusion: Option 2 is to be used.

Requirement reference	Potential solution(s)
Requirement 4	This requirement contains two sub-requirements. One is related to the content and structure of the task to be created, and the other is related to the logic of allocating/assigning these tasks to third-party agents. The first sub-requirement can be solved in multiple ways, including the following. • Option 1: Use the standard Task object, which includes most of the desired fields. The drawback of this approach is that you must be aware of the standard Task object's limitations, such as the inability to link another object to the Task object via a lookup. However, the standard Task object has built-in functionalities that integrate well with the rest of the Salesforce platform, such as a reminder icon at the top right corner of the Salesforce screen. • Option 2: Create a custom object to represent a task. This will give you complete control of the behavior of this object but at the cost of losing some of the standard configurable functionalities built within the platform. Conclusion: This is a tricky decision that the design authority might need to validate other requirements to conclude. For simplicity in this book, option 1 will be used. The second sub-requirement can also be solved in multiple ways. • Create a flow with logic to query the third-party users and distribute the tasks to them. • Create an Apex class with logic to query the third-party users and distribute the tasks to them. You are likely to invoke the logic from the flow that will be built to handle requirement 3; both solution options are valid, and choosing between them will depend on the skills available within your team and other external factors such as commitments, timeline, and strategy. Conclusion: For simplicity, option 1 will be used.
Requirement 5	This requirement contains two sub-requirements. One is related to restricting the task status to particular values. This can be easily met using a picklist field; the field already exists as part of the standard Task object. There is no need for a design decision for the first sub-requirement. The second sub-requirement can be solved in multiple ways, including the following. • Option 1: Create an *autolaunched flow with a record trigger* that gets fired upon saving a task record with a specific status value. The *flow* will check the value and determine if a follow-up task needs to be created (and assigned to the same user or another user) or not. • Option 2: Create an *Apex Trigger* to do the same logic mentioned in option 1. Conclusion: Option 1 is to be used.

Requirement reference	Potential solution(s)
Requirement 6	This is an interesting requirement that consists of two separate sub-requirements. The first is to count the number of failed reach-out attempts, and the second is to check the number of failed reach-out attempts and stop auto-creating activities based on the check and instead mark the Contact as unreachable. The first sub-requirement can be solved using the following approach. • Option 1: Create a custom hidden field on the *Contact* object to store the number of failed reach-out attempts. This field should not be visible to any user and only be used by the system. Then an *autolaunched flow with a record trigger* or *Apex Trigger* code can be used to increase the value in this field by one whenever a *Task* record related to a *Contact* is set to *deferred*. The value of the custom hidden field should be set to zero whenever the status of a *Task* record related to a *Contact* is set to *Completed*. Conclusion: Option 1 is to be used, which will rely on a *flow*. Considering that this requirement has only one solution option (assuming there is no need to compare using a flow vs. Apex trigger), there is no need for a design decision. The second sub-requirement can be solved using the following approach. • Option 1: Update the *flow* that will be introduced as a solution for *requirement 5* to check the value of the hidden field that will store the number of failed reach-out attempts, and if the number is above five, then update the field **Data_refreshment_status__c** in the related *Contact* to a value indicating that the *Contact* is unreachable. The same logic can be achieved using an *Apex Trigger*; however, it makes sense to stick with *flows* and avoid unnecessarily mixing between *flows* and *Apex* (as that could negatively impact performance under certain circumstances). Conclusion: Option 1 is to be used, which will rely on a *flow*.
Requirement 7	This requirement can be solved using the following approach. • Option 1: Update the *flow* that will be introduced as a solution for *requirement 5* to update the fields **Data_refreshment_status__c** and **Last_data_refreshment_date__c** in the related *Contact* to indicate that the contact has been reached out to and updated successfully. The same logic can be achieved using an *Apex Trigger*. Conclusion: Option 1 is to be used, which will rely on a *flow*.

Requirement reference	Potential solution(s)
Requirement 8	This solution to this requirement should consider the wireframe designed in *Figure 3.3*. The solution and the wireframe are related and dependent on each other and should be developed in parallel. From the wireframe in *Figure 3.3*, you can see that there is a need to develop a custom UI/screen to capture the input from the user, including the answers to the asked questions. The custom UI/screen should also query the latest version of the available questions from the object **Data_Refresh_Question__c** and display them. The custom UI/screen should also create the relevant **Data_Refresh_Answer__c** records and link them to the *Contact*. This custom UI/screen can be built in multiple ways. • Option 1: Using a Screen Flow. However, the UI is complex and will be a stretch for Screen Flows. • Option 2: Using a Lighting Component. This option will give the ultimate control over the UI and the best performance. • Option 3: Using a Visualforce page. This option will give the ultimate control over the UI and a good performance Options 2 and 3 are closely matched. The difference in performance is negligible for such UI. Option 2 is more future proof considering that *Lightning Components* is the technology that Salesforce invests more in while *Visualforce* is retained for backward compatibility only. You could choose option 3 over 2 if there were some non-technical restrictions, such as a limitation with the available skillset within the team. Conclusion: Option 2 is to be used.
Requirement 9	The proposed data model and the **Is_Active__c** field on the **Data_Refresh_Question__c** object already address this requirement to a good extent. You need to ensure that only one set of **Data_Refresh_Question__c** records (that has the same version number) can be marked as active. This can be achieved in multiple ways, including the following. • Option 1: You can introduce an Apex Trigger to ensure that the one and only set of records are active. • Option 2: You can rely on manual user validation, considering that this table is not going to be updated frequently (bi-annual). The design authority must discuss such design decisions to ensure that all points of view are considered. For this example, you can assume that the design authority preferred option 2. Conclusion: Option 2 is to be used.

Table 3.1: Salesforce editions

You might have noticed that some of these design decisions directly impact the data model design. This is correct and expected. Designing the data model happens simultaneously while creating and validating some of the design decisions. They are not sequential but somewhat parallel and support each other.

Design decisions are taken by the *design authority* (also known as *the architecture review board)*, which is an organizational structure you must consider forming within your application developing team. Smaller applications might require simpler structures. The following diagram illustrates the different layers that a design authority could include. Additional layers might be needed for highly sophisticated applications. A design authority regularly gathers (such as daily, weekly, or bi-weekly) to discuss, challenge, validate, and select a solution for a given requirement. Please refer to the following figure:

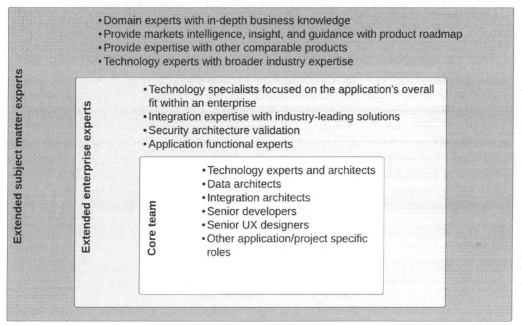

Figure 3.6: *A sample design authority structure*

After several iterations of development, validation, and rectification, your Salesforce application should be ready for deployment.

Deploy the application

There are several ways to deploy a Salesforce application, depending on the complexity of the application and its intention. Suppose you are a professional working for an enterprise and building an application your employer will use exclusively. In that case, you can use the simple change sets, a more sophisticated deployment via metadata (deployed via an IDE such as **Visual Studio Code**), or a more scalable deployment mechanism using a **Source Code Management (SCM)** tool such as **GitHub** and a **Continuous Integration/ Continuous Delivery (CI/CD)** setup.

The following diagram shows a typical deployment setup using *change sets*:

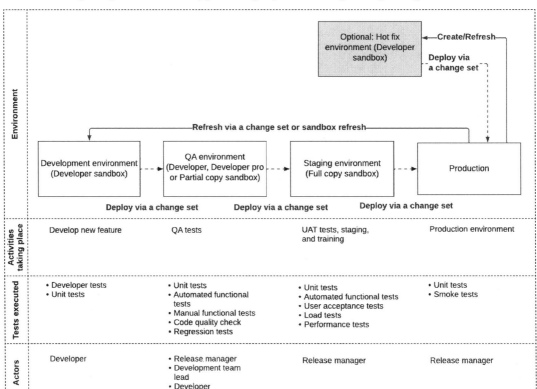

***Figure 3.7**: Typical setup for deployment via change sets within a company Salesforce org*

You can read more about using *change sets* and their limitations from the following link.

https://help.salesforce.com/s/articleView?id=sf.changesets.htm&type=5

If you are a professional working for a company that builds Salesforce applications to be sold to and deployed to other enterprises. In that case, you will probably consider options such as deploying via *unmanaged packages* or the **AppExchange**.

The following diagram shows a typical deployment setup using *unmanaged packages*:

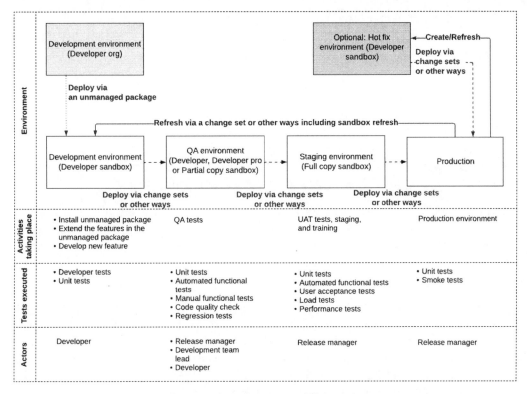

***Figure 3.8**: Typical setup for installing an unmanaged package and then deploying changes within a company Salesforce org*

You can read more about *unmanaged packages* from the following link.

https://developer.salesforce.com/docs/atlas.en-us.packagingGuide.meta/packagingGuide/packaging_developing_unmanaged.htm

Deploying a managed application via **AppExchange** is a long topic and will not be covered in this book.

You have now learned about the application lifecycle of a Salesforce application. Next, you will learn about several gaps that were missed/left unaddressed and can cause future application difficulties or limit the future growth plans for your application.

Identified gaps and lessons learned

You managed to solve all the requirements shared by PWT. You even extracted additional requirements that were missed from the original list. You ensured that the end-to-end process was clear and understood by everyone by creating a BPMN diagram. You created a detailed solution for each requirement and associated some with a design decision that was socialized and validated by a design authority. You also ensured that your application runs on an optimized data model with a robust design validated by different experts from the design authority. You have already identified and successfully closed many gaps that could have been missed, so what are the additional gaps that have been missed?

The software industry is sophisticated, with a broad spectrum of success levels for an application. Take instant messaging applications as an example; there are dozens of applications in the market that belongs to different generations. Many can be considered successful, but only one was sold for a whopping $16 billion. Why? There are many reasons that will require long research to uncover. However, one of these reasons, without a doubt, is that the application brought solutions for problems that were unidentified before by its predecessors or came up with a better solution to known problems.

Creating a successful application is both a process and an art. The structured and organized process can help you close 80% of the possible gaps. This process is something that you need to learn and master with experience. You have already seen an example in this section where you combined activities, tools, and artifacts to ensure your solution is designed with minimal mistakes. You will also see more examples throughout this book.

The remaining 20% is the art you can learn by keeping an observant eye and an open mind to learn from the leading software applications and experts. You need to be a dreamer who can think like a machine and imagine how users' end-to-end experience would look under certain conditions. You must look for the details and ensure you do not leave a stone unturned. And once you formalize an idea, you need to put it on paper/on a system to socialize and validate it with other experts and stakeholders.

If you go back to the PWT application example and think of the end-to-end experience, you can identify some gaps, such as.

- How will the third-party users pick up their assigned tasks? Are they expected to go to a specific list view where they can click on the tasks one by one? These agents could have tasks of other types also assigned to them; what would be the impact of mixing the different types of tasks on the user experience? You can probably create multiple list views and expect the user to switch between them. This is an accepted solution, but can a better one be offered? If you put yourself in the user's shoes, would it help if you could see a screen with all the different tasks assigned to you grouped by type (and probably highlighted differently to make it easy for the eye to identify them at a glance)? The screen can get very crowded and busy in that case. Perhaps a subset of the records of each type should be shown with the ability to expand/collapse sections to view additional details.

- How many clicks do the agent require to pick a task, execute it, close it, and pick another? How many screens will pop up in the process? If you put yourself in the user's shoes, would it help if you could open a single screen to handle a task, and when you close it, the next task is automatically brought up next without the need to close the screen and open another? Would it also help to have the ability to have a list of the pending data refreshment tasks that can help you immediately jump to a specific task without leaving the screen? You might think these ideas are for the UX designers to uncover; this is both right and wrong. Remember that the success of an application is the responsibility of all team members. Although the UX experience is expected to be led by UX designers and product owners, you are also responsible for thinking, imagining, and dreaming of the end-to-end solution. Every team member is responsible for identifying gaps and raising them with the stakeholders.

- What should PWT do with unreachable contacts? Should they be simply deleted, or are there other channels that can be used to update them? How will the PWT management be informed about these contacts? If you put yourself in the PWT management's shoes, would it help to get a weekly report with these contacts to plan your next steps accordingly? Would it help if you also can run that report at any time and from any device to get an up-to-date list with critical figures?

- What is the optimal device for the PWT third-party agents to execute their assigned tasks? If you put yourself in the user's shoes, would it help if you could do that from a mobile device? Would it help if the answers to the questions asked could be automatically filled in by interpreting the transcript of the call? Would it help if you could get some hints about the customer and any past experience with them before you start the call?

Closing some of these gaps in an optimal solution could be the difference between a successful and outstanding application that can reach different heights of success.

Summary

In this chapter, you came across your first Salesforce application. You started by receiving and understanding requirements shared by a hypothetical client, and you managed to read between the lines and extract additional detailed requirements that were missing initially. You then followed a structured and repeatable process to design, socialize, and document your solution to minimize the chances of mistakes and increase the chances for your application success.

You had an early look at some of the valuable artifacts that can help you design your application efficiently. You will learn more about these artifacts and understand why and how to use them in *Chapter 5, Understand the Supporting Tools and Artifacts*. You also briefly learned about the different ways to deploy your Salesforce application. Finally, you discovered what it takes to design and build a successful application.

This chapter gave you a practical glimpse of the Rapid Salesforce Application Development lifecycle. You will learn more about it in the next chapter and understand its differences compared to the classic software development lifecycle.

Join our book's Discord space

Join the book's Discord Workspace for Latest updates, Offers, Tech happenings around the world, New Release and Sessions with the Authors:

https://discord.bpbonline.com

CHAPTER 4

Learn the Salesforce Application Development Lifecycle

Introduction

This chapter will continue building on what you have learned in the previous chapters about the **Rapid Application Development (RAD)** lifecycle for Salesforce applications. You will be briefly introduced to the classic Web Application Development lifecycle (inherited from the software development lifecycle) and learn about the differences between it and RAD. You will then know more about RAD for Salesforce, in particular. This knowledge is crucial for you as a professional who wants to learn how to build Salesforce applications. It can help you adapt quickly to other foundational technology changes in the future.

You will then dive into the details of RAD for Salesforce and spend some time learning each of its components in detail. You will not only learn the *what* and the *how* but also the *why*, which will equip you with a solid foundation of knowledge that can adapt and change in alignment with the technology shifts in the future.

RAD requires an optimized usage of a combination of no-code/Low-code tools and full-code elements when needed. This helps utilize the team's diverse skillset and ensure you spend as much time as possible delivering value to your business rather than overcoming technical obstacles. You learned in the previous chapters that the primary concept of RAD is to develop and deploy applications fast, which helps realize the application's **return on investment (ROI)** quickly. And you also learned that a suitable software development framework is required to develop applications in that way, ensuring that an adequate level of governance, documentation, and design thinking is still followed.

In this chapter, you will learn more about setting up the RAD processes in your workplace and overcoming the commonly known challenges. This chapter will cover the theoretical knowledge behind the practices, decisions, and activities you have experienced in *Chapter 3, Develop a Sample Salesforce Application - PbP Phonebook*.

Have a look next at the structure of this chapter.

Structure

The chapter covers the following topics:

- Introduction to the web application development process
- Rapid Application Development: The Salesforce philosophy
- Define the problem you are solving
- Design the application's blueprint
- Wireframe/prototype the application
- Build and validate the application
- Test and rectify the application
- Deploy and gather feedback

Objectives

By the end of this chapter, you will gain a deep understanding of the RAD lifecycle for Salesforce applications. This will help you set up a successful set of processes and procedures to help you build successful Salesforce applications that can grow and scale without leaving a trail of technical debt behind. You will gain an in-depth understanding of each step of RAD for Salesforce applications and learn from practical examples.

Introduction to the web application development process

Before the internet boom and the introduction of Web Applications (An application hosted on a remote computer/server and accessed via a client/thin client connected to the internet. Web applications do not need to be downloaded.), a structured approach to developing software application has taken shape in the late 1970s and early 1980s. This approach was called the **Systems Development Life Cycle (SDLC)**, while others referred to it simply as the Software Development Lifecycle. The SDLC brought the concept of splitting the software development process into clearly distinct phases with a specific set of activities in each.

The SDLC adoption increased to become the benchmark and standard for software development as it offered an easy-to-follow and repeat framework with all steps required to build software. Overall, the SDLC significantly improved the software development lifecycle management and opened the door for more sophisticated and capable software to be developed.

Web application development brought a different challenge and demanded a more streamlined process as the time that can be offered to developers is shorter, and the number of involved stakeholders is higher. In the web applications world, the stakeholders (taking part in building the web application) include business analysts, UI/graphic designers, UX designers, multimedia designers, security experts, customers, developers, architects, database designers, and more. The structure of the web development team has changed, and it was roughly divided into 30% software engineers, 30% UX/UI/Graphics/Creative designers, 20% management team, and 20% business and domain experts. Also, due to the nature of web applications and the ever-increasing customer expectations, the time schedules for development became relatively short.

The Web application development lifecycle was updated to include the following seven distinct phases.

1. **Requirement gathering:** This phase is usually initiated by ideas from entrepreneurs or business owners about the desired web application. These ideas get validated and compared to market data and other relevant data to determine the feasibility of the ideas in general. The ideas are then further developed into one or more documents with goals, vision, desired features, supporting technology, market proposition, and future plans. These documents give the development team a good understanding of the desired web application and its objective, including critical elements such as the target audience, focus industry (if any), main rivals, and budget.

2. **Planning and blueprinting:** The outcome of the previous phase is used to create the roadmap of the web application. The roadmap consists of detailed requirements that could be grouped into one or more features. One of the known pain points for this phase was that it used to take much time to create a detailed requirement that may need to be revised (sometimes significantly) at later stages. At this stage, developers/architects create a software blueprint that includes artifacts such as flowcharts, BPMN diagrams, and even sketches to help determine the overall structure of the web application.

3. **Designing:** This phase focuses on the UX/UI elements of the web application and all relevant graphics and multimedia. The UX designers create graphics, icons, color themes, buttons, templates, and more elements. The UX designers create

wireframes and interactive mockups of the website, which can help illustrate the overall navigation experience. The developers and architects would fine-tune the artifacts they made in the previous phase and share concerns and ideas with the UI/UX team. The architects also create a logical (sometimes physical) representation of the underlying data model. The wireframes and interactive mockups are then validated with clients/stakeholders and adjusted based on their feedback. This activity is repeated until a particular client/stakeholder satisfaction level is achieved. Some development activities from phase 4 can also overlap with this phase as the development team might already start creating some of the web application's components.

4. **Developing/Programming:** This phase is all about developing and programming the features and requirements defined in the previous phases. Developers and architects would create frameworks, code, APIs, business logic, security layers, integration interfaces, and many more. This phase is known to be the most prolonged and most time-consuming, although some technologies can speed up a few tasks. The experience and skills of the technical team played a crucial role in the speed and quality of the delivered items in this phase. While developing, a basic level of testing is also included.

5. **Content creation:** The content of a web application is as crucial as its functionalities. Many web applications thrived mainly due to their high value and quality content. This stage focuses on finalizing the labels, captions, flow of information, and any other text content within the application. **Search Engine Optimization (SEO)** optimization and content creation can also occur at this stage. Part of the application technical documentation also occurs at this stage with collaboration between the content authors, developers, and architects. Technical documentation has always been a crucial element in the software lifecycle; without it, the lifespan of an application and its ability to adapt and grow in the future is significantly reduced. The creation of technical documentation starts as early as phase 2 (planning and blueprinting).

6. **Testing and releasing:** Testing the application before releasing it is crucial. A solution full of bugs is destined for failure. Several types of tests could occur at different stages of the development lifecycle, including unit, functional, integration, user acceptance tests (UAT), load, performance, and smoke tests. Failed tests could re-trigger the developing/programming phase.

7. **Application maintenance:** After releasing the application, there will be a need to maintain it, add new enhancements, and fix any minor reported bugs. Introducing major functionalities could trigger a completely new development cycle.

Several software companies and individuals introduced additional phases to detail specific activities that were part of the original seven phases. The following diagram illustrates the seven main phases of the web application development lifecycle:

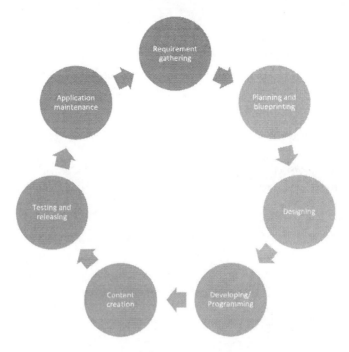

Figure 4.1: The web application development lifecycle

SDLC offers a solid and structured framework for building and releasing applications. However, it does not offer a competitive time to market value. This is why RAD was invented. In comparison, the standard RAD contained only four stages. RAD reduced the planning time and focused more on the iterative prototyping concept. The RAD's four distinct phases are the following:

1. **Requirements gathering and planning:** Combines and condenses activities from phases 1 and 2 of the SDLC. During this phase, stakeholders determine the project's scope and the key requirements to be addressed.

2. **Design/User design:** RAD proceeds directly to development once the requirements are scoped out. Prototypes are created and refined iteratively until reaching an agreed maturity level. This phase is the heart of the RAD lifecycle and where the most significant part of the success or failure of the project is determined. The client/end-user works closely with the development team and gives quick feedback on the developed prototypes. The requirements are tested in an iterative fashion and at a much faster pace compared to SDLC. The developers and UX designers would adjust the prototype multiple times until a satisfactory design was reached.

3. **Rapid build:** This phase focuses on converting the prototypes and beta version work done in the previous phase to a fully working solution. The developers can develop the solution quickly at this stage, as most of the questions and challenges

were answered/resolved at the previous stage. This is a significant advantage compared to classic SDLC. During this phase, the developers and testers develop and test the application (including multiple types of testing such as unit tests, integration tests, and system tests). The client/end-user is still involved in rapid feedback gathering at this stage. Content creation also takes place in this phase when relevant.

4. **Releasing and application maintenance:** Similar to classic SDLC but more condensed. The application is released/deployed, and the application maintenance activities take over. Introducing major functionalities could trigger a completely new development cycle.

The following diagram illustrates the four main phases of the RAD lifecycle:

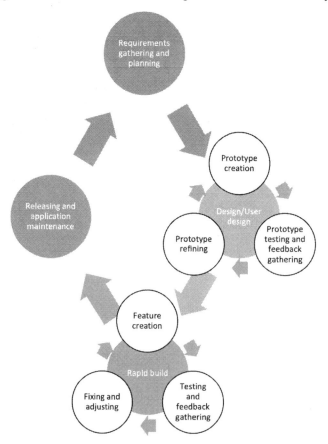

Figure 4.2: The RAD lifecycle

The most challenging aspect of RAD is also its most distinctive feature. With the rapid development, change, and re-change, the design of the under-the-hood components of the solution could get messy. Moreover, due to the speedy nature of this software development approach (particularly phases 2 and 3), documentation is usually skipped to speed up prototyping and building, eventually creating a poorly documented solution that is difficult to maintain.

Worth mentioning that RAD is usually adopted hand in hand with the agile delivery methodology. The difference between a software development lifecycle and a delivery methodology is challenging to articulate. Still, you can think of the first as the set of activities required to build and support an application, while the latter includes the entire process of rolling out a particular software to its users. That includes shared activities with the software development lifecycle but can also extend to procuring additional software/license activities, data migration, marketing campaigns, and more. A software development lifecycle focuses on the software, while a delivery methodology focuses on tackling and solving challenges to deliver (or build and deliver) software to the end users.

Both SDLC and RAD offer clear benefits and have their disadvantages. Considering the nature of the Salesforce platform, there was a need to create a software development process that could provide value without leaving a trail of expensive technical debt.

Rapid Application Development: The Salesforce philosophy

The Salesforce platform offers a ton of configurable features that are ready to be used by most of its customers straight away. Using a flexible and speedy delivery methodology such as the **Agile Methodology** to deliver this software is an obvious choice. However, most of these customers will also discover that they must introduce multiple customizations to their implementation to fit their needs. Several customers will build sophisticated applications on the Salesforce platform, including all different customizations. The flexible nature of the Salesforce platform makes it very attractive for rapid build and change. However, the continuous design changes and the lack of governance mechanisms to ensure these changes are done correctly inevitably lead to creating a hard-to-maintain solution that is slow to change and adapt to the customer needs.

On many occasions, a Salesforce implementation would end up with several black boxes that no one knows how they work or operate. That fragmentation in the solution and the vision of building the solution to start from strips away much of the benefits that can be extracted from Salesforce, one of the most modern and powerful tools available in the industry today.

This is why it is essential to have a solid software development lifecycle to power and support your Salesforce delivery methodology. The Salesforce RAD lifecycle addresses this by combining concepts from SDLC and RAD in an agile-compatible manner.

The Salesforce RAD lifecycle includes the following distinct phases.

1. **Requirement gathering and market benchmarking:** This phase aims at creating an overall strategy and high-level roadmap items. The ideas of the desired application get validated and compared to market data, competitors, and other relevant data to determine the feasibility of the ideas in general. The contents of the AppExchange can be beneficial at this stage as some similar products might exist already; comparisons against these products can help determine either to drop the idea of the application altogether or help inspire the newly developed application. By the end of this phase, one or more documents will be created containing information such as goals, vision, desired features, supporting technology, market proposition, and future plans.

2. **Blueprinting:** Blueprinting (sometimes called pre-game) is a phase where the application roadmap is defined and high-level solution architecture elements are designed. The outcome of the previous phase is used to create the application roadmap. The roadmap consists of brief-but-descriptive requirements that could be grouped into one or more features. Compared to SDLC, the main difference in this phase is that the requirements are expected to be partially (not fully) detailed. However, they should have enough details to explain the functionality to any. One of the common pitfalls that could lead to significant rework at later stages is oversimplification. The requirements at this stage should not be high-level nor very detailed but somewhere in between. The requirements should have enough details to allow the rest of the team (and members from outside the team) to understand what this requirement is all about and what value it would add to the application. The BAs and architects are the main actors at this stage, ensuring that every requirement is clear. The architects and senior developers should be able to read the requirements and start imagining how the application would work and create a high-level solution design. Multiple key artifacts are expected to be created at this stage, including 70-80% of the overall solution requirements, a set of BPMN diagrams explaining the main processes within the system, a draft data model diagram (logical level), a draft landscape architecture diagram, a log of design decisions, an agreed governance model, and a preliminary design of the data sharing and visibility model. The Salesforce RAD lifecycle should welcome changes at any stage of the lifecycle, and all the outcomes of this phase should not be considered final as they will get updated at later stages. However, all efforts should be made to ensure these artifacts are as close to their final version as possible.

3. **Detailing, designing, and prototyping:** The requirements from the previous phase should be fine-detailed at this stage. This will be the primary focus of the BAs, with some help from the architects. Designing and prototyping take place in a similar fashion to standard RAD, where the focus is on creating low-fidelity prototypes that can be validated and tested by the end users to gather feedback that can help adjust the solution. The prototypes can be interactive or non-interactive wireframes. The prototypes can even be a working module developed in development environments (such as Sandboxes or Salesforce Developer org). Clients/end-users are closely

involved in this phase, and their feedback is used to adjust the prototypes quickly. All requirements must pass through this phase. Some might quickly move on to the next phase, while others must undergo several iterations before proceeding. Developers can try things out at this phase and build working prototypes to ensure a specific functionality or platform capability is tried and tested even at this stage. For example, a developer might need to be sure how a particular Salesforce functionality would operate under certain conditions. A prototype can help nail down a **Proof of Concept (PoC)** to determine potential limitations early on. This prototype can then be used to inspire the end solution. One significant difference of this stage compared to RAD is the need to extend the prototype concept, sometimes beyond a UI/UX wireframe and into a small PoC that can be used to test the concept with the end users and demystify any potential system limitations early. The cost of change at this stage is minimal compared to later stages. Several artifacts, such as the data model diagram, the landscape architecture diagram, and others, are expected to mature further during this phase. These artifacts must be kept up to date and never be left to be updated at later phases. All design decisions must be validated by the design authority set up in the previous phase as part of the governance structure. Design decisions should be detailed and logged into a design decision log.

4. **Developing/building and testing:** This phase focuses on converting the detailed requirements, prototypes, and beta version work done in the previous phase to a fully working solution that meets the requirement's acceptance criteria. Some of the solution artifacts might require an update at this stage. However, this is expected to be minimal. Requirements can transition between this phase and the previous depending on findings revealed during developing/building the requirement. For example, a requirement can return to the design phase if the team discovers the original design had flaws during the build. The developers are expected to build the solution quickly, as most questions and challenges were answered/resolved at the previous stage. The testers can use the acceptance criteria defined for each requirement to build their test suits. The clients/end-users are involved at this stage, and their feedback is used to adjust the built solution. Content creation also takes place in this phase when relevant.

5. **Deploying/releasing:** Further tests might be required before releasing an application (or a particular set of functionalities within an application), such as load and performance tests. Once the application or the set of features to be released reaches an acceptable level of quality and passes all acceptance criteria, they are released to production. Release notes should be created and published as part of the release, and a track of the release version must be kept. Techniques such as CI/CD can be used to limit the risk of bugs created due to parallel working by different development teams.

6. **Application maintenance and live feedback gathering:** After releasing the application, there will be a need to maintain it, add new enhancements, and fix any

minor reported bugs. Introducing major functionalities could trigger a completely new development cycle. A live and continuous feedback-gathering loop should be introduced to ensure the voice of the clients/end-users is heard. The feedback loop must be transparent to instill trust within the feedback providers and therefore increase its utilization and value.

What is important to highlight is that several of the Salesforce RAD phases are not finish-to-start phases where one has to wait for the previous phase to end before it can start but more smoothly fluid phases that transition between each other. The following diagram illustrates the main phases of the Salesforce RAD lifecycle:

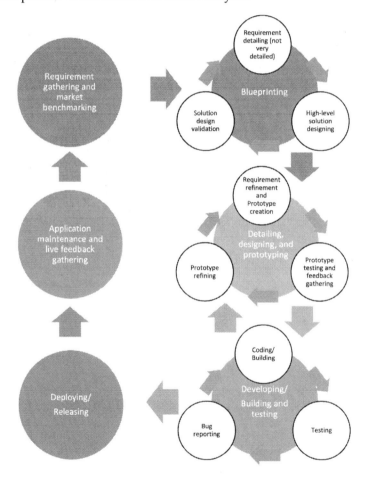

Figure 4.3: *The Salesforce RAD lifecycle*

Now that you are familiar with the Salesforce RAD lifecycle and can point out its differences compared to the classic SDLC and RAD, move on to gain a deeper understanding of each of the Salesforce RAD lifecycle phases.

Define the problem you are solving

The first phase of developing a Salesforce application is to define the problem that the application will be solving. The chances of success for an application that does not solve a real problem are slim.

Imagine opening a fancy new restaurant that offers a non-popular cuisine in the town. This is an example of solving a problem that did not exist. In most cases, the restaurant will shut down. It is also essential to understand that the nature of problems is transitory. This means that what is perceived today as a problem might differ from the next week or year. A good understanding of the problem will help you understand its roots and longer-term needs. Problems are actually opportunities. Think of all the innovations in humankind's history; they were all created out of necessity to solve problems.

Attempting to solve a problem too quickly can sometimes be worse than not solving it at all. While failing to address some problems quickly enough might exponentially increase the size of the problem. Striking the right balance between reacting quickly enough to solve a problem and taking enough time to analyze it properly to create an optimal solution is the goal that most enterprises strive for.

Concluding into the problem definition too quickly is human nature. However, it is also one of the main reasons for a project failure, as the cost of wrongly defining the problem or discovering a missing problem later is much higher compared to doing so at the early stages.

Jumping to early problem solutions is also a human nature that can steer the development team in the wrong direction and drive a series of changes that increases the application cost and reduces its reliability and maintainability. However, it should not be treated as absolute evil as some seasoned experts might be able to spot the root of the problem much earlier than others and offer a solution that significantly cuts down the time to market. Seasoned experts would also know better than running to early conclusions is risky (and could create excessive or incomplete solutions), but having an appetite to take some calculated risks occasionally is okay too. Such personnel might not exist as part of every software development team. The structured way of problem-solving adds organization and governance that can help the team build a successful application even without such experts.

The first stage of solving a problem is by first understanding what the problem is. This is what is usually referred to as *problem analysis*.

Problem analysis is a set of activities to understand and reveal the problem. Solving the problem is identifying the potential solutions for a given problem and selecting the most suitable amongst. Problem-solving is not part of the problem analysis.

Problem analysis has the following five main steps.

The first step: Define the problem

The first step to start with is defining the problem. If you cannot describe the problem, you will naturally be unable to solve it. Defining the problem is more complicated than it sounds, as people have different perspectives, motivations, and priorities. Some individuals might influence their perspective of the problem and distract the team's focus from the actual root of the problem. The following activities can help you define the problem and avoid distractions:

- **Write the problem down:** Writing the problem down helps clarify it for all relevant stakeholders. Standardized process documentation tools such as BPMN diagrams can significantly help at this stage and deliver a thousand words in a single image.

- **Gather multiple perspectives:** People naturally have different views and perspectives on the problem to solve. Getting more perspectives can help you learn more about the problem and get closer to understanding its root cause.

- **Dig deeper and aim for the roots:** The problem on the surface might be the top of the iceberg, with many more lurking in deep. Focusing on the problems on the surface could be an attempt to fix the symptom but not the actual condition. Keep digging deeper, as you could reveal more related problems.

These three activities would help you define the problem. Next, you should try to reveal the root cause.

The second step: Figure out the root cause

A problem could have one or more root causes. Understanding the root cause can be thought of as revealing the problem behind the problem. Root cause analysis is an activity followed to reveal root cause problems where questions such as the following are asked.

- Is there a primary problem? Challenging the described problem and asking for more details about the existence of a primary problem that should have been reported earlier?

- What are the contributing factors? What factors could have a role in causing the targeted problem? The impact of these factors could vary. However, identifying and understanding the contributing factors can significantly help understand a problem's root cause.

- Who can provide more details? Who are the people that can give more information and offer other perspectives on the problem?

The fishbone chart is an excellent tool to document and describe the main problem and its contributing factors. The diagram below is an example:

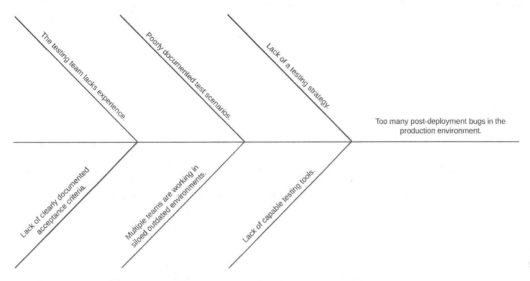

Figure 4.4: *The fishbone chart can be used to describe the main problem*

In the previous diagram, the main branch represents the main problem. While each contributing factor is represented as a branch. The third step is to identify the impacted stakeholders.

The third step: Identify the impacted stakeholders

Different problems can impact different people. Each impacted person can offer a different perspective on the problem and share other concerns. This set of people is considered stakeholders. Stakeholders can have positive or negative stakes. Having a positive stake means that the person would gain from solving it. The opposite is true for the negative stake. For example, some people might see resolving a problem as a threat to their job security, and this is an example of a negative stake. The problem's stakeholders could include the project sponsor, the end user, the customer of the end user (if applicable), the management team, and others.

Once the impacted stakeholders are identified, you need to define the boundaries of your solution.

The fourth step: Define the solution's scope

The solution scope forms the boundaries you can operate within while solving a problem. The scope includes the addressable areas within your control, and it is important to be defined to ensure you do not endeavor into an area that is not part of your responsibility. The problem might impact several other areas, internal and external, and it is important to be clear on what you can target with your solution and what requires support from other parties.

Once the scope is defined, you need to assign a priority to the problem. Multiple factors can determine the problem's priority, which differs from one company/situation to another. But generally, problems are prioritized based on severity and potential impact (in the short term and the long run). There are several frameworks used to prioritize the problem. You should use a consistent framework across the project lifecycle. Finally, you need to define the solution constraints.

The fifth step: Define the solution's constraints

Solution constraints are barriers/blockers that could stop/prevent you from solving a problem or could have a negative impact on the delivery time. Constraints can be addressed once identified; ignoring them could have a significant adverse effect at later stages. Constraints could be a lack of resources (money, people, and other resources), a lack of particular expertise, political challenges, compliance requirements, technological limitation, or others. Partial constraint reliefs should be expected and accepted in the absence of better choices. Sometimes, the constraint might be out of your control and should be accepted as it is.

After defining the problem and partially/fully generating documents such as goals, vision, desired features, supporting technology, market proposition, and future plans, you can move to the blueprinting phase, which is sometimes considered the most critical phase of your project.

Design the application's blueprint

This phase focuses on creating a product roadmap and an overall solution design. In *Chapter 3, Develop a Sample Salesforce Application - PbP Phonebook*, you learned that requirements could be written in multiple formats. One of the common ways to write a requirement (which reduces the chances of missing any part of it) is to write a requirement as a *user story*.

A **user story** is a way to write a requirement using natural language. The requirement is described from a persona perspective (such as an end-user), highlighting what this persona wants, why, and the acceptance criteria of a solution addressing the requirement. A set of user stories can be combined to form an *epic*. An *epic* is usually released to the end users as a *feature*. However, multiple epics could be linked to a single feature and vice versa. A rich backlog of features is the backbone of your product roadmap. Next, you will learn how to create a user story for the Salesforce RAD lifecycle.

Creating a backlog of user stories

User stories offer a simple way to capture requirements where the requirements' who, what, and why are clearly articulated. User stories also encapsulate information that used to be scattered across multiple documents and link personas to their requirements and acceptance criteria. Most importantly, user stories are designed to allow quick and efficient partial capture of the requirement at early stages while enabling additional details to be added later incrementally.

Misunderstanding the minimal details that should be captured in the user story early can lead to missing an excellent opportunity to leverage it. User stories in the Salesforce RAD lifecycle should be detailed enough to allow other team members to create a preliminary end-to-end solution design for the application (or, at least, the feature included in the related epic).

The standard user story should be short, capture the essential elements of the requirement, and have the following format.

As a *[persona/role]*, I want to *[action describing the requirement]* so that *[value gained/benefit]*.

Here are some details.

- The *persona/role* should refer to an actual persona that will be using the system. Members of the development team do not qualify as a persona/role.

- The *action describing the requirement* is usually unique per user story. The action should be written in an active voice.

- The *value gained/benefit* can be shared between multiple user stories and could impact other personas than the one mentioned in the user story.

The acceptance criteria can be added later and are not part of the core part of the story. Remember that the story is expected to be detailed incrementally. Acceptance criteria are usually difficult to identify at earlier stages.

Here are three examples of user stories.

- As a *[customer]*, I want *[to be able to create a complaint online]* so that *[I can easily raise a complaint from anywhere]*.

- As a *[customer]*, I want to *[receive a notification about my complaint status]* so that *[I can get timely information about any progress]*.

- As a *[manager]*, I want to *[execute a report]* so that *[I can understand the type of complaints raised]*.

The first story is very high level and could become an epic. The second is short and concise but needs more details about the desired notification channel. The fourth can be elaborated further to add details about the desired report, but even at this stage, there is a need to describe the report in more detail as this could impact the proposed solution.

The second and third user stories can be detailed further to become similar to the following.

- As a *[customer]*, I want to *[receive an email notification about my complaint status immediately after it gets updated]* so that *[I can get timely information about any progress]*.

- As a *[manager]*, I want to *[execute a report covering all complaints received in the past 30 days]* so that *[I can understand the type of complaints raised]*.

Without clarifying that the desired notification is a real-time email notification, the architects and senior engineers could miss the need for a mechanism to send emails in real-time upon the complaint's status update. And without defining the targeted reports' timespan, the architects and senior engineers might miss the need to handle a considerable amount of records in their reports.

The user stories get further detailed (this activity is called grooming) in the next phase (detailing, designing, and prototyping). However, it is required to create a high-level end-to-end solution at this stage, and this will only be possible with detailed enough requirements.

You can only create a rough blueprint of a building if you know basic information such as the number of floors, the type and size of apartments included, and the desired building usage. Similarly, your application blueprint would lack crucial details that should exist at this stage if you do not have detailed enough requirements.

BPMN diagrams are very useful for detailing processes that span across multiple user stories. BPMN diagrams can also be incrementally defined and are usually grouped into as-is and to-be diagrams. You will learn more about BPMN diagrams in *Chapter 5, Understand the Supporting Tools and Artefacts*.

While the requirements are being defined and detailed, another parallel activity of defining the governance structure/body occurs. The governance body helps validate the design decisions raised during the designing/architecting of the solution.

Defining a governance body

You learned about the design authority as a governance body in *Chapter 3, Develop a Sample Salesforce Application - PbP Phonebook*, and you came across *Figure 3.6*, which illustrates a possible design authority structure.

The design authority (or a similar structure) is a must-have to govern the development of any software solution. This is particularly true for Salesforce applications for the following reasons.

- Salesforce is a platform that promotes low-code or no-code development. However, many of its clients end up creating a lot of code to extend its features. Sometimes the decision to develop code is the right decision. However, some Salesforce customers/application providers might perceive it as a wrong decision due to bad personal experiences. The hyper allergy of custom development is a challenge that the design authority can address. Moreover, a design authority can act as a quality gate to validate and document the design decision of custom-developing a particular feature.

- The Salesforce platform can be a home for highly sophisticated solutions and applications. On several occasions, teams could end up developing the same feature multiple times. The lack of a well-documented solution is one root cause of this. The lack of a governing body that can validate and cross-check a proposed new solution against the existing landscape is a significant contributor.

- The Salesforce platform offers excellent performance if configured correctly. Customized features could underperform due to their bad design. A tool is as strong as the person using it. Similarly, a solution designed by a single person and has never been validated has more chances of going wrong compared to a solution that multiple people have thoroughly validated. Adding more brains around the table should always be welcomed as long as there is an agreed mechanism to use them best.

- The Salesforce platform is based on shared tenancy, as you learned in *Chapter 1, Introduction to the Salesforce Platform*. This means that governor limits are imposed to ensure fair usage of the platform. A well-architected and validated solution can avoid hitting the governor's limits (which is not a pleasant experience).

- A well-architected solution should be flexible and easy to change or extend. A poorly designed solution might address today's obvious needs and completely miss tomorrow's potential needs. A successful application would go into evolutions, not revolutions in its lifespan. The design authority ensures that more brains are used to develop the most optimal solution in the long run.

During the blueprinting phase, the structure of the governance body must be agreed on. The structure can evolve and change in later phases. But the decision to change it must go through the preliminarily agreed governance body.

The governance body/design authority validates design decisions raised by architects, senior engineers, and other team members at different application lifecycle stages. The design authority will start doing this activity as early as the blueprinting phase.

Design decisions have the following characteristics.

1. A design decision is only needed where there is more than one realistic potential solution for a problem. There is no point in listing out non-realistic solutions as options.

2. They must clearly articulate the problem with enough details to make it clear and simple to understand even by an outsider/non-team member.

3. A design decision must be as summarized as possible but includes all the necessary details to help the design authority make a final decision.

4. The design decisions should list the pros and cons of each approach in a summarized and clear way to allow the design authority (which might include

members not part of the day-to-day team activities) to take calculated risks and make decisions.

5. Design decisions could have dependencies but should not overlap or contradict each other.

6. A design decision must have an outcome and must list the decision-makers.

Design decisions have the following high-level structure/template:

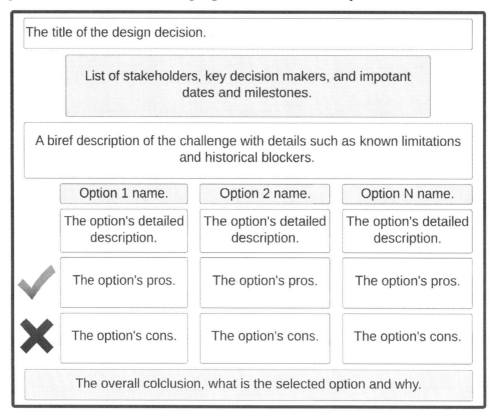

Figure 4.5: Design decision sample template

The structure could slightly differ from one team to the other.

Design decisions are used to guide the high-level end-to-end solution architecture that will also take place during this phase.

Creating an end-to-end solution architecture

The third essential activity in this phase is the design of the high-level end-to-end solution architecture. The word high-level can have several interpretations and is, to a good extent, an abused term in the market. The value you can gain from designing the high-level end-to-end solution architecture will vary depending on the level of detail included in your design. There is also a common misunderstanding that the solution architecture can be encapsulated in a single diagram. To set things straight, there is no single standard diagram that can be used to represent a solution architecture. The diagram misused mostly to represent solution architecture is the landscape architecture diagram. The landscape architecture diagram is indeed part of the artifacts that can describe the solution architecture, but it is certainly not enough by itself.

The high-level end-to-end solution architecture can be represented using a set of artifacts that combine to give a high-level yet complete understanding of how the solution will be built. The following artifacts are commonly used to create and document Salesforce application solution architecture.

1. **A list of actors, personas, and licenses**: This artifact describes the actors (roles of users or other systems within the solution), personas (archetypical instance of an actor), and licenses that can be summarized in a list. However, it is common to see some personas described using multiple pages.

2. **The landscape architecture diagram**: This artifact shows your application's logical and physical structure. The landscape architecture diagram can also be extended to include information about multiple applications or the entire enterprise landscape. The landscape architecture diagram shows information such as key capabilities offered by an application (or a specific module of it) and the used technologies and middleware, all along with integration interfaces that connect the different parts of the solution. In some cases, this diagram will also include details about the relevant databases and their physical locations.

3. **Process flows diagrams**: This artifact is usually a set of BMPN diagrams representing the different processes the solution covers. You came across some examples already in *Chapter 3, Develop a Sample Salesforce Application - PbP Phonebook*.

4. **The data model diagram**: Also known as an ERD (Entity-relation diagram). This artifact is the most crucial for your application architecture design. The quality of the underlying data model of an application could be the determining factor for its success or failure. This diagram helps you design, socialize/communicate, and validate the structure of your application's underlying data structures.

5. **A list of integration interfaces**: This artifact includes full details about all the integration interfaces used in a particular solution. An extended version of this artifact can include a complete list of the integration interfaces used across the enterprise.

6. **A development lifecycle diagram**: This artifact shows the different environments and tools used to build and deploy an application.

7. **A role hierarchy diagram**: This artifact illustrates the role hierarchy of actors in a particular Salesforce solution. Unlike the other artifacts in this list, this is a

Salesforce-specific artifact rarely used in classic applications' solution architecture designs. It can be considered optional in some cases, even for Salesforce solutions.

8. **A capability map diagram**: This artifact is optional and sometimes merged into the Landscape architecture diagram. However, a standalone capability map diagram can reflect a different angle of the interconnections between the different capabilities offered by a solution which is required particularly for more complex solutions.

You will learn about these artifacts in detail in *Chapter 5, Understand the Supporting Tools and Artifacts.*

The main benefit of the high-level end-to-end solution architecture is to provide unified-vision technical guidance for the whole team throughout the application lifecycle. The solution architecture will draw the initial boundaries of the solution and its components. It will express the technical vision in a common tongue language that can be understood by other developers, architects, BAs, and technology professionals. An application lacking a clear technical vision can become a difficult-to-manage and maintain solution due to its non-harmonized components/modules built using different principles and standards.

Lacking a technical vision could have even more severe impacts, such as broken user journeys and experiences.

The application blueprinting phase can contain multiple iterations to create and fine-tune its outcomes. The iterations would continue until an agreed level of outcome detail and quality is reached. The next phase of the Salesforce application development lifecycle can include a partial overspill of some non-complete outcomes from the blueprinting phase, such as unfinished work from the high-level solution architecture.

The next phase mainly focuses on creating low-fidelity wireframes/prototypes to get early end users' and stakeholders' feedback about the application.

Wireframe/prototype the application

The main focus in this phase is to create a low-fidelity prototype of your application's key elements to convey your ideas and the proposed solutions for the given requirements and gather quick feedback from the end users. Prototyping saves time, effort, and money as it is much easier to change a prototype than a working application that developers have spent hours building. Prototyping also ensures the involvement of the stakeholders in the solution design and, therefore, increases their association and adoption of the application. And on top of that, prototyping brings easy-to-understand visuals to the developers that can help them clearly understand the application's expected behavior.

So far, the terms wireframing and prototyping have been used interchangeably in this book for simplicity. But the terms refer to different things despite the significant overlap between them.

The simplest-to-spot difference between the two is that a wireframe is low-fidelity while a prototype is high-fidelity. The wireframe is a high-level view of what the application would look like. A simple wireframe has the following characteristics.

- Wireframes are simple and quick to create; they can be a sketch on paper or simple black-and-white digital images.

- Wireframes contain placeholders for content, usually using the generic *Lorem ipsum* text. You can learn more about the *Lorem ipsum* text from the following link **https://www.lipsum.com/**

- Wireframes use simple placeholders for images.

- A wireframe is unlikely to be interactive.

A wireframe can be created using multiple tools, including a pen and paper. Today, several tools in the market can create digital wireframes quickly (some can even create fully interactive prototypes). You learned about some of them in *Chapter 3, Develop A Sample Salesforce Application - PbP Phonebook* such as **Figma**, **Adobe XD**, **Marvel**, **Justinmind**, and **Lucidcharts**. The following is a sample wireframe:

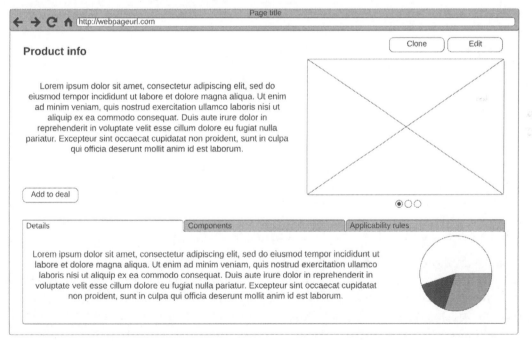

Figure 4.6: *A sample wireframe*

On the other hand, a prototype is a high-fidelity version of the proposed application design. A prototype can look very similar to the final application and even act interactively with the testing users. Prototypes are much more time-consuming to create, but they provide a much richer experience for gathering user feedback. Some tools can even offer the capability to test a prototype with a mass number of users and monitor their interaction with each element of the prototype to help gather analytical data about the design's usability and intuitiveness.

The following is a sample prototype:

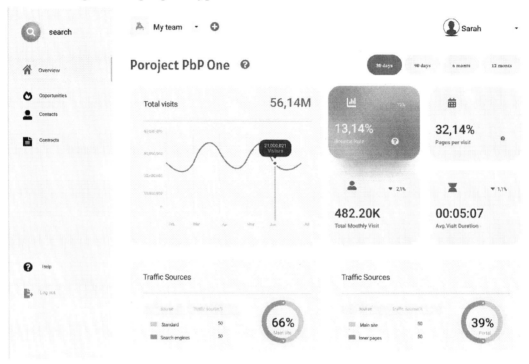

Figure 4.7: A sample prototype

A middle ground between a wireframe and a prototype is sometimes referred to usually as a *mockup*. A mockup focuses on the UI more and aims to finalize the application's look. But it does not extend to the usability testing as the prototype covers that.

Salesforce applications can be created faster than classic applications. The Salesforce UX designers are more likely to rely on wireframes to convey the design to the end users and developers and gather feedback quickly. Then proceed with building the actual version of the actual functionality/application/module/page, as the difference between the efforts required to make an interactive and fully working prototype and the actual functionality is negligible in most cases. Prototypes are still created for more complex functionalities/ modules of a Salesforce application that require significant custom development.

PoCs are also built in this phase whenever needed to ensure that a particular solution would scale without the risk of potentially violating one of the Salesforce governor limits.

Once the wireframes/prototypes are created, validated, and matured to an agreed level, the iterative application build starts.

Build and validate the application

Multiple iterations occur at this stage to build, present, and validate the solution. The iterations are usually called sprints, a terminology coming from the agile delivery methodology, which you learned is favored by the Salesforce RAD lifecycle. To ensure an efficient building and validation process, the user requirements prioritized for the sprint must have *acceptance criteria* defined before the development team can start working on them.

The acceptance criteria are predefined conditions that must be met to consider a particular user story completely resolved and ready to be deployed. Acceptance criteria define the scope of the requirement that the development team should deliver, and therefore they are sometimes referred to as the *definition of done*.

BAs or product owners write acceptance criteria and must meet the following standards.

- **They must be clear and concise**: The acceptance criteria should not be lengthy, yet they must reflect the precise expectations of the stakeholders. The acceptance criteria should be clear and straightforward without missing any critical information. If the acceptance criteria cannot be understood by everyone (particularly the developers and testers), then they are rendered useless.

- **They must be testable**: The developers must check if what they have developed is good enough to close the requirement before handing it over to the testers. The lack of a complete list of testable acceptance criteria is the most common cause of low-quality outcomes by the developers, which can cause a delay in the delivery timeline due to multiple avoidable iterations of fixing and retesting. Moreover, the lack of a complete list of testable acceptance criteria limits the efficiency of your testers as they would need to spend much time figuring out the missing acceptance criteria rather than focusing on finding out quality issues and automating tests as much as possible.

- **They must provide the user's perspective**: The acceptance criteria should reflect the user's standpoint for a given user story/requirement/problem. Writing the acceptance criteria this way makes them easier to understand, test, and reevaluate based on feedback.

Acceptance criteria cannot be written in a hurry, considered a good-to-have accessory, or be considered obvious or known already to the team. A well-defined list of acceptance criteria per user story is the first line of defense against low-quality outcomes and all the problems they bring to the success of the project and the application. Adding well-defined acceptance criteria to a user story must precede any development activities against that story (except for PoCs).

The acceptance criteria format usually uses a *scenario/given/when/then* structure to fit the format and structure used to create the user stories. The *scenario* describes some preconditions followed by a detailed description of the acceptance conditions.

For example, the user stories you came across earlier in this chapter under the section *Creating a backlog of user stories* can have the following acceptance criteria.

- User story: As a [*customer*], I want to [*receive an email notification about my complaint status immediately after it gets updated*] so that [*I can get timely information about any progress*]. [*Scenario*]: The customer raises a complaint about a missing order, and the order is assigned to a support agent. [*Given*] that the agent updated the status of my complaint. [*When*] the changes to the complaint record are saved. [*Then*] the email notification informing me about the update and the new complaint status is sent to me immediately.

The following user story is another example.

- User story: As a [*manager*], I want to [*execute a report covering all complaints received in the past 30 days*] so that [*I can understand the type of complaints raised*]. [*Scenario*]: The system has been running for more than 30 days and has complaints received during that period of time. [*Given*] that the manager can access a system with live data and has already set the report to filter the complaints to show only the past 30 days. [*When*] the manager clicks on a button to run the report. [*Then*] the report is displayed immediately, showing live data retrieved from the system.

Well-defined acceptance criteria leave little to the imagination and help to put the whole team on the same page. However, the acceptance criteria themselves could need refinement and updates during the iterative build in this phase. Understandably, such changes could lead to reevaluating the proposed solution for this requirement. The single iteration in this phase could look like the following:

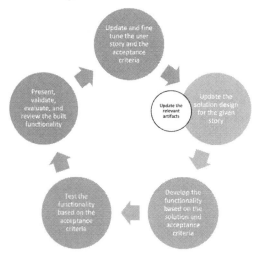

Figure 4.8: Iterative building and validation

This phase overlaps with the next phase. The more agile and rapid the development is, the more overlap can happen.

Test and rectify the application

In some online RAD references, you might find that this phase merged/combined with the previous phase. This is because there is a natural overlap between the two. However, although many test and rectification activities happen during the build phase, other distinctive test activities occur in this phase.

In *Figure 3.7* of *Chapter 3, Develop a Sample Salesforce Application - PbP Phonebook,* you saw an example of a development and release environment setup where multiple development environments are used for different purposes. This approach is usually called a multi-layered environment strategy.

In the multi-layered environment strategy, the functionalities related to user stories are developed in low-level (typically called developer environments) and promoted to higher layers of development environments after meeting specific conditions, mostly related to passing certain quality gates. This approach is used extensively in classic software development and is easier to achieve within the Salesforce platform. The separation of development environments/layers provides a needed level of separation of concern that helps to avoid and resolve conflicts between the different team members.

Think of the example where the developers and testers work in the same environment. Testers could be stumbling across features still under development and confuse them with genuine bugs. This confusion could generate unnecessary tension and waste valuable time reporting and resolving problems that did not exist from the beginning.

Another example is where updates from multiple developers working in parallel on the same functionality could override each other's work, which will again waste precious time and resources.

Separating the development environments provide each team with the most suitable setup to do their work. The classic setup is to have at least three layers of environments.

1. **Development environment:** Where the new functionalities are being built and tested by the developers themselves before handing them over to the QA team.

2. **Testing environments:** Where the ready-to-be-tested functionalities are made available to the testing/QA team to verify if they meet all the acceptance criteria under the specific scenarios and fit into the bigger end-to-end processes in the application. This is also the environment where crucial **User Acceptance Testing (UAT)** occurs, where some end users are involved in testing the new features before releasing them.

3. **Production environment:** The environment where tested and ready-to-deploy functionalities are made available to the end users.

The Salesforce platform offers more flexibility and makes environment management a breeze compared to other classic software development setups. Therefore, it is common to see more layers added to the three-layer setup to provide further separation of concern and ease of execution. The additional environments could be.

- **A build environment:** This environment is introduced between the development and testing environments. The built environment allows the developers to merge changes that took place in multiple development environments and resolve any code conflicts without risking any impact on the test environment. Early automated regression test scripts can also be executed at this stage to ensure new functionalities are compatible with existing functionalities even before testers further test the functionalities in the testing environment.

- **A pre-production/staging environment:** This environment is introduced between the testing and the production environments. Staging environments usually contain a full copy of the production data (although anonymized to avoid data privacy risks), allowing the testers to test using data very similar in type and quantity to production data. Moreover, staging environments usually use an infrastructure similar to the production environment, which makes them ideal for performance and load tests.

- **A hot-fix environment:** This environment is used to fix a production error quickly, bypassing the whole deployment chain. This environment is separate from the rest of the deployment chain, and any change in it is merged with lower development environments as soon as possible.

The following simplified diagram illustrates the common environment setup used in building Salesforce applications:

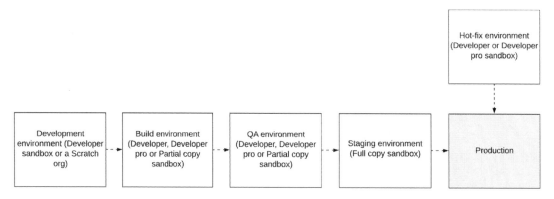

Figure 4.9: Salesforce application's multi-layered development environments

To understand the full benefit of such a structure, you must understand the different types of tests your application might need.

Understanding the different types of tests

Creating a bug-free application requires rigorous testing, which goes far beyond testing a set of application functionalities. The following table contains a non-exhaustive list of the tests that could be needed for an application:

Test type	Description	Tools
Unit test	This type of test is very granular and is used to test a particular functionality (such as a developed Apex code). This test is the first line of defense against bugs, and it should incorporate tests to cover as many acceptance criteria as possible. This test will form one of the crucial building blocks for the regression test suite. Unit tests should be automatically executed whenever a new functionality (code or configuration) is introduced.	Apex test classes and methods.
Functional test (Manual/ automated)	This test validates a specific functionality and ensures it meets all the defined acceptance criteria. Functional tests can be executed manually or automatically via specialized automated test suits. Automated tests provide more consistency and therefore preferred to build a solid regression test suite. Functional tests include test elements that the unit tests could not cover, such as testing the UI layout, UI-based validation, and a few other functionalities that cannot be tested via unit tests.	Manual and automatic test suits.
Integration test	This test validates if all parts of an integrated distributed solution work together as expected, including testing any integration interfaces. This type of test is essential for complex applications with many externally integrated entities.	Manual and automatic test suits.
User acceptance test (UAT)	You have come across this type of test already. This test validates if a functionality meets business requirements and if the end-user accepts it.	Manual (usually guided by the QA team).

Test type	Description	Tools
Load test	This test gauges the overall application performance while fully loaded (or overloaded) with data. The test is executed under normal performance conditions (the expected number of users at the same time or the expected number of API calls in a predefined period), but while the system is loaded with a vast amount of data. This test is instrumental in validating the design of the data model and the CRUD operations while dealing with massive data. Databases cannot scale infinitely, and this test aims at finding if they can scale to certain limits without significant impacts on performance.	Manual and automatic test suits.
Performance test	This test aims at gauging the application performance under usual and unusual conditions. For example, it measures the overall performance when a specific pre-agreed number of users are using the application concurrently. Then the test measures the performance when the number of concurrent users increases (slightly or dramatically) until a particular breaking point is identified. This test generates one of the major documentation that should accompany your application which describes the performance under normal conditions (and what these conditions are) and the performance under irregular conditions with a defined breaking point.	Manual and automatic test suits.
Smoke test	This crucial test ensures the overall system stability at any given time. Note that this test is not necessarily performed as part of a release cycle, but it could be continuously executed at any given time to ensure the system's health. This test is usually executed in the production environment and works simply by running a suite of the most commonly used functionalities and ensuring they work as expected. The results are monitored and immediately reported if abnormal behavior is observed. The name of this test is derived from the simple concept of periodically turning on machines and observing if any smoke comes out of them.	Manual and automatic test suits.

Test type	Description	Tools
Penetration test	Also known as Pen-test, this test aims to validate your application's security measures by simulating a cyber-attack attempt. The pen-testers would use all that is in their arsenal to break the security of your application; the test is successful if all their attempts fail. This test can reveal vulnerabilities such as unsensitized inputs and poor integration security mechanisms.	Manual and automatic specific tools.
Regression test	This is a suite of tests rather than a single test type. A regression test suite could include multiple other tests, such as unit tests, functional tests, UAT, performance tests, and others, depending on the nature of the application.	Manual and automatic test suits.

Table 4.1: *A non-exhaustive list of application tests*

Next, you will learn how to deploy your application after ensuring it is bug-free and meets all the desired business needs. You will also learn how to establish a lively channel with your end users to gather their feedback and incorporate it into your application roadmap.

Deploy and gather feedback

In *Chapter 3, Develop a Sample Salesforce Application - PbP Phonebook*, you have already learned about possible setups to deploy/release your Salesforce application, including releasing it via an unmanaged package, a change set, metadata, or publishing it on AppExchange.

What you need to learn more about is the role of **source code management (SCM)** tools such as **GitHub** in your release strategy and how you can use such tools to build a lively release cycle or what is usually called a **CI/CD (Continuous Integration /Continuous Delivery)** setup. Finally, you will learn how to implement an active feedback mechanism to enrich your application requirement pipeline.

Understanding source code management tools and their usage

A *source code repository* is a storage location (such as a directory or storage folder) where a copy of a code being worked on by a development team is stored. A source code repository may contain several archived copies of the code besides the live version.

Tracking changes to a source code repository is done through special tools called **source code management (SCM)**. SCM tools have undergone multiple evolutions in recent years; most modern SCM tools (such as GitHub, Bitbucket, and GitLab) support the **git** protocol. You can learn more about the git protocol from the following link.

https://git-scm.com/book/en/v2/Git-Internals-Transfer-Protocols

The git protocol provides commands that make pushing or pulling code to a source code repository easy.

The SCM keeps a record of modifications made to a code base in a source code repository and provides functionalities that can help resolve conflicts caused by attempts to merge updates done by multiple contributors. **Version control** is another term for SCM.

The need for SCM tools increases with the increase in the size of the development team (the contributors) and the complexity of the application.

Git-based SCM tools utilize a branching strategy to track the different versions of the code the team is working on simultaneously. One branch could contain the latest update from team A while another could have the latest updates from team B, while a third branch could include an older version of the code being tested by the QA team. The SCM facilitates merging these branches at one point and resolving conflicts (such as changes made by different teams to the same Apex class).

The latest version of the production code is stored in the *main* branch. At the same time, there are usually branches for each lower environment (such as the staging environment, the QA environment, and the built environment). A *feature branch* is associated with every developer environment.

The following diagram is an updated version of *Figure 4.9*, highlighting the interactions between the environments and their associated SCM branches. The Hot-fix environment and branch were removed for simplicity:

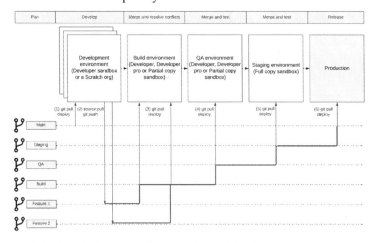

Figure 4.10: *Salesforce deployment using multi-layered development environments and SCM*

The following steps are illustrated in *Figure 4.10*:

1. An initial git command is used to refresh a development environment using the latest code available in the **Main** branch. Please note that multiple development environments could co-exist.

2. A git command creates a **Feature** branch for a specific development environment. This command can be executed multiple times in case of the existence of multiple development environments.

3. A git command is executed to pull changes in the **Feature** branch to the **Build** branch and then deploy the changes to the **Build environment**. At this stage, code conflicts should be detected and resolved.

4. A git command is executed to pull changes in the **Build** branch to the **QA** branch and then deploy the changes to the **QA environment**.

5. Once all tests are completed in the **QA** environment, a git command is executed to pull changes in the *QA* branch to the **Staging** branch and then deploy the changes to the **Staging environment**.

6. Once all remaining tests are completed, including UAT, a git command is executed to pull changes in the **Staging** branch to the **Main** branch and then deploy the changes to the **Production** environment. The release manager usually does this last activity.

There are specialized Salesforce release management tools that help simplify the whole deployment lifecycle. These tools have become very popular in recent years. Examples of these tools are **Copado, Flosum**, and **AutoRABIT**.

This book is not going into the details of the git protocol and its commands and usages in release management but instead provides a brief overview of a potential setup. It is worth mentioning that the highlighted environment setup and interaction with SCM represent one example, and there could be several other setups to use.

Understanding CI/CD

The multi-layered development environment structure, SCM tools, and release management tools have become popular due to the value they offer development teams (particularly big teams). The term CI/CD was coined to describe modern software development practices where **Continuous Integration (CI)** stands for the practice of making frequent incremental code changes and merging them into a code repository to resolve conflicts early and ensure the developers are always working on the latest possible version of the code. The CI process usually triggers automated build-and-test steps.

The CD process then promptly delivers the code in an automated or semi-automated fashion. CI/CD setup facilitates the delivery of incremental code changes from the developers' machines to production quickly.

A version number is assigned whenever a new code version is deployed to production, and a release note is simultaneously issued to the stakeholders. The version number is a unique identifier that can be used to refer to a specific version of the code. A release note is detailed documentation that can be used to inform the stakeholders and end users about the details of the released functionalities.

The version number has the format of *[major].[minor].[patch]* such as *1.12.3*. Here is a description of each of these parts:

- **The major version number:** A major version includes significant changes to the existing functionalities. A major version is usually released every month or quarter.

- **The minor version number:** A minor version includes noticeable changes to the existing functionalities without drastic changes. A minor version is usually released weekly or bi-weekly.

- **The patch version number:** A patch version includes all other changes to the application, including hotfixes. Patch versions could be released once a day or even multiple times every day.

Introducing a smoothly running development and release cycle is essential to manage development activities efficiently. However, it is equally important to maintain a healthy pipeline of requirements and desired features, preferably those requirements coming from your end users or customers. You can achieve that by introducing an active feedback-gathering process, which you will learn next.

Active feedback gathering

Getting to the top is hard, but staying there is even harder. A successful application might not hold its position at the top for long without enough support. The support can take multiple shapes and forms, such as active promotional campaigns, world-class customer support, and license discounts.

One of the effective methods to stay on top is to listen to your users, get feedback from them, curate it, and eventually include the suggested enhancements and features into your application roadmap. Many companies claim that they base their roadmaps on data gathered from their customers. However, only a few live up to that claim.

Establishing a live feedback loop from the end users/customers is easier said than done. The lessons learned from the best companies who do that indicate that the following conditions must be met:

- **It must be easy to participate and share feedback:** The form/method used to gather the user's feedback should be simple, easy to access, and not very elaborate. Complex processes where the user needs to reach out to someone, arrange a meeting, and try to convince that person with an idea are too complex and will deter many. Such elaborative processes were common in other industries in the mid-twentieth century. The core value of such methods is to ensure the idea is thoroughly validated before it is even considered by higher management. The drawback is that it creates much dependency on the person validating ideas. The model works only if that person is creative enough and is open to ideas. Even when such a person existed, retaining a consistent performance from the same person for several years was challenging. This model was partially successful in the past, but it does not fit today's fast-paced nature of the software industry. A modern process must welcome feedback and makes it as easy and seamless as possible.

- **It must be accessible from anywhere:** The feedback-gathering method must be accessible from anywhere at any time. You cannot expect the users to be in a specific location (such as being logged into the company intranet) or participate at a strict time window (such as during working hours). The feedback-gathering method must be available on the go for all relevant stakeholders at any given point in time. Online forms (authenticated or non-authenticated) are a good example.

- **Promoted and adopted:** There is no point in building the fanciest feedback loop if no one uses it. User adoption is crucial; prepare to promote the tool until you build enough momentum and trust to continue without further promotions. Promotions can occur in multiple ways and on different channels, such as email, social media, events, and webinars.

- **Genuine and trusted:** Before spending time and money building feedback loops, you need complete buy-in from the department that will support it. This team must have clear KPIs and be held to them by their managers. The end-users must trust the feedback-gathering loop; they should feel that the feedback provided is being processed by someone and not ignored or treated as a low priority by default. For example, several modern applications provide a mechanism to report a bug. Yet, very few users do because they have done so in the past many times, and nothing changed. The process has lost trust, which is tough to regain once lost.

- **Transparent:** One of the critical enablers of trust is transparency. Speaking the truth is always a safe bet. The feedback providers should transparently know the status of their idea. They should also know who is validating it, whether it has been selected, and why. A clear and transparent process will encourage the end users to provide their feedback so they can monitor its progress. Moreover, they will feel that their feedback has equal priority compared to others.

- **Must support two-way communication:** The feedback-gathering loop must support two-way communication between the end users and the team validating their ideas. This will help clarify some ideas and strengthen the impression that the feedback is handled with care by a team, not hiding behind walls.

These conditions and many more have been implemented by market leaders in different industries, the software industry included. Salesforce has dominated the CRM market for more than a decade for a reason. The feedback-gathering loop introduced by Salesforce (called the **Salesforce Ideas** website) embodies several of the mentioned conditions and more. You can experience the Salesforce Ideas website from the following link

https://ideas.salesforce.com

The gathered ideas feed the very first phase of the RAD lifecycle for Salesforce applications. An application could go through many cycles in its lifetime. Some applications have successfully retained their position at the top of their market segments for over twenty years. Your application could become one of them.

Summary

You covered information in this chapter. You started by understanding the classic Web Application Development lifecycle. Then you learned about the **Rapid Application Development** (**RAD**) lifecycle and how Salesforce applications can be developed rapidly and efficiently using a modified version of RAD. You learned about the different phases in RAD for Salesforce applications and dived deeper into the activities taking place at each stage.

You are now ready to proceed and learn more about the artifacts required to design and document your solution. You had a brief intro about these artifacts while exploring the *Blueprinting* phase. You will now dive into more details, learn how to create these artifacts efficiently, and make that a second nature while creating your Salesforce applications.

Join our book's Discord space

Join the book's Discord Workspace for Latest updates, Offers, Tech happenings around the world, New Release and Sessions with the Authors:

https://discord.bpbonline.com

CHAPTER 5

Understand the Supporting Tools and Artifacts

Introduction

This chapter will focus on the Blueprinting phase of the Salesforce RAD lifecycle. In *Chapter 4, Learn the Salesforce Application Development Lifecycle,* you learned that this phase includes activities such as creating a backlog of user stories, defining a governance body, and creating an end-to-end solution architecture. This chapter will mainly focus on creating the solution architecture and the artifacts needed. Designing the right solution architecture is considered by many the most important technical activity during an application lifecycle. The right solution architecture can ensure your application is extendible, flexible, future-embracing, performant, maintainable, and secure. The tools and artifacts discussed in this chapter will help you ask the right questions and validate the most crucial topics to design a successful application foundation.

In *Chapter 4, Learn the Salesforce Application Development Lifecycle,* you were briefly introduced to a set of artifacts that can help you both design and document your solution, such as the landscape architecture, process flows, and data model diagrams. In this chapter, you will look deeper into how to create each artifact and its value.

As you also learned in *Chapter 3, Develop a sample Salesforce application - PbP Phonebook,* the best practice is to use standard tools and techniques to generate your artifacts (such as using standard diagrams) as there is a significant value in using battle-tested techniques that have evolved over the years rather than inventing your own. Moreover, standard diagrams and artifacts represent a common language that can easily convey ideas to others. Because these artifacts are standard, there are endless resources on the internet on how to create them. However, it will take considerable time to master the skills required to generate each artifact. This chapter will teach you the basic skills and knowledge needed to create these artifacts.

Have a look next at the structure of this chapter.

Structure

The chapter covers the following topics:

- Demystify the need for documenting software architecture
- What needs to be documented and when
- Introducing UML diagrams
- Introducing the Context diagram
- Define actors, personas, and licenses
- Design the process flows
- Detail activities using sequence diagrams
- Create a landscape architecture diagram
- Define the integration interfaces
- Create a data model diagram
- Create supporting diagrams

Objectives

By the end of this chapter, you will gain knowledge to create the set of artifacts needed to design and document an end-to-end solution. You will learn the value of each artifact, what information is expected to be conveyed using it, and when you should aim at creating it during the RAD application lifecycle. You will gain practical experience that will set you up to start designing a performant, extendible, and secure Salesforce applications architecture.

Demystify the need for documenting software architecture

Software architecture is highly crucial to the success of an application. A solid architecture helps you lay down the foundations to deal with challenges such as system performance, scalability, flexibility, extendibility, maintainability, and reliability. Software architecture describes the foundations of a particular system, such as its design principles, relationships, structural elements, and more.

While designing an application, you need to have a vision of how it will react to increased usage growth (for example, by having more users using it or more data flowing into it) and how easy it will be to extend it with future capabilities. You will likely need help from others (internal or external team members) to validate decisions and ensure you are on the right track. A clear and easy-to-follow software architecture ensures you have the right tools to use for communication.

There is a very famous quote from the brilliant late *Danny Thorpe* that says:

Programming without an overall architecture or design in mind is like exploring a cave with only a flashlight: You don't know where you've been, you don't know where you're going, and you don't know quite where you are.

Documentation is not something that many enjoy doing; that can be attributed to multiple factors, including:

- **Confused understanding of what needs to be documented, by whom, and when:** Do you need to document the module's design, the steps to configure it, or the relevant meeting notes? Who should be documenting what and when?

- **Confused understanding of the different types of documentation and their purpose:** The word documentation immediately triggers the image of a lengthy manual that describes how to use every system feature. Creating such a document is seen as a nightmare for developers and architects. However, they are not expected to create it. Such confusion between the different types of documentation and who should be creating them is very common. It generates somewhat of an allergic reaction when people hear the word *documentation*. You will learn about the different types of documentation, their purpose, and when they are expected to be created later in this chapter.

- **Bad experiences from the past:** The unfortunate experiences gathered from working in a place with a suboptimal setup and procedures might leave the wrong impressions on a professional and leave them with certain misleading opinions. Sometimes people get affected by other people's views even if they have never encountered such a bad experience.

- **Lack of support, guidance, and tools:** The professionals working in the software industry come with different skill sets and backgrounds. Some might need to learn about some standards. Documentation requires support from leadership, which takes multiple shapes and forms, such as ensuring the professionals are getting enough time to document, their artifacts are reviewed and validated by someone more senior, and they have access to the right tools. Using suboptimal tools can make the documentation process much more complex and time-consuming.

Several enterprises struggle to maintain their solutions due to the lack of *useful documentation*. Some solutions might have very long documentation, leaving the impression that they are *well-documented*. However, it is common to find that much of this documentation is useless either because it is outdated or unsuitable for the purpose.

Generally, you can classify application documentation into the following four categories.

- **Product documentation:** Documents in this category are used to document and communicate items related to the product specifications. Some of these documents are updated more frequently than others. Documents such as user stories, **Key Performance Indicators** (**KPIs**), tracked metrics, product roadmap, capability maps, wireframes, and others are usually managed by the product owner's team.

- **Technical documentation:** Documents in this category are used to detail the technical design of the application. Examples of this category are solution architecture documents, design decisions, and release notes. The technical team owns and manages these documents. The solution architecture documents are going to be the focus of this chapter.

- **Public documentation:** Documents that are created with the purpose of sharing them publicly. Example documents from this category are the user manual, administrator manual, and training materials. The public-facing section of the release notes also belongs to this category. The documentation team usually owns documents in this category with support from other teams.

- **Operational documentation:** These documents are used in the day-to-day life of an application and are not covered by the other categories already, such as estimate documents, project updates, project schedules, project plans, minutes of meetings, standards, policies, how-to, who is who, and others. Documents in this category are usually owned by the project delivery team with support from other teams.

This is a technical book; therefore, the focus will be mainly on the technical activities and outputs. Next, you will learn more about what needs to be included in the technical documentation and when.

What needs to be documented and when

You need to document the core components of your architecture in enough detail that allows your team, extended team, and potential new joiners to understand all the major functionalities within the system, how they are built, and why they have been made that way. The documentation must be self-explanatory, easy to follow, and understandable without additional help.

In many companies, new joiners spend months trying to find out more about a particular solution by setting up dozens of meetings with existing team members. These meetings will consume time and effort from both the new joiners and the existing team members, in addition to the distraction and frustration that the whole experience comes with. All of that is a cost that you can avoid with good documentation. Good documentation should be thought of as an investment rather than a burden.

You will probably not document every code and configuration change in the end-to-end solution architecture documentation. However, you should definitely document significant changes. Moreover, you should always link these changes to their relevant decisions. Doing so will inform the reader about *what has changed* and *why*.

It is vital to recognize that the solution architecture design documentation is created in two stages, before and after building the functionality. Documentation that takes place before building a functionality is usually referred to as **forward design**, while the documentation after building a functionality is referred to as **backward design**. Documentation generated in each of these stages has different values and specifications. Here are more details.

- **Forward design:** Designs and documentation created at this stage help the team visualize and validate the solution while still in the early stages. Forward designs also help the designer (architect, developer, or others) mature their thoughts and clear their vision. Designs at this stage should be considered tools that can help the solution designers do their work.

  For example, designing the data model of your application will help you think about what data is going to be created at each transaction, calculate the expected data volume, and validate if there are any data redundancies or inconsistencies that could lead to data discrepancies or losses.

  The list of integration interfaces is another good example of a forward design that can be used as a tool as it helps the designer determine the interactions between the application and external applications. Furthermore, it helps clarify what will be required from those external applications (such as supporting a specific authentication standard).

- **Backward design:** Designs and documentation created after building the actual feature ensure the initial documentation is updated to reflect the actual implementation. It is very optimistic to assume that the initial forward design will completely match what will be built at the end. For example, you can miss a few lookup tables in your data model or a few fields. These missing objects and fields will be spotted and introduced during the build. You need to ensure that the documentation and artifacts you created are up to date; failure to do so could impact their trust in them and, therefore, their overall value.

It is worth noting that other factors impact the usability of your documentation, such as:

- **Accessibility:** Even good documentation is useless if inaccessible. The documents and artifacts must be available and accessible to all team members. Moreover, these artifacts must be easy to find and discover. The adoption of the documentation, and therefore its value, can be impacted if the document is accessible through a complex setup only (such as via a VPN). Workers in the software industry today have different expectations from those who worked in it twenty years ago. Today's professionals are expected to access their data anytime from anywhere via any device.

- **Ability to share:** It should be easy to share the documents and artifacts with other team members, ideally via live and up-to-date links, rather than sharing copies of the documents.

- **Ability to collaborate:** It should be possible for the readers to provide comments and suggest changes to the document. Ideally, some readers should be able to do tracked and controlled modifications.

- **Consistent style and structure:** The readers should be able to use your document straight away. They should not explore how it is structured or figure out the meaning of specific styles or color codes used inconsistently between the pages. Your documentation should be created as it was a book that needs to be published. It must ensure consistency across all its components.

- **Maintaining a single source of truth:** Latest changes must occur in the central repository accessible to everyone.

In this chapter, you will learn about diagrams and artifacts forming the core of your solution architecture documentation. These diagrams should be used in both forward and backward designs. But before exploring these diagrams and artifacts, it is good to learn about the standard **Unified Modeling Language (UML)** diagrams, as you will use some to document your Salesforce application solution architecture.

Introducing UML diagrams

The **Unified Modeling Language (UML)** is a diagramming language/notation that became an ISO standard in 1997. UML allows you to create artifacts (in this case, diagrams) to visualize systems. Since 1997, UML had several updates to support the market demand and new tech.

There are 14 main types of UML diagrams that are grouped into two categories. Each diagram is used for a different purpose. You can use them all to document your solution thoroughly. However, a few would be particularly useful in documenting your Salesforce application without compromising the RAD concepts.

The two main categories for UML diagrams are structure diagrams and behavior diagrams.

Introducing UML structure diagrams

Structure diagrams are good for showing the relationships between the different system parts and their internal structure. There are seven main structural UML diagrams. Out of them, three diagrams are helpful for designing Salesforce applications. You will learn about each of the seven UML structural diagrams briefly and dive deeper into the three particularly relevant to Salesforce applications.

The seven UML structural diagrams are:

- **Class diagram:** Classes are the main building blocks for **Object-Oriented Programming (OOP)**. The class diagram enables you to design and document the structure of the classes used within a system. Class diagrams are the most widely used UML diagram due to their simplicity and publicity within the technical community. This diagram represents a class as a rectangle with three main sections: a class name, class attributes (fields), and class behaviors (methods). Inheritance between classes is represented with a closed-head arrow. Here is a simple example:

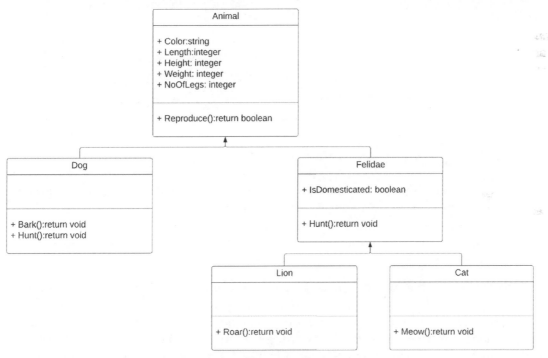

Figure 5.1: Example of a UML class diagram

Class diagrams are not very popular in the Salesforce ecosystem. Although Apex is an OOP language, its developers are usually more focused on building business functionalities rather than optimizing the structure of classes. The class diagram is still used, though, when the class is sophisticated or needs a more advanced class setup involving inheritance.

- **Object diagram:** In OOP, classes are data types, and objects are instances of them. This diagram shows examples of data structures for a specific use case or at a particular time. The **object diagram** is very useful as it offers an example of how the data can look; a variant of it is even used to represent how the data in your data model would look. Here is a simple example where the diagram provides an example of table/object values in a database for a given use case:

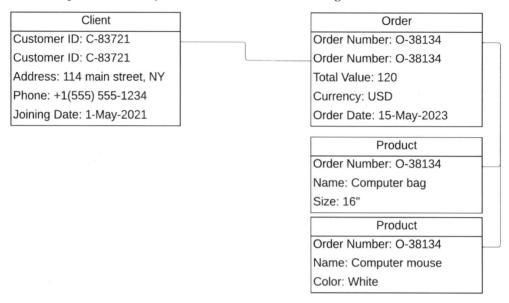

Figure 5.2: *Example of a UML object diagram*

Object diagrams are used in Salesforce mainly to illustrate how the data in the database would look under specific circumstances or for a given use case. This is one of the essential diagrams for your toolset as a Salesforce specialist, particularly while illustrating complex use cases that require a data example to make them more comprehensible.

- **Deployment diagram:** This type of diagram helps you visualize how the different components of your solution are deployed. For example, you can use this diagram to show that parts of your solution will be deployed on specific hardware (called nodes). Native Salesforce platform applications are deployed on the platform itself, making this diagram more straightforward. Salesforce professionals usually use an environment and release management diagram to cover both the environment setup and the target release nodes. You learned about this diagram in *Chapter 4, Learn the Salesforce Application Development Lifecycle,* and came across an example in *Figure 4.10.* Hybrid Salesforce applications (where external elements are part of the solution, such as a backend hosted on **Heroku**) would require more details added to the diagram.

- **Component diagram:** This diagram visualizes the relationships between the different solution modules and classes. This diagram lets the developers know each component's exact role and behavior in your software. This diagram is particularly useful for complex solutions that need to break down a system into smaller components.

This diagram is not commonly used with Salesforce applications since the platform handles many of the complexities. Think of the Salesforce data sharing and visibility module, which consists of multiple layers that offer different services (such as the ability to hide/show specific objects, fields, or even records of specific objects under certain conditions). Such a complex solution would require a component diagram. However, Salesforce professionals get all these capabilities out of the box, which helps them focus on solving the business problem only without worrying about other complexities.

- **Composite structure diagram:** This diagram is rarely used in software applications as it becomes handy for detailing the internal structure of complex classes, the relation between the internal class components, and how they interact with external environments. Most software applications (Salesforce applications included) usually do not require such a level of detail.

Keep in mind that UML is not meant only for software applications. For example, the composite structure diagram is handy for documenting the internal components of the hardware.

- **Package diagram:** This diagram is used to visualize the relations and dependencies between the solution's different groups of components. Each group is referred to as a package. Packages can also include other packages. The following figure represents a simple example of the package diagram:

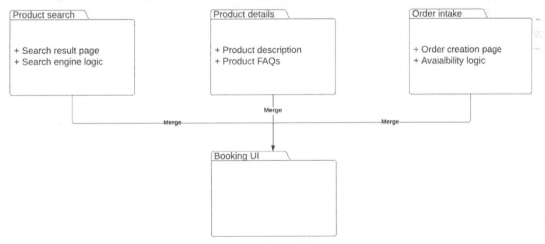

Figure 5.3: Example of a UML package diagram

This diagram is rarely used in Salesforce applications.

- **Profile Diagram:** This diagram is used to extend existing UML notations. This diagram is rarely used in software development.

Now that you are familiar with structural UML diagrams, move on to learn about the second category of UML diagrams.

Introducing UML behavior diagrams

Behavior diagrams are good for showing the system's interactions with users and other systems and entities. There are seven primary behavior UML diagrams. Out of them, three diagrams are helpful for designing Salesforce applications. You will briefly learn about each of the seven UML behavioral diagrams and dive deeper into the three particularly relevant to Salesforce applications.

The seven UML behavioral diagrams are:

- **Use case diagram:** This diagram is crucial to analyze and document functional requirements. It has three main parts, functional requirements represented as **actions** (also known as *use cases*), **actors** (users or systems), and **relationships**. While designing your Salesforce application, you must also consider the licenses used by each actor. Salesforce professionals use a different adaptation of this diagram called **actors and licenses**. You will learn more about that diagram later in this chapter under the *Define Actors, Personas, and Licenses* section. The standard use case diagram could look like the following:

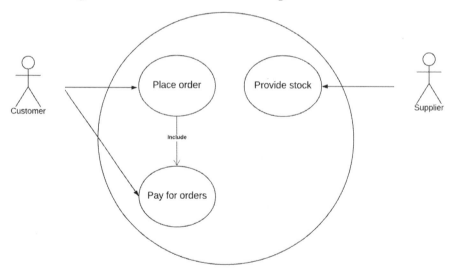

Figure 5.4: Example of a standard use case diagram

As you can see, the actions/use cases performed by the actors are represented as a circle/ellipse, such as paying for orders. All actions are contained in a bigger circle/ellipse. You can also see some dependencies between the different actions.

- **Activity diagram:** This diagram is one of UML's most commonly used. It is useful to design and document business processes and describe the different activities included and the flow between them. This diagram also shows the different actors/entities involved and attributed actions to each. This diagram has similarities with both simple **Flow Charts** and the more sophisticated **Business Process Model and Notation (BPMN)** diagrams. In *Chapter 3, Develop a sample Salesforce application - PbP Phonebook,* you came across *Figure 3.1,* which represents a simplified business process diagram. BPMN is more commonly used in the Salesforce ecosystem as it provides richer content than the UML Activity diagram. You will learn more about BPMN diagrams later in this chapter under the *Design the Process Flows* section.

- **Sequence diagram:** This diagram (also known as an event diagram) is one of the most crucial UML diagrams and is very popular in the software industry. Sequence diagrams describe the sequence of events and interactions between different actors (users/systems). All communications are shown on this diagram using their chronological order. This diagram is widely used to describe the sequence of events, such as an authentication flow, but it can also be used to describe a business process. Actors are represented as boxes (also called objects) or icons at the top of the diagram, interactions between the actors are represented using arrows that link between different boxes (also called activation boxes), and the time used to complete an interaction determines the size/length of each box. Salesforce professionals widely use this diagram, and you will learn more about it later in this chapter under the section *Detail activities using sequence diagrams.*

- **Interaction overview diagram:** This diagram is technically an *activity diagram* made of multiple other activity diagrams. This diagram is not popular in the software industry due to its complexity.

- **Timing diagram:** The main focus of this diagram is to represent the relations between objects across a linear timeline. This diagram does not focus on object interactions but on how objects and actors act across time. Here is an example:

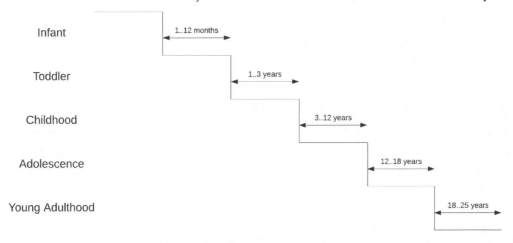

Figure 5.5: Example of a timing diagram

This diagram is not popular in the software industry.

- **State machine diagram:** This diagram describes the behavior of a particular entity by highlighting its different states and the sequence of events that it can go through, which would move it from one state to the other. Here is an example:

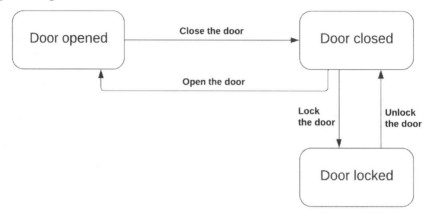

Figure 5.6: Example of a state machine diagram

This diagram is rarely used in Salesforce applications. However, it has significant usage in other types of software, such as describing the actions taken by the **Internet of Things (IoT)** devices upon certain events.

- **Communication diagram:** This diagram (also called the collaboration diagram) shows how the different entities connect through messages within the system. This diagram is not widely used in the software industry.

You can learn more about the UML diagrams from the following link:

https://www.uml.org/

Now that you are familiar with both structural and behavioral UML diagrams, move on to learn about the **context** and **container** diagrams.

Introducing the context diagram

The **context** diagram is part of the **C4 model**. C4 stands for **context, containers, components, and code**. The C4 model includes a set of diagrams that can be used to document software architecture. These diagrams detail different levels of information to the various audiences. For example, managers, executives, and key stakeholders are usually after high-level information about the software, such as what it is and who would be using it.

Salesforce professionals use different standards and diagramming annotations to design and document their Salesforce applications. As you learned previously, not all diagrams apply to the nature of Salesforce, and some are not even designed for software.

As a Salesforce professional, you will likely use the context diagram out of the C4 model to design and document high-level information about your application without diving into details.

The context diagram illustrates information such as general system description, what other system it interacts with, and who uses it. You will find that some of this information is covered in more detail with other diagrams, such as the *actors, personas, and licenses diagrams* and the *landscape architecture diagram*. However, the key benefit of the context diagram is its simplicity, making it easy to understand at a glance by nontechnical people.

This level is where your diagrams give your audience a bird's eye view of the entire system. The details of the system's inner workings and technologies are not important in context diagrams. These diagrams should be a general description of the system—what it does, who uses it, and the other systems it interacts with.

This diagram consists of box shapes representing systems (your system would usually be at the center). Each system is described using three parameters, 3 parameters: a key, a title, and a description. The diagram also includes shapes representing the actors who interact with the systems. Arrow-head lines are used to establish relationships between the entities, with annotations to describe the type of the relationships. The following diagram is an example:

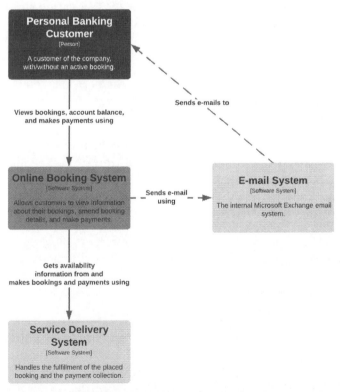

Figure 5.7: *Example of a context diagram*

Other diagrams from the C4 model are commonly used in the software industry but not necessarily with Salesforce applications; therefore, they will not be covered in this book. Now that you learned about some of the foundational diagrams used in the software industry move on to learn more about those particular diagrams you will use to design and document your Salesforce application and solutions.

Define actors, personas, and licenses

This is one of the first diagrams you create upon designing your Salesforce application. You already learned that this diagram is based on the UML use case diagram with some additions that will make it more relevant to the Salesforce world. The diagram must include the actors and the licenses but can optionally include an addendum detailing the personas.

Personas can be misdescribed as actors. The two terms are related but different. A persona describes a person who would use the system; it can be considered an archetypical description of a system user. Personas help design the system to fit the needs of a specific user. Personas are usually given names such as Lisa Smith or Person X and represent fictional people based on knowledge gathered from existing or potential real users.

On the other hand, actors describe a role played by a user, a set of users, or even a system. It is common to have actors such as customers, vendors, payment processors, and so on. An actor can be described with a short sentence, such as describing a customer as an individual who does business with a company.

So, while an actor could be described as a customer, the personas would take that further and elaborate on describing the archetypical instance of the actor by detailing several different types of customers.

Describing a persona using one or two pages of documentation is common. Personas bring the system users to life, making them much more understandable to the team designing and building the application. This is particularly important for designing highly personalized systems and journeys. Personas can even include fictional photos and their fictional names to bring them even more to life.

There are several best practices to follow while creating a persona. However, this book will not cover that, as the main focus is on all the artifacts needed to help you design and build rapid Salesforce applications. And while the actors and licenses diagram is one of these artifacts, the personas definition is not part of it.

The actors and licenses diagram is essential because it allows you to plan and communicate the required Salesforce licenses needed for your application/solution, including any third-party licenses. This diagram makes Spotting the required licenses easier as you can link the actors to their relevant use cases; some use cases depend on specific standard Salesforce objects, such as the Opportunity or Case, which require a particular type of license to access. By understanding what the actors will do, you can plan and determine what type of licenses they will need.

The benefits of this diagram include the following:

- Identify the main use cases within your application and associate them with their relevant actors.

- Identify each actor's required licenses, including feature and third-party licenses. This is particularly important in the Salesforce world as the cost of your solution increases by the number of licenses used. It is important to communicate such expectations upfront to your stakeholders and eventually to your customers.

- Design the foundations for your data access, sharing, and visibility strategy, as most actors can be turned into user profiles.

- Provide an easy way to understand who is using the system and how. Such information is usually lost with time as the complexity of the Salesforce solution grows.

Some Salesforce professionals use a table instead of a diagram to describe the actors and licenses. Both ways are acceptable, but a diagram gives a more appealing view to the reader and is usually quicker to comprehend in a nutshell.

The following diagram is an example of a actors and licenses diagram for a Salesforce application. Note how similar it is to *Figure 5.4:*

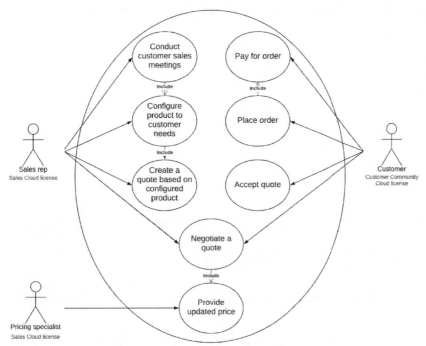

Figure 5.8: *Example of an actors and licenses diagram*

You can see that the diagram illustrates more than just the names of the actors and the actions they do. It also shows the dependencies between some of these actions. For example, according to the diagram, a customer sales meeting includes configuring the product to customer needs and creating a quote. This means that a quote is generated as part of the product configuration activity, which also takes place during a customer sales meeting. The quote generation can still occur independently, but you now know some of the relationships and dependencies between these activities.

You can learn more about the standard UML use case diagram from multiple resources on the net, including the following.

https://www.uml-diagrams.org/use-case.html

The Salesforce actors and licenses diagram also shows the type of licenses used (or expected to be used) by each actor. For example, you can see that the sales rep is expected to use the Sales Cloud license. This means that there is an assumption that the sales reps will be accessing the standard sales objects in Salesforce, such as Opportunity and Opportunity Product. The solution could be designed to rely entirely on custom objects, and in that case, the required license could be a lightning platform license. Such information is easy to document and communicate using this diagram.

Next, you will learn about the diagrams used to design and document process flows.

Design the process flows

There are several ways to design and document process flows. The simplest is to use a flowchart. Flowcharts are easy and quick to create and can be easily understood by many as it is taught in many schools and institutes worldwide. Flowcharts have the following basic elements:

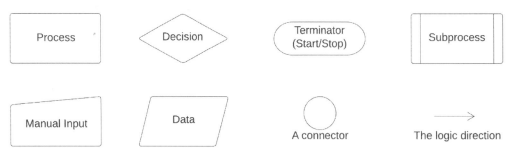

Figure 5.9: Flowchart's basic elements

The following example illustrates using a flowchart to document a simple process to cross the road:

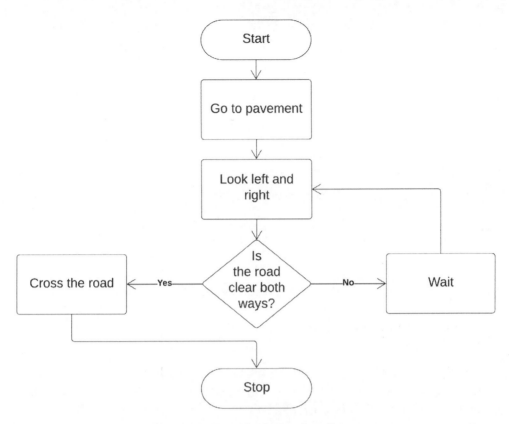

Figure 5.10: *Example of a flowchart diagram*

Due to their simplicity, flowcharts are unsuitable for describing the business flow in detail. Several other diagramming and notation standards, such as the **Business Process Model and Notation (BPMN)**, can be used. The **Business Process Management Initiative (BPMI)** developed BPMN, which is currently maintained by the **Object Management Group (OMG)**. Following their merger in 2005, updates to the BPMN standard have been released. The most recent version, BPMN 2.0, was introduced in 2011, bringing unified specifications and additional levels of detail.

BPMN 2.0 is preferred to design and document your Salesforce application's business processes due to its popularity, simplicity, and thoroughness.

BPMN 2.0 has an abundance of elements. The following figure shows a basic set of them; numbers have been added next to the upper left corner of each element for easy reference:

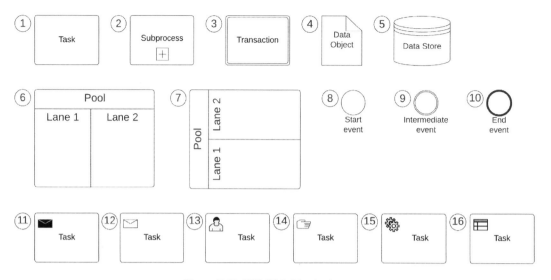

Figure 5.11: BPMN 2.0 basic elements

Here is a short description of each element:

- **Task:** Represents a single action in a business process.
- **Subprocess:** A set of tasks grouped together as a subprocess.
- **Transaction:** Represents a set of activities that must be performed atomically (that is, as a single unit. All pass or all fail)
- **Data Object:** Represents data required by a process.
- **Data Store:** Represents a data store, such as a database.
- **Vertical swim lane pool:** Multiple swim lanes are used to represent the different business process participants (systems/actors). It can be represented as a vertical or horizontal pool of swim lanes.
- **Horizontal swim lane pool:** Multiple swim lanes are used to represent the different business process participants (systems/actors). It can be represented as a vertical or horizontal pool of swim lanes.
- **Start event:** Represents a start of an event.
- **Intermediate event:** Represents an intermediate event.
- **End event:** Represents an end of an event.
- **Send task:** Represents the activity of sending a message to another element. The task is considered complete upon sending the message.
- **Receive task:** Represents an activity that relies on an incoming message. The task is considered complete upon receiving the message.
- **User task:** Represents a task performed by a user/person. This task usually cannot be broken into smaller tasks.

- **Manual task:** Represents a task done by the user manually outside the application / solution.

- **Service task:** Represents an automated task or web service.

- **Business rule task:** Represents services maintained by a business rather than IT.

Worth mentioning that the decision element from the flowchart diagrams can also be used in BMPN diagrams.

You came across an example of a simple BPMN diagram in *Chapter 3, Develop a sample Salesforce application - PbP Phonebook*, illustrated in *Figure 3.1*. You also learned that it is a best practice to use a horizontal flow whenever possible and try to fit the BPMN diagrams on one page. However, the width of the printed book will restrict us from following these best practices. The following figure is an example of a BPMN 2.0 diagram:

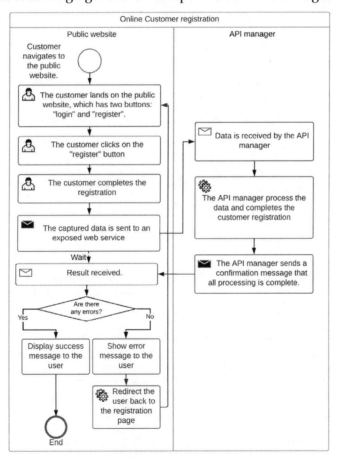

Figure 5.12: Example of a BPMN 2.0 diagram

Use the BPMN diagrams to design your processes or to document an as-is process with the aim of re-engineering it. BPMN diagrams are one of the most valuable tools for *forward design* activities. You might need to detail a specific process or transaction further so that even the most technical reader would find the level of detail they seek. This is where sequence diagrams become handy.

Detail activities using sequence diagrams

Sequence diagrams are popular in the software industry. The main focus of a sequence diagram is the interactions between objects across time. The sequence diagram describes how your system's different actors/objects interact and in what order. This diagram is used in the software industry to detail an existing process or to describe a particular requirement.

The following figure shows a basic set of elements and symbols used to draw sequence diagrams; numbers have been added next to the upper left corner of each element for easy reference:

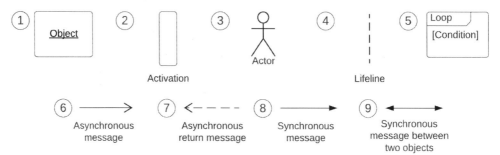

Figure 5.13: *Sequence diagram basic elements*

Here is a short description of each element/symbol:

- **Object:** Represents an actor (usually a system). The sequence diagram shows the behavior of objects across their lifeline and the messages exchanged between them. The object is illustrated on the diagram with a lifeline connected to it.

- **Activation:** Represents the task the object must complete upon receiving a message. The length of the activation box is determined by the time required to complete the task.

- **Actor:** Represents an actor (usually an external entity or a user) interacting with the system.

- **Lifeline:** Represents the time passage during the illustrated process. The lifeline symbol extends downwards, beginning with an object or an actor symbol and ending with them (optional).

- **Loop:** This symbol is also known as the *option loop* symbol and represents if/then scenarios.

- **Asynchronous message:** This symbol represents a message that does not require a response from the recipient. Such as *fire-and-forget* messages sent from one system to the other.

- **Asynchronous return message:** This symbol represents a response message that does not require a response from the recipient.

- **Synchronous message:** This symbol represents a message that requires a response from the recipient before it can proceed further. Such as *blocking calls* where the sender expects a confirmation message from the recipient.

- **Synchronous message between two objects:** This symbol represents a bi-directional message between two systems that requires interaction from both objects, such as an interactive input form.

The following figure is an example of a sequence diagram that illustrates a user login mechanism with two-factor authentication:

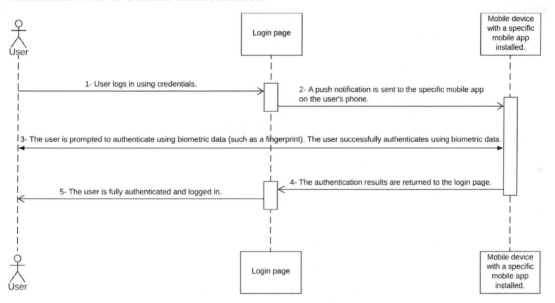

Figure 5.14: Example of a sequence diagram

Notice that you can add as many details as required to this diagram. It is a flexible diagram that is also easy to read and follow. However, due to the time needed to detail this diagram, it is usually used in limited use cases where the need for details justifies the efforts. Next, you will learn about a very popular diagram in software architecture, the landscape architecture diagram.

Create a landscape architecture diagram

The landscape architecture diagram (also known as the system landscape diagram) is familiar and popular in the software industry. It helps illustrate the entire landscape of your solution by showing the different applications and systems included and they interface with each other.

Today, enterprises are using much more sophisticated solutions compared to the past. These solutions would likely span multiple systems and applications. Such type of solutions is usually referred to as distributed solutions. Distributed solutions are the natural progression of simpler monolithic solutions. Today, even a single application can consist of multiple distributed parts that are seamlessly integrated. For example, your application could have modules built on the Salesforce platform and others built on Heroku with seamless integrations developed to provide a continuous, unbroken experience to the user; this example can be considered a distributed application. A distributed solution can include two or more applications or distributed applications.

The landscape architecture diagram helps explain your solutions landscape; it will likely be a progressively evolving diagram requiring regular and timely updates. This diagram is also the entry point for you to define the list of your application's integration interfaces (which you will learn more about in the next section under the section *Define the Integration Interfaces*).

The landscape architecture diagram is likely to be the main diagram in addition to the context diagram you use to explain the high-level details about your solution to a non-technical audience.

You can have multiple versions of the landscape architecture diagram, each with a different level of detail to suit the target audience. However, the following level of detail is recommended for Salesforce applications:

- Include all the applications and systems relevant to your solution. Do not attempt to boil the ocean and document applications more than two layers away from the scope of your solution. For example, your solution could involve a Salesforce platform org, an integration middleware (such as **Mulesoft**), and an **Enterprise Resource Planning (ERP)** solution like SAP. Your landscape architecture diagram should include all of them. However, you might find that documenting the additional applications that SAP connects to is unnecessary. A complete landscape architecture diagram is usually the focus of enterprise architects, where every major system and application in the enterprise is illustrated. However, as a Salesforce application designer and developer, you don't need to go beyond the scope of your application/solution.

- Include the applications/systems you plan to retire as part of a new application release. Your system landscape architecture diagram should reflect the latest version of your solution. During the lifetime of your application/solution, you might retire some modules/systems or even other applications (in case you are building distributed applications); your landscape should reflect that and show the retired systems/applications. You will likely keep multiple versions of your system landscape architecture; the standard practice is to reflect retiring systems/applications for at least one major version.

- Include the names/codes of your integration interfaces. If the diagram is not complex or cluttered, you can even add some details about these integration interfaces, such as the data sets they transfer. The reader can then go to the detailed list of integration interfaces and, using the integration name/code, find additional information.

The following figure shows a basic symbol used to draw landscape architecture diagrams; numbers have been added next to the upper left corner of each element for easy reference:

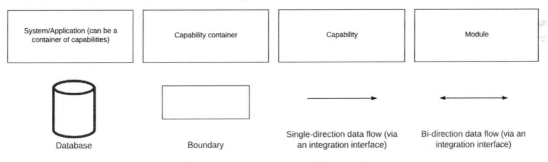

Figure 5.15: *The landscape architecture symbols*

Here is a short description of each element/symbol:

- **System/Application:** Represents an actor (usually a system) that can contain modules, capabilities, or capability containers.
- **Capability container:** A box that provides a way to group related capabilities.
- **Capability:** Represents a business capability covered by the container system/application.
- **Module:** Represents a module/sub-module within a system/application.
- **Database:** Represents a database or a data store.
- **Boundary:** This symbol creates boundaries that group related systems/applications, such as grouping on-premise applications.
- **Single-direction data flow:** This symbol represents a data flow in a given direction.
- **Bi-direction data flow:** This symbol represents a bi-directional data flow.

The following figure is an example of a landscape architecture diagram that illustrates a distributed application with three main components, a Salesforce org, a Heroku org, and a custom-built website:

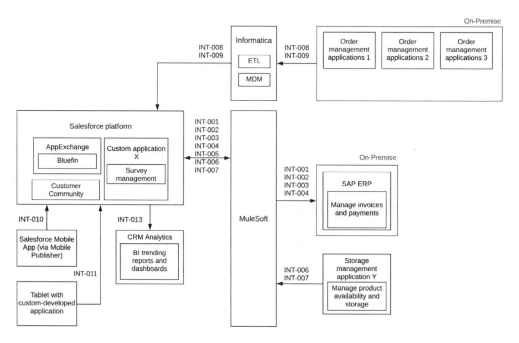

Figure 5.16: Example of a landscape architecture diagram

The landscape architecture diagram is likely one of the first diagrams you will start developing for your application. Next, you will learn about a supporting and related artifact, the list of integration interfaces.

Define the integration interfaces

In today's rapidly expanding enterprise landscape, Salesforce is rarely used in isolation from other systems. Integration is now more straightforward than ever before, making distributed solutions the norm. However, the successful implementation of enterprise software solutions is still heavily dependent on the effectiveness of integration.

The integration interfaces are crucial to your overall application/solution architecture. It is both a *forward* and a *backward* design artifact, as it provides essential information before building the application and important references for the application maintenance phase and beyond.

This artifact is usually a table rather than a diagram. However, you can still document it as a diagram. There is no standard diagram to document integration interfaces; the nearest possible option is to add additional details to the landscape architecture diagram.

The following information is required per integration interface:

- **Integration interface name/code/number:** A unique identification for the integration interface that is easy to reference and use. Usually, an incremental interface number with a predefined naming convention is used to generate a unique interface code. A naming convention such as *INT-[number]* can be used for regular integration interfaces, while something like *SSO-[number]* can be used for **Single Sign On (SSO)** interfaces. The interface number would auto-increment for each integration interface.

- **Source and destination:** You must define the source and destination for every integration interface, even if the source or destination is a middleware (such as an API Manager). The documented interfaces are always between two systems. You should break an interface that involves more than two systems into multiple interfaces. For example, an interface from Salesforce to SAP ERP via a middleware should be split into two interfaces, the first between Salesforce and the middleware and the second between the middleware and Sap ERP.

- **Integration layer:** Applications are generally organized using three layers, **User Interface (UI)**, **Business Logic (BL)**, and **Data**. Integration can occur at any of the three layers. A good example of UI-layer integration is the usage of Google Maps in your web application. You can embed a Google Map straight into your web page and pass it parameters (such as a location pin) to show a specific picture on a map. An example of BL-layer integration is when you click a button in an application that invokes a remote web service from another application, pass it some data, then return results. Web services are a very popular mechanism to expose business logic that could be consumed by other applications these days. An example of Data-layer integration is the overnight batch data synchronization that could happen between two systems. The data would be replicated directly from one data store to another without invoking any business logic. Your documentation can simply indicate which layer this integration interface operates on.

- **Integration pattern:** Six common integration patterns are used in the Salesforce ecosystem. These patterns are generally used in software technology but might have slightly different names. Integration patterns describe strategies of common integration scenarios. You will learn more about the six common Salesforce integration patterns later in this section.

- **Description:** A short but thorough description of the integration interface. The description should be detailed enough to help any reader understand what this integration interface is about and how it works. Here is an example: This interface retrieves four financial health indicator values about a user from the ERP system, which is then displayed on the user UI. Salesforce would invoke a web service exposed by the ERP system and pass it information, such as the unique user identifier.

- **Security:** Securing data in transit while sending or retrieving is crucial, and you must always consider how you will achieve this. A common way is to use a secure connection; over the web, this is usually a **Hypertext Transfer Protocol Secure**

(**HTTPS**) connection secured using a **Transport Layer Security (TLS)** certificate. Another common approach is to use a two-way TLS certificate for better security. This book will not detail the specifications and differences between one-way and two-way TLS security as it is beyond the scope.

- **Authentication:** While integrating into other systems, it is essential to ensure that any actions can be attributed to an asserted actor/user/entity. Authentication is the act of proving that an entity is genuine. For example, when a remote system attempts to invoke a Salesforce web service to retrieve data, it has to authenticate itself to ensure that it is allowed to invoke the service and retrieve the desired data. This usually takes the form of authentication as a Salesforce user. Similar to what you do when you log in to your Salesforce org, the remote system needs to provide details that uniquely identify it and prove that it is what it is claiming to be. Standard authentication mechanisms in the software industry are also supported by Salesforce, such as **Security Assertion Markup Language (SAML)**, **Open Authorization (OAuth)**, and **OpenID Connect**. There are also less secure standards, such as simple authentication (where a username and password are passed as part of the authentication process). You need to specify which authentication mechanism will be used in your integration interface. This book will not detail the specifications and differences between the authentication standards as it is beyond the scope.

Before proceeding with an example, it is worth spending some time learning the six integration patterns commonly used in Salesforce solutions. The following list contains a short description of each:

- **Remote Process Invocation—Request and Reply:** The source system invokes a remove system process and waits for completion. Once completed, a response is retrieved by the source system. During the process, the source system will be blocked and unable to start other processes unless it was designed to support multithreading. An example of this pattern is when you click a button in Salesforce that invokes a remote web service, invokes a process, then returns the results to be displayed on the user's UI. During this process, an icon is displayed on the UI to indicate a process happening in the background. This pattern is used when Salesforce is the source system, there is a similar pattern used when Salesforce is the destination system, and it is called **remote call-in**.

- **Remote Call-In:** An external source system invokes a Salesforce API to **Create, Retrieve, Update, Or Delete (CRUD)** data in Salesforce. All Salesforce APIs return results within the same context of invocation. Therefore, this pattern is considered similar to **Remote Process Invocation—Request and Reply** but takes place in the opposite direction (from external systems to Salesforce rather than the other way around). An example of this pattern is when a remote system invokes the **Salesforce REST API** to retrieve specific data, such as a list of Accounts.

- **Remote Process Invocation—Fire and Forget:** The source system invokes a remove system process but does not wait for completion. Instead, the destination system acknowledges receiving the request, and the source system continues operating without waiting for the result of the process. A modified version of this pattern includes a callback mechanism where the destination system would call back the source using the Remote Call-In pattern to hand over the results of the process upon completion. An example of this pattern is when Salesforce invokes a remote web service to send data to a target system and returns immediately after receiving a confirmation that the data has been received and without waiting for any potential results processing that data. Another example of this pattern is when Salesforce emits a Platform Event. Salesforce does not wait to know who consumes the raised platform events and what is the result of that. This pattern is very popular in **event-driven architecture**, where events are used to build loosely coupled solutions.

- **Batch Data Synchronization:** This is a data-layer integration pattern where data in a source system is created or refreshed in batch based on updates from an external system or vice versa. Data synchronization can take place via multiple methods. For example, the **Salesforce Batch API** can be used. This pattern is particularly useful for mass data transfer and synchronization.

- **UI update based on data changes:** The UI of a system is automatically updated (without a need for page postback/refresh) due to changes in its underlying data. For example, the UI could show live figures of the number of Opportunities at different stages. The figures should automatically change (in real-time) based on the changes happening to the Opportunity records across the Salesforce org by other users.

- **Data virtualization:** The source system accesses and displays external data on-the-fly without persisting any of that data in Salesforce. This is a UI-layer integration pattern, and mashups are a good example, such as the example you came across earlier in this section about using **Google Maps** on a web page (or a Salesforce Component or Visualforce page). This pattern is lightweight and usually easy to set up.

There are other less modern integration patterns, such as **file transfer**, where a file containing data (in a specific format, such as **CSV, XLS, ZIP**, or others) is shared with a remote system, usually via a channel such as directory storage of **Secure File Transfer Protocol (SFTP)** storage. These patterns were not mentioned for brevity especially considering that they are not popular in the Salesforce world.

The following table is an example of a list of integration interfaces:

Interface name	Source/ destination	Layer	Pattern	Description	Security and Authentication
INT-000	Salesforce -> Marketing Cloud	Data	Batch Data Synchronization	Synchronize Contacts and Leads from Salesforce to Marketing Cloud using the Marketing Cloud Connector	OAuth 2.0 Client Credentials flow, secured using HTTPS
INT-001	Salesforce -> MuleSoft	Business Logic	Remote Process Invocation— Request and Reply	Invoke a web service exposed by MuleSoft to place an order in application X (custom order handling solution). The web service is invoked from a button within a custom Lightning Component in Salesforce. Once the button is clicked, an Apex controller invokes the MuleSoft web service and waits to get the result.	OAuth 2.0 web-server flow (then refresh token flow), secured using two-way TLS

Interface name	Source/ destination	Layer	Pattern	Description	Security and Authentication
INT-002	MuleSoft -> Application X	Business Logic	Remote Process Invocation— Request and Reply	Invoke a web service exposed by application X (custom order handling solution). The web service is invoked from MuleSoft's web service and passed a pre-agreed data structure. Once the order is successfully placed, an order number is returned to MuleSoft. An error message and code will be returned otherwise. MuleSoft will wait until a result is received.	Simple authentication (username/ password), secured using one-way TLS
INT-003	Salesforce -> Heroku	UI	Data Virtualization	Invoices, invoice line items, and payments stored in Heroku are displayed in Salesforce as External Objects using Salesforce Connect.	OAuth 2.0 web-server flow (then refresh token flow), secured using one-way TLS
SSO-001	Salesforce -> Azure Active Directory	SSO	SSO	SSO for Salesforce using Azure Active Directory as an IDP and identity store	SAML 2.0 SP initiated flow, secured using one-way TLS

Table 5.1: *Example of a list of integration interfaces*

Having hundreds of integration interfaces for highly sophisticated distributed applications is normal. Please do not attempt to reduce the number of interfaces by merging them; this is an area where a high level of detail is more important than the ease of reading. Next, you will learn about one of the most crucial artifacts of your application, the **data model diagram**.

Create a data model diagram

Data modeling is an extremely valuable technique for designing and documenting the structure of the underlying data structure of your solution. Data modeling involves creating **entity relationship diagrams (ER diagrams)** that represent the structure of your database tables (Salesforce objects) and how they relate to each other. An ERD visually represents your database and its tables/objects. It simplifies validating and describing the data structure and can be easily transformed into a relational schema by database professionals. The ERD has three main, *entities, attributes* and *relationships*. Here is a description of each:

- **Entities:** Represents the basic objects or entities in your database, such as Accounts, Contacts, Products, Opportunities, and so on. An entity's instance represents a specific example of an entity. Technically, an entity instance is called a database **record**.

- **Attributes:** Represents the details of an entity, such as an Account Name, Type, Address, and so on. Attributes are also called *table columns* in a database table and *fields* in Salesforce objects. The primary key and the foreign keys are special types of attributes. The former is an attribute or more that uniquely identifies an entity's instance (a record), while the latter is a key used to link more than one table/object together. All Salesforce objects have a primary key field called *ID*. It is auto-populated and maintained by the Salesforce platform. Lookup relationships and master/details relationships establish foreign keys between the child object and the parent object. External keys are also referred to as alternate keys in data modeling, and they represent a unique external identifier that can be used to identify an entity's instance (a record).

- **Relationships**: Represents the way tables/objects are linked together. Relationships are sometimes described using verbs and represented on a diagram using multiple techniques, including the popular **crow's foot symbols** (you will see examples next). **Cardinality** is an important concept used to describe relationships, and it represents the number of occurrences of one entity associated with occurrences of another entity.

A relationship cardinality can take multiple forms, such as:

- A one-to-one relationship, such as having one account associated with one mailing address.

- A one-to-many relationship (or many-to-one, depending on the relationship direction), such as having one Opportunity associated with multiple opportunity line items, all those opportunity line items have a single related Opportunity.

- A many-to-many example relationship, such as the relationship between Opportunities and Products in Salesforce. Opportunities can be associated with multiple Products; at the same time, Products can also be associated with multiple Opportunities. Many-to-many relationships are usually broken by a **bridge object** (sometimes also called a *junction object*), such as the opportunity line item.

The following symbols represent these three relationship cardinalities on an ERD diagram:

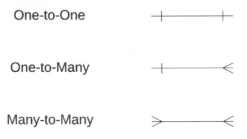

Figure 5.17: Standard relationship cardinality

As described earlier, you are unlikely to see the many-to-many relationship as it is usually broken by a junction object.

Relationship cardinality can also have constraints that indicate the minimum and maximum occurrences that apply to a relationship, such as the following:

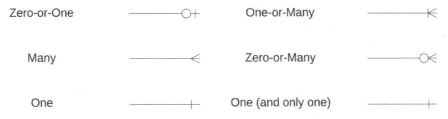

Figure 5.18: Cardinality constraints for a relationship

Here is an example of an ERD that shows the following information:

- One customer can book one or more appointments

- An appointment can be booked by one and only one customer

See the following representing ERD:

Figure 5.19: *An ERD example*

Worth noting that foreign keys are not shown in the previous diagram, but you will see that in later diagrams after you learn about the three different layers of data models.

The ERD was created using the crow's foot notation. In this notation, the following symbols are used:

- Entities/tables/objects are shown as boxes with attributes listed inside.

- Relationships are drawn as solid lines linking entities.

- Cardinality and cardinality constraints are shown using a symbol similar to the crow's foot.

A data model can have three different layers, conceptual, logical, and physical. Here is a description of each.

- **The conceptual data model:** This is the highest-level view of your data model, which is meant for non-technical audiences. You can skip this layer for smaller applications.

- **The logical data model:** Contains more details about the data model, such as the type of the attributes/fields in each entity/object. This layer provides a high-level view of the data structure without being bothered by the technology used to implement it.

- **The physical data model:** This model contains all the required technology details to enable the developers and database specialists to create the database. The physical data model must also include details such as primary keys, foreign keys, alternate keys, and indexes. It can also contain information such as constraints and triggers. When drawing the physical model, you usually list all the object's attributes/fields. However, you can create summarized versions of your physical data model with a subset of the attributes/fields. A sophisticated application may have multiple physical data models, each showing a specific group of related objects. For example, Salesforce has complete documentation of the standard objects grouped by category (sales data model, service data model, and so on).

While creating your Salesforce data model, you will usually use the physical data model but not necessarily list all fields in the object. The following diagram illustrates an example Salesforce data model diagram.

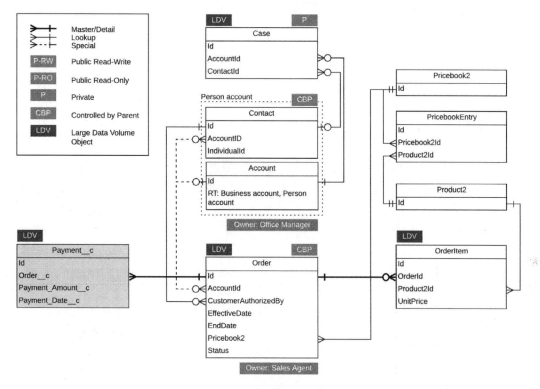

Figure 5.20: Example of a Salesforce data model diagram

You will note that the following information is highlighted on the diagram:

- Standard objects are differentiated from custom objects using the object name (custom objects end with __c) and, optionally, color. A similar approach can be followed to differentiate external objects and custom metadata types.

- Some objects are marked with the tag **LDV; this** indicates that the particular object is considered a **Large Data Volume** object. LDV objects either have many records stored in them, or they get a massive amount of records added, deleted, or updated regularly. Identifying and mitigating LDV objects' risks is vital for all databases regardless of the technology, as no database system can scale infinitely. LDV object identification and mitigation strategies are beyond the scope of this book.

- **Organization-Wide Defaults (OWD)** tags are added to some objects (**P** for Private and **CBP** for Controlled by Parent). This practice is only relevant to the Salesforce platform due to its scalable and flexible sharing and visibility capabilities. You learned about OWD in *Chapter 2, Deep Dive into Key Building Blocks and Tools*.

- The concept of the Person Account in Salesforce is unusual for traditional relational databases as it combines two objects (Contact and Account) to create one. This is why it is modeled nonstandardly using a dotted line.

- Similar to person accounts, the record type concept is also unique to the Salesforce platform. Record type fields are modeled as standard fields with the label RT.

Such information is specific to Salesforce only. However, practices such as adding tags to identify LDV objects can also be used with other database solutions.

Now that you learned about the data model diagram look at additional useful supporting diagrams you can create.

Create supporting diagrams

You came across several diagrams in this chapter; most are mandatory to design and document your Salesforce application properly. However, there are additional useful diagrams that you might find helpful for specific use cases and purposes. Here are some of them:

- **Development lifecycle diagram:** You came across several examples of this diagram, such as *Figure 3.7* and *Figure 3.8* from *Chapter 3, Develop a Sample Salesforce Application - PbP Phonebook*. This diagram is necessary for any application that is not considered too simple.

- **A role hierarchy diagram:** This diagram is specific to the Salesforce platform and illustrates the role hierarchy used in a solution or the role hierarchy required by an application. Here is an example Salesforce role hierarchy diagram.

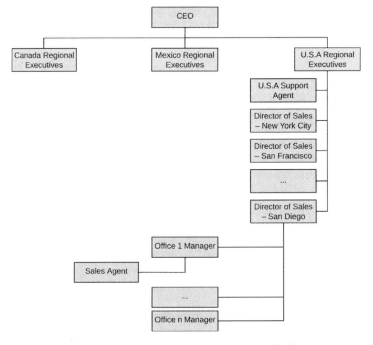

Figure 5.21: Example of a Salesforce role hierarchy diagram

The role hierarchy can also be represented as a simple table, although the diagram is easier to read.

- **A capability map diagram:** The landscape architecture diagram can be created without the business capabilities illustrated on it. Instead, a separate diagram is created to list each system's different capabilities in the landscape. Most Salesforce architects merge the two diagrams, as you saw earlier in *Figure 5.20*.

There are several other valuable diagrams, such as data flow diagrams and data migration diagrams. However, this book will not cover them as they are not necessarily related to Salesforce RAD activities.

Summary

You started this chapter by learning about the need for documenting software architecture and understood what needs to be documented, at which level of detail, and when. You learned new design concepts, such as forward design and backward design. You came to know the importance of using standard diagrams to design the solution before developing any major feature. You learned that the time spent during the design phase is not wasted and definitely not against the RAD concepts but an investment to avoid future rework and costly changes. You then learned about the standard UML diagrams and had a deeper dive into particular diagrams used to design and document Salesforce applications. You learned that the following diagrams are a must for all Salesforce applications.

- The context diagrams
- Actors and licenses diagram
- Process flow diagrams
- Wireframes
- Sequence diagrams (when needed)
- Landscape architecture diagram
- List of integration interfaces
- Data model diagram

And you also learned about some other diagrams that can be useful under some conditions, such as the role hierarchy and the development lifecycle diagram. In the next chapter, you will start practicing the knowledge you gained in this chapter and the previous chapters. You will be introduced to a hypothetical application scenario and start developing it step by step using the artifacts and tools you are now familiar with.

Join our book's Discord space

Join the book's Discord Workspace for Latest updates, Offers, Tech happenings around the world, New Release and Sessions with the Authors:

https://discord.bpbonline.com

CHAPTER 6

Create a Sample Application: Define and Refine the Requirements

Introduction

This chapter will help solidify the knowledge you gained from the previous chapters using a practical example. You encountered something similar in *Chapter 3, Develop a sample Salesforce application - PbP Phonebook,* where you created a simple phonebook application on the Salesforce platform. However, this chapter will use a more complex scenario and clarify the activities in more detail. The aim is to help you live as close as possible experience to developing a real-world Salesforce application. This chapter will introduce the scenario and the application idea. You will then use the techniques you learned in the previous chapters to read the requirements between the lines, spot gaps, and propose missing requirements. You will then create user stories to describe your requirements in detail and add suitable acceptance criteria. You will also create supporting artifacts as needed throughout the process, such as **Business Process Model and Notation (BPMN)** flows.

Building such an application takes a considerable amount of time, even using **Rapid Application Development (RAD)** tools and technologies. It is not possible to list all activities included. Still, you will go through the majority in *Chapter 7, Create a Sample Application - Solve and Build the Application - Part One, Chapter 8, Create a Sample Application - Solve and Build the Application - Part Two,* and *Chapter 9, Create a Sample Application - Test and Deploy the Application.*

Have a look next at the structure of this chapter.

Structure

The chapter covers the following topics:

- Introduction to the way this scenario is created
- High-level requirements
- Reading between the lines, derived requirements
- Creating and validating the high-level process flows
- Defining the actors and licenses
- Designing the preliminary solution blueprint
- Creating and Validating the User Stories

Objectives

By the end of this chapter, you will gain knowledge to validate application requirements, read between the lines, and spot requirement gaps. You will gain practical experience creating user stories and supporting artifacts to communicate the project scope and requirements to the various stakeholders. By the end of this chapter and the following three chapters, you will have gained enough experience to start your journey of rapid SaaS application development using the Salesforce Platform.

Introduction to the way this scenario is created

The scenario in this chapter represents a real-world challenge that many companies have created applications to solve. The scenario was intentionally chosen to be close to the reader's experience, as selecting a scenario that represents an uncommon business would make it more difficult for the reader to understand the different business processes included. This is why, in the real world; domain experts provide immense value to the application lifecycle and the technology experts. Domain experts, such as healthcare, shipping and logistics, finance, and other domain experts, provide practical domain knowledge to business analysts and technology experts, who can turn it into detailed requirements ready to be built.

The scenario was chosen to reduce the dependency on domain experts as much as possible and turn the focus to application design and building instead. The scenario had to have enough challenges to give the reader the desired level of experience, but it had to also fit into a book. Therefore, several advanced real-world requirements have been intentionally skipped. Smaller companies could possibly use the outcome application, but it is by no means designed to be used by bigger enterprises with much more sophisticated requirements.

You will notice that several artifacts will change multiple times during the application design and build. This reflects the reality as many of these artifacts are meant to be living items that undergo various changes throughout the application lifecycle. You will also notice that creating these artifacts becomes easier and quicker with time as you develop your muscle memory for making them, just like driving a car which feels like a tough task at the beginning but becomes second nature with time and practice.

You will occasionally notice some repetitive text and elements when there is a need to organize details across the chapter.

The following list of tools will be required for this chapter and the three to follow:

- A tool to capture user stories. This could be an advanced tool like **Jira** (by **Atlassian**), but in the simplest forms, this could be an **MS Excel** sheet.

- A tool to create various design artifacts. You will need a capable diagramming tool such as **Lucidchart** (by **lucid**). You can sign up for a free edition that contains most of the required diagram symbols. There are some other similar tools, such as **MS Visio**, **SmartDraw**, **Asana**, and more. Moreover, there are specialized tools that are more capable of creating specific types of diagrams (such as **erwin Data Modeler** and **ER/Studio** for creating data model diagrams). The choice is yours.

- At least one **Salesforce Developer Edition** org. It is recommended to sign up for a brand new one for this chapter and the three following chapters.

- A tool to document design decisions and host other artifacts. This tool is preferably a live collaborative tool such as **Confluence** (by **Atlassian**), but in the simplest forms, this could be an **MS Word** document.

It is recommended that you try configuring Salesforce and creating each artifact yourself using the relevant tool and then compare that to the samples in the book. This will give you hands-on experience that will improve with time and practice. Feel free to interactively jump back and forth between the tools and the book; some readers prefer to focus on reading first and then practice using the tools. Use the best approach that suits you; what is essential at the end of the day is to gain hands-on experience across the application lifecycle.

The following section will introduce you to the hypothetical scenario of the Salesforce application to build.

High-level requirements

PbP Software Designers (PSD) is a small software development house that builds and sells different types of software. In the past, PSD developed applications using multiple technologies, including **Java** and **Python**. Recently though, the company started to show interest in the Salesforce ecosystem as the idea of a low-maintenance distributed application targeting Salesforce clients became more appealing to PSD's founders.

PSD did market research and considered different ideas for Salesforce applications. Based on the research, PSD identified that within the small-medium enterprise segment, there is a market need for user-friendly recruitment software.

PSD's market research also identified several competitors in the market. PSD focused on competitors who offered their services on the Salesforce platform (or have a connector to allow using their software directly from within the platform) and aimed at identifying the winning features that the new PSD application must have. The following winning points were identified:

- The application must natively integrate with the Salesforce platform. As the targeted customer segment are existing Salesforce customers, the application must integrate seamlessly with their orgs.

- The application must not depend on any of the higher-cost Salesforce licenses. Accessing some standard objects (such as Case and Opportunity) requires the costlier Salesforce licenses (such as Sales Cloud and Service Cloud). The application targets small and medium enterprises and should be financially competitive.

- The application must focus on simplicity in favor of feature completeness. Several advanced functionalities can be introduced to a recruitment application. However, more features would usually complicate the solution. The application must balance feature completeness and simplicity with a preference for the latter.

- The application must be extendible by the customer. The application should be shipped with a predefined set of functionalities but must allow a level of extendibility to the buying customer.

- The application must be distributed via the **AppExchange**. This strategy will ensure that AppExchange markets the application and simplifies the updates.

PSD did a feasibility study that helped them plan a rough estimate of the license cost. PSD also managed to create a list of high-level application requirements. At the end of the requirement gathering and market benchmarking phase, PSD created a set of documents with the following information:

- Goals and vision

- Desired features

- Proposed solution

- High-level imaginary demo

- Market proposition
- Future plans

Here are the details of each.

Goals and vision

The following problem statements were identified as part of the market benchmarking activity:

- **Lack of internal development capability:** Most companies do not want to reinvent the wheel by building their own recruitment software. They would like to use a proven, battle-tested application that meets their needs (or at least the majority of them) without breaking the bank.

- **Unresponsive agents and candidates:** Recruitment is a time-sensitive activity, especially in today's competitive market. The more proactive and interactive recruiters are, the more likely they will be able to find the right candidate. The same applies to candidates, who usually respond quickly. However, candidates in high-demand segments might be less responsive. The software should aim at keeping both user segments engaged.

- **High competition:** The market condition means that the software must give the recruiters an edge over their competitors. Technology has always been considered a company's differentiator, and recruitment is no exception. The application should provide the recruiters with better tools to win the right candidate, including automation tools, transparent reports, real-time data and interactions, and using **Artificial Intelligence (AI)** whenever applicable.

- **Long interview process:** One of the common reasons for candidates to drop off an interview is the lengthy interview process. The tool should help minimize that as much as possible, although it should also be configurable to allow the customer to set up their interview process.

- **Counteroffers:** The market research indicated that counteroffers are one of the main reasons for losing talents at the last stages of the interview process. The software should aim at addressing this concern.

- **Not enough internal recruiters:** Most companies do not have enough recruiters, particularly recruiters with field experience who can do the initial market screening. The software should provide tools to support the recruiters during this process and aim to automate their work as much as possible.

- **Standardization:** The market research indicated that the recruitment process and experience could differ from one country/region to another and even from one recruiter to another. The application should standardize the process and elevate all types of recruiters to become recruiting rockstars.

The application should address most of these concerns in its first release, as there will be a risk of losing customers if launched without some of these capabilities. In parallel, the team must build and communicate an ambitious roadmap ahead to message our customers that this software will grow into something more capable with time. Still, it will never become another complex recruitment software.

Desired features

The first version of the software should have the following features:

1. Ability to create multiple job posts for different departments.

2. Ability to maintain a unique record per candidate.

3. Ability to maintain a complete history of a candidate's application submissions.

4. Ability to capture details about the candidates such as their personal details, resume, and their current and expected salary.

5. Ability to conduct multiple interviews per job application and systematically capture the interview's outcome.

6. Ability to inform the candidate of updates happening to their application, at what stage it is, and the expected next steps.

7. Ability to define multiple interview processes and use one for each requisition.

8. The application should help save time by suggesting a pay range based on the position's pay scale.

9. The application must be accessible on browsers and mobile phones.

10. The application must provide a way to configure pre-defined activities for each position type.

11. If a candidate is lost, the application should allow capturing reasons for the loss.

12. The application should help remind agents and candidates of tasks expected to be completed.

13. The application should provide a set of reports for management to track and spot any abnormal situation.

14. The application should calculate the commission of external recruiters if used.

15. The application should allow candidates to apply using PSD's website. The candidate should be able to upload their resume and provide a cover letter.

16. The application should automatically parse the uploaded resume and use it to create a detailed candidate profile in the system.

17. The application should allow tracking of the history of each recruiter and show key indicators such as the total number of successfully recruited candidates vs. the number of lost candidates.

18. The application should allow tracking of the history of each interviewer to show their participation in the past.

19. The application should show indicators such as the positions that take the longest to recruit and in which countries.

20. The application should allow the creation of a profile of each candidate with their skills and level of expertise.

21. The application should allow an internal candidate search to fill a position using a known candidate who initially applied for a different position. The application should also enable inviting the found candidate to apply for the new job.

22. The application should have a configurable data refreshing exercise to allow a specific team to update the candidate details.

An advanced recruitment application would probably have ten times more requirements than what has been identified in this hypothetical scenario. However, the aim is not to build a full enterprise-scale application, as that would take multiple books to document.

Proposed solution

The following high-level points describe the proposed solution:

- Utilize the Salesforce platform to build the application.

- Design the application to avoid dependencies on the Salesforce Sales and Service licenses.

- Design the application to utilize the Salesforce mobile app whenever relevant.

- The application's unique selling points should be the ease of use and the ability to configure the application to meet different customer needs.

- The application should be installed via AppExchange as a managed application.

- The application architecture should be simple and easy to maintain. The architecture should also aim to avoid using additional platforms as much as possible to simplify the billing process.

You will notice that the proposed solution at this stage offers very high-level information about the application. This will be detailed at later stages. Keep in mind that at this stage, PSD is still deciding what they are trying to build and how.

High-level imaginary demo

The high-level imaginary demo can contain sketches of how PSD envisions the application to look. These sketches can be drawn by hand on paper, on a whiteboard, or using professional wireframing applications. The aim at this stage is to explain the idea using the easiest-to-use tools and with the least possible effort. More detailed wireframes will be created at later stages.

The following sketch represents the envisioned homepage:

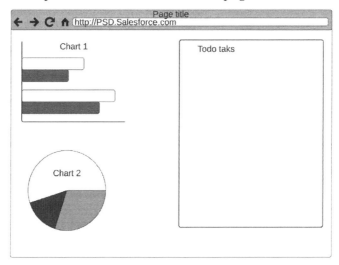

Figure 6.1: *The application's sketches (homepage)*

The following sketch represents the envisioned application's main screen:

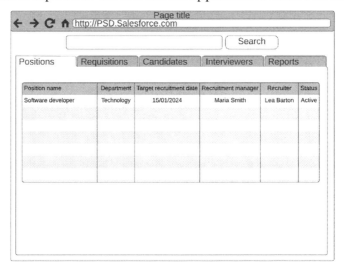

Figure 6.2: *The application's sketches (main page)*

Keep in mind that the creator of these sketches might have no previous knowledge about Salesforce applications. These are simple sketches that can be used to illustrate the envisioned solution.

Another potential outcome of this stage is the context diagram. As you learned in *Chapter 5, Understand the Supporting Tools and Artifacts*, the context diagram illustrates information such as general system description, what other system it interacts with, and who uses it to technical and non-technical audiences such as managers, executives, and key stakeholders which makes it ideal for this stage where there is a need to explain the application to the whole team. The context diagram could look similar to the following:

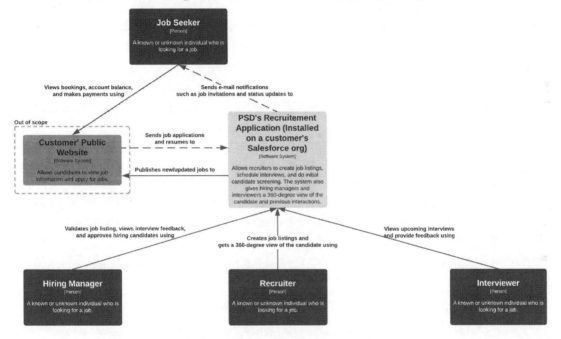

Figure 6.3: *The application's context diagram*

You might wonder about the value of creating such a diagram at this stage and if it can be replaced with a short paragraph. Here are a few pieces of information that are designed and communicated on the diagram that could cause confusion if missed:

- The application does not include a public website. However, it should be designed to support a customer who does.

- The application is designed to be the source of truth for job applications. Once an application is approved for listing, it should show up on the public website in real-time (the diagram highlights the relationship using a continuous, which reflects a synchronous activity rather than a dotted line representing an asynchronous activity).

- The website is not supposed to send any sort of email to the job seeker/candidate. All email notifications are expected to be sent from the application itself. The website's role is to show the jobs and allow the candidate to apply to them.

- The website is a public website rather than an authenticated portal. However, it is out of the application's scope and has only been added to the diagram for clarity. It is up to the customer to use a public website, an authenticated portal, or both.

- The interviewer must log into the system to view their upcoming interviews. At this stage, there is no planned integration with any email clients (such as **MS Outlook**).

- The application will be the single source of truth to communicate and review interview feedback. No feedback is expected to be shared over any other channel (such as email).

Diagrams are very powerful tools as they communicate a whole story in a nutshell. Moreover, they allow you to design forward and clear your thoughts while creating them.

Missing information, such as the fact that the application should be the only communication point with the candidate, could have sent the team in a completely different direction and resulted in wasted efforts building email-sending mechanisms from the website (including integration with SMTP servers) and at the end delivered a suboptimal solution that misses the value of having a single solution managing all communications with the candidate. Such miscommunications are the main reason for project delays and for the creation of applications that do not live up to their potential.

As part of the outcome of this phase, PSD created a market proposition statement.

Market proposition

PSD created the following initial market proposition and marketing strategy:

- The application is designed for small and medium-sized companies.

- The application should not be presented as a competitor to the more advanced enterprise-scale solutions but as a simpler and more cost-efficient option for smaller companies or companies with more straightforward needs.

- The application is sold as-is with a few accepted modifications, but the customer should be responsible for any significant changes.

- PSD will offer limited implementation services (professional services). Major customizations have to take place via a partner.

- PSD will partner with a set of implementation service providers and will train them on the product.

- The application will be exclusively sold via AppExchange. The right keywords, descriptions, and demos should be created and used on AppExchange.

- The application should be a native Salesforce application, as this will simplify the contracting activities with the customers and the internal billing activities.

- A limited marketing campaign will be launched to promote the application on **LinkedIn**.

- The application should be priced to target small and medium companies with limited budgets.

- The marketing department will work with three potential customers (that we already have good relationships) to test and validate the application. These customers will get the application with promotional prices to build success stories and logos that can help us promote the application further.

Expect the market proposition and marketing strategy to look much more detailed and expanded even at this early stage. Some complex marketing strategies could easily fill in a small book. The above should help you understand what such a document would usually contain. PSD also created future plans to help them maintain their competitive advantage, including an exit strategy.

Future plans

PSD created the following future plans to maintain competitive advantage:

- Continue monitoring the Salesforce updates and newly introduced features and develop additional capabilities that make use of them.

- Create and publish articles on the potential use of AI in recruitment, mainly using Salesforce products such as **Einstein Next Best Action**, **Einstein Prediction Builder**, and **Einstein Language** (**Einstein Intent** and **Einstein Sentiment**).

- Develop open-source connectors to enable integrating the application with other standard website-building/digital experience technologies like **Sitecore**.

- Follow a three-major-releases strategy similar to Salesforce and stagger it to occur a month after the Salesforce releases.

An exit strategy is usually part of the application's business plan (an outcome of the requirement gathering and market benchmarking phase). An exit strategy is triggered when a company wants to abandon the project and mitigate potential damages. PSD created the following exit strategy:

1. Sell the application with its source code and complete ownership to one of the companies that own enterprise-scale recruitment applications as a simplified recruitment application that would help them penetrate the small and medium companies' market.

This concludes the requirement gathering and market benchmarking phase. Developers are less likely to participate in this phase as the main actors would usually be product owners, entrepreneurs, sales and marketing specialists, senior architects, analysts, and subject matter experts.

The next phase is the *blueprinting/pre-game* phase, where the focus is on detailing the requirements to the level that allows the rest of the team (and members from outside the team) to understand what the requirements are all about and what value they add to the application. This is followed by a series of design activities led by the business analysts and supported by the architects and business experts to define and detail the key application processes (as BPMN diagrams), which will enable architects and developers to start designing the solution and create supporting artifacts such as a draft actors and licenses diagram, a draft data model diagram, a draft landscape architecture diagram, and a log of design decisions.

Move on to the next section to start practicing these activities.

Reading between the lines, derived requirements

The first activity of the *blueprinting* phase is to detail the application requirements further. PSD's product owners, business analysts, and senior architects are expected to review the shared initial requirements and conduct workshops with the business experts/subject matter experts to understand further the functionalities expected from the application. This will also help in reading between the lines and surfacing any missing requirements.

Go through the requirements one by one and try to read between the lines, and extract uncommunicated requirements. Starting with the following requirement:

- Ability to create multiple job posts for different departments.

    The requirement indicates the need to support multiple departments. There should be another requirement about the ability to define different departments in the system. The other question you might ask here is *what would the process of creating a job post look like*. This will help you detail the process and surface the need for a status/stage field in the job post, probably combined with an approval process. However, assuming that all job posts will require approvals is unrealistic as you are designing an application that should be shipped and adopted by multiple other customers. It is better to include the core functionalities only in the application and then utilize the standard Salesforce functionalities (such as the standard Salesforce approval process) to deliver customer-specific requirements. Such configurations will be part of the application implementation activities. However, what you need to cater to as part of the application is the need for a status/stage field for job posts.

Here is how that requirement can turn into after the extraction of the uncommunicated requirements:

- Ability to define multiple departments.

- Ability to define a different recruitment process per department.

- Ability to have multiple statuses/stages per job post to allow different activities to occur at each stage.

- Ability to create multiple job posts for each department.

  Could a single department have multiple recruitment processes? Could the recruitment process be derived from the job role rather than the department? Or from both? All of these are valid questions that should be asked at this stage. The hypothetical scenario in this chapter is simplified compared to real-life challenges. Move on to the next requirement.

- Ability to maintain a unique record per candidate

  You should ask yourself, *how can I create a unique record per candidate? How can I ensure it is not duplicated by mistake?* Such questions would lead to surfacing the definition of a unique individual and the de-duplication requirements. Here is how that requirement can turn into:

- Ability to define de-duplication rules to ensure no duplicate candidate records are created

- Ability to maintain a unique record per candidate where a unique candidate is identified using their email address.

  Later, the architects and product owners might decide to keep this requirement out of the application scope and include it as part of the configurations/customizations during the implementation activities for each customer to avoid shipping a de-duplication rule that might enforce an undesired behavior to the customer. However, at this stage, the focus should be on gathering and refining the requirements rather than solutioning them. Move on to the next requirement.

- Ability to maintain a complete history of a candidate's application submissions.

  There is little to add to this requirement. One common question to ask whenever words such as *complete history* are mentioned is *how long is the application supposed to retain the data?* However, you are designing an application in this hypothetical scenario, which means you do not own the data stored within the application. You are not responsible for maintaining it. The customer installing and using the application should determine what to do with the data and how long it should be retained within Salesforce. Move on to the next requirement.

- Ability to capture details about the candidates such as their personal details, resume, and their current and expected salary.

Candidates could be applying from multiple locations with different currencies, so there is a need to capture the currency of the salary and its amount. While validating this requirement, you also uncovered that posted jobs could target multiple countries/locations; the solution should cater to that. Here is how that requirement can turn into:

- Ability to capture details about the candidates such as their personal details, resume, current and expected salary, and relevant currencies.

- Ability to post the same job across multiple countries/regions.

Requirements 5, 6, 7, 8, and 9 are straightforward and can remain as is. However, requirement number 10 is worth stopping at. The requirement is:

- The application must provide a way to configure pre-defined activities for each position type.

  The requirement is vague and can be interpreted in multiple different ways. The mentioned activities could be tasks assigned to the recruiter or the candidate. The activities could simply refer to a different set of interviewers for each position. The requirement must be clarified further to remove ambiguity, as the wrong understanding of the problem would likely lead to incorrect implementation. In this scenario, assume that the requirement got discussed with the subject matter experts to become the following:

- The application must allow defining a set of interview types for each position. Suitable interviewers should get assigned to the interview sessions. For example, a developer should be interviewed by a peer developer, a senior developer, and an engineering director. In comparison, a senior developer should not be interviewed by someone more junior such as a developer. The application should allow defining a template of interviews for each position type.

- The application must allow defining a set of activities that need to be completed by the recruiter for each position type. For example, executive positions require far more preparation and market research than regular positions. The system should allow defining a template of activities that get assigned to the recruiter depending on the position type.

While creating a requirement, try to stick to a format (such as the user story format, which you will convert these requirements to later on in this chapter). However, always strive for clarity and completeness, even if that creates a less-than-ideal format for a given requirement. For example, in the two previous requirements, there was a need to clarify them further; therefore, an example was added to each. So far, No other requirement has an example added, which means these two requirements will look odd. However, clarity and completeness should always trump format and good-looking.

Requirements 11, 12, and 13 are straightforward and can remain as is for now. Check on requirement 14:

- The application should calculate the commission of external recruiters if used.

  While validating this requirement, you should ask yourself *what an external recruiter is. This is the first time I have heard about this actor. Can you elaborate more, please?* The updated version of this requirement could look like this:

- The application should support defining internal and external recruiters.

- The application should provide clarity on the recruitment agency that each external recruiter works for and allow reporting on each recruitment agency.

- The application should allow defining a specific commission rate for each recruitment agency.

- The application should calculate the commission of external recruiters if used.

  These requirements can be elaborated even further as commission modules can become complex. But the requirement will not be elaborated further in this chapter for simplicity.

  The next requirements are all straightforward up until requirement 20. Have a look at it next:

- The application should allow the creation of a profile of each candidate with their skills and level of expertise.

  To maintain good data quality and consistency, the candidate should be able to pick a skill out of a list rather than typing it. Pickling a skill from a list provides more consistency and removes the risk of typos. The requirement can look like the following:

- The application should allow defining a set of skills that can be used to describe both the skills required for a position and the skills possessed by a candidate.

- The application should allow the creation of a profile of each candidate with their skills and level of expertise.

  Move on to the following requirement, which is the following:

- The application should allow an internal candidate search to fill a position using a known candidate who initially applied for a different position. The application should also enable inviting the found candidate to apply for the new job.

  The requirement is detailed to a reasonable extent. However, you should try to imagine how it would work and ask questions if you have any doubts. For example, you could ask *how the search is expected to take place?* Salesforce global search provides great flexibility, but it will likely create a suboptimal experience as it is meant to search for keywords across multiple objects. The recruiter may want to search using various parameters such as the position, skills, location, previous feedback, and last update date. What is needed is a mechanism to search based on multiple provided parameters effectively. The requirement could look like the following:

- The application should allow an internal candidate search to fill a position using a known candidate who initially applied for a different position. The application should also enable inviting the found candidate to apply for the new job.

- The application should allow recruiters to search for internal candidates using multiple search parameters such as location, salary expectations, previous feedback, previously applied positions, skills, and last update date.

The extracted requirement is significant as it would likely lead to introducing a differentiator feature. Remember that no requirement should be skipped at this stage because it is considered advanced. Prioritization will happen later. At this stage, the aim is to reveal as many requirements as possible with enough detail.

The last requirement requires defining the data refreshing process. You saw an earlier example in *Chapter 3, Develop a sample Salesforce application - PbP Phonebook*, and learned that such an activity could become sophisticated. In real life, you are expected to detail such requirements similar to what you did with the other requirements. This particular requirement will be skipped in this book for brevity.

The requirements now have enough details to allow the rest of the team to start designing the application blueprint. Here is the updated list of requirements:

1. Ability to define multiple departments.

2. Ability to define a different recruitment process per department.

3. Ability to have multiple statuses/stages per job post to allow different activities to occur at each stage.

4. Ability to create multiple job posts for each department.

5. Ability to define de-duplication rules to ensure no duplicate candidate records are created

6. Ability to maintain a unique record per candidate where a unique candidate is identified using their email address.

7. Ability to maintain a complete history of a candidate's application submissions.

8. Ability to capture details about the candidates such as their personal details, resume, current and expected salary, and relevant currencies.

9. Ability to post the same job across multiple countries/regions.

10. Ability to conduct multiple interviews per job application and systematically capture the interview's outcome.

11. Ability to inform the candidate of updates happening to their application, at what stage it is, and the expected next steps.

12. Ability to define multiple interview processes and use one for each requisition.

13. The application should help save time by suggesting a pay range based on the position's pay scale.

14. The application must be accessible on browsers and mobile phones.

15. The application must allow defining a set of interview types for each position. Suitable interviewers should get assigned to the interview sessions. For example, a developer should be interviewed by a peer developer, a senior developer, and an engineering director. In comparison, a senior developer should not be interviewed by someone more junior such as a developer. The application should allow defining a template of interviews for each position type.

16. The application must allow defining a set of activities that need to be completed by the recruiter for each position type. For example, executive positions require far more preparation and market research than regular positions. The system should allow defining a template of activities that get assigned to the recruiter depending on the position type.

17. If a candidate is lost, the application should allow capturing reasons for the loss.

18. The application should help remind agents and candidates of tasks expected to be completed.

19. The application should provide a set of reports for management to track and spot any abnormal situation.

20. The application should support defining internal and external recruiters.

21. The application should provide clarity on the recruitment agency each external recruiter works for and allow reporting on each of these agencies.

22. The application should allow defining a specific commission rate for each recruitment agency.

23. The application should calculate the commission of external recruiters if used.

24. The application should allow candidates to apply using PSD's website. The candidate should be able to upload their resume and provide a cover letter.

25. The application should automatically parse the uploaded resume and use it to create a detailed candidate profile in the system.

26. The application should allow tracking of the history of each recruiter and show key indicators such as the total number of successfully recruited candidates vs. the number of lost candidates.

27. The application should allow tracking of the history of each interviewer to show their participation in the past.

28. The application should show indicators such as the positions that take the longest to recruit and in which countries.

29. The application should allow defining a set of skills that can be used to describe both the skills required for a position and the skills possessed by a candidate.

30. The application should allow the creation of a profile of each candidate with their skills and level of expertise.

31. The application should allow an internal candidate search to fill a position using a known candidate who initially applied for a different position. The application should also enable inviting the found candidate to apply for the new job.

32. The application should allow recruiters to search for internal candidates using multiple search parameters such as location, salary expectations, previous feedback, previously applied positions, skills, and last update date.

33. The application should have a configurable data refreshing exercise to allow a specific team to update the candidate details.

The requirement does not need to be in a user story format yet. You will turn these requirements into user stories later in this chapter in the *Creating and Validating the User Stories* section. For now, proceed with creating the different blueprinting artifacts, starting with process flows.

Creating and validating the high-level process flows

Identifying, validating, designing, redesigning, and documenting process flows is expected to be done by business analysts. Developers and architects should be able to read and contribute to the created BPMN diagrams, but they are not likely to own them. In real life, you might need to step into some other colleagues' shoes from time to time to deliver the job. This is why it is crucial to possess the skills of creating and validating process flows, even if you are a developer or an architect.

Business processes are usually categorized into five levels, they are:

1. **Level 1, categories:** this level contains the core business functionalities of the enterprise, such as finance and human resources.

2. **Level 2, process groups:** this level contains the value chain of each category, such as manufacturing, shipping, sales, and marketing.

3. **Level 3, processes:** represents the operations and responsibilities within each process group, such as account management, contact management, and opportunity management for the sales process group.

4. **Level 4, activities:** contains a detailed description of each process.

5. **Level 5: tasks:** contains an even further detailed description of a single activity.

There are predefined processes (level 3) for each process group that most enterprises would simply copy. However, enterprises could have a set of differentiator processes that they define themselves. This book is not going to dive deeper into the process design topic. What you need to learn is the ability to identify a process from a set of requirements and design and document it.

PSD's shared requirements point to multiple distinct processes, including the following:

1. Job listing

2. Internal/external candidate sourcing

3. Online job application submission

Business process details can be gathered by analyzing the shared requirements and conducting interviews/workshops with business stakeholders and subject matter experts. If you go through the shared requirements, you will find that requirements 3, 9, 18, and 20 are related to the job listing process. Requirements 15 and 16 are also relevant as they describe a set of activities that accompanies job listing.

You can start documenting the business process using a simple numbered list. The job listing process can look like the following:

1. The hiring manager creates a job requisition from an existing position allocated to their team.

2. The system automatically allocates a recruiter based on the department, job type, and target location.

3. Multiple job requisitions can be created to target different locations. Each job requisition can have a different assigned recruiter.

4. The created job requisition starts with a *draft* status.

5. Once a job requisition is assigned to a recruiter, a set of activities is automatically generated based on the template defined for the given job type and assigned to the recruiter.

6. The recruiter should get an email notification once assigned to a requisition.

7. The assigned recruiter is expected to pick up the requisition record and start completing the assigned tasks.

8. The recruiter should validate the requisition record and ensure all required information exists. Once completed, the recruiter should update the requisition status to *interview panel selection*.

9. Once a job requisition is updated to the status *interview panel selection*, interview sessions should be automatically created.

10. The recruiter is expected to define the interviewer of each interview session manually. Once an interview session has a confirmed interviewer, its status should be automatically updated to *interviewer selected*.

11. The selected interviewer should get a notification email once an interview session status is updated to *interviewer selected.*

12. When all the interview sessions have an assigned interviewer, the recruiter can update the requisition status to *recruiting.*

13. Once a requisition is updated to the *recruiting* stage, it should become visible on the website. The application is not going to handle any publishing activities, however. This process ends upon updating the requisition's status to *recruiting.*

Several other activities could be included in this process, particularly for bigger enterprises. However, this level of detail will suffice as an example.

After defining and documenting the business process using a numbered list, you can quickly turn it into a BPMN diagram. While doing so, you will notice that the diagram will allow you to embed several other details and will summarize the process in a simple-to-read format that can be understood with one glimpse rather than a long list of text that could be written with different levels of detail and accuracy depending on who creates it.

The BPMN of the job listing process can look like the following:

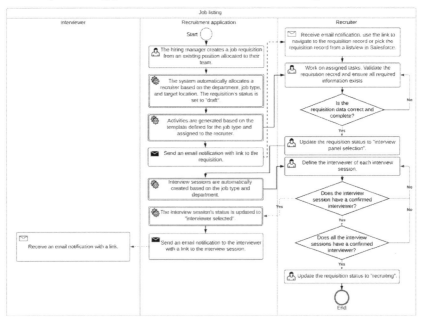

Figure 6.4*: The job listing process diagram*

Remember that in real life, you will not have restrictions on the diagram size, and you can draw it using a horizontal layout and extend it as needed. You do not necessarily need to define the recruiter and the interviewer as separate swim lanes as long as you call out each activity's actors.

Following the same approach, the internal/external candidate sourcing process could look like the following:

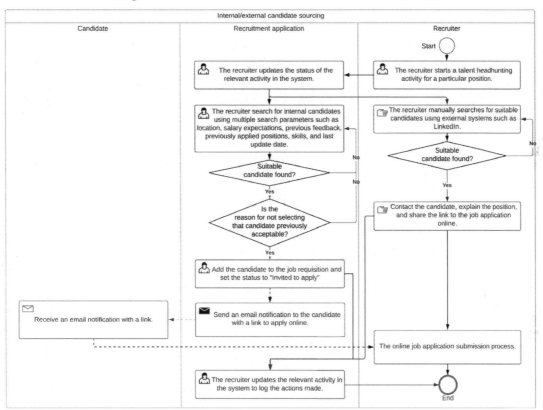

Figure 6.5: *The internal/external candidate sourcing process diagram*

You can add other details to the diagram that were left out for brevity, such as the need to continue the sourcing activities until the requisition is closed. You can also include the reminders the application should send to the recruiter. You may even want to extend the application to record every contact with a potential candidate as a separate activity to allow more transparent reporting. You could end up with multiple versions of the BPMN diagram, one representing the ultimate desired business process and the other illustrating interim phases. For example, PSD might want to integrate with external systems (such as **LinkedIn**) to search for talents from within the application. However, this activity might continue to be done manually for several releases.

RAD is all about developing and releasing applications quickly. However, that does not remove the need to invest enough time to design and document the solution in detail. You need to balance your activities so you do not over-engineering or over-document the solution. All activities and all team members involved in a RAD activity should embrace the principles of RAD and use them while doing their daily work. Your application should be analyzed, designed, built, released, documented, and tested quickly. All solution elements, including your design and created artifacts, are subject to change and improvements.

The online job application submission process could look like the following:

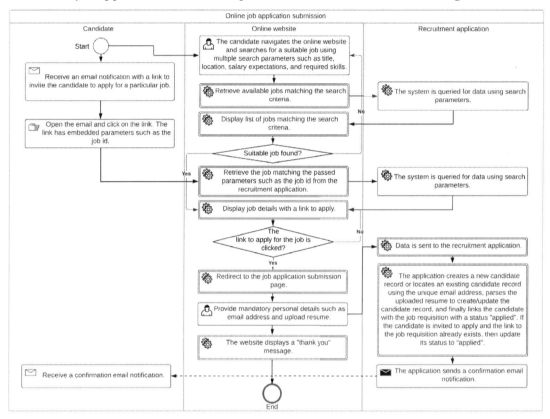

Figure 6.6: *The online job application submission process diagram*

There are other processes communicated within PSD's requirements, such as the candidate interview process, that will not be documented in this chapter for brevity. You are encouraged to try to design and document this process yourself.

While the team is designing and documenting the different business processes, other activities, such as defining the actors and licenses, could occur in parallel.

Defining the actors and licenses

The shared requirements are the primary source to identify potential actors. Initially, it will be impossible to define suitable licenses for each actor. But this will be possible at later stages while the solution design progressively develops. Research and UX analysis are other activities that can reveal additional actors. Research can occur in parallel at a suitable time to ensure information completeness; simultaneously, the application team can work with the already-known information to make non-regrettable design decisions. The RAD methodology is all about making the right decisions on what to spend time to elaborate (and to which level of detail) and what not.

Go through the shared requirements and try to identify as many actors as possible. While doing so, also try to identify the use cases/activities they would be doing in the application. For example, the *Recruiter* is one of the actors. This actor is expected to be involved in the following use cases:

- Review a job requisition

- Post a job online

- Define the interviewers of a job requisition

- Headhunt for internal/external candidates

- Send job invitations to known candidates

- Create and maintain the candidate profile

- Maintain and update the job requisition record throughout its lifetime

- Arrange interview sessions

Similarly, you can identify other actors and use cases. Your actors and licenses diagram could look like the following:

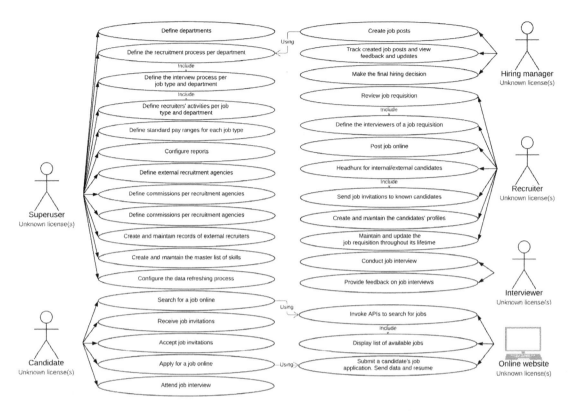

Figure 6.7: The online job application submission process diagram

The standard oval shape that contains all use cases has been removed due to the limited available space on the page. In real life, you would not have such restrictions.

It is worth mentioning that the *System administrator* is an actor usually omitted from this artifact/diagram as it can theoretically do everything in the system. The *Online website* was included as an actor, despite not being part of the application, because the application is expected to provide all the needed APIs to allow integration with an external website. Considering their simplicity, some use cases, such as receiving notifications and reminders, were not included for brevity.

At later stages, once the solution design is further detailed, you will know which objects and standard functionalities each actor will access. Based on that, you can update this diagram with each actor's suitable license(s).

In parallel, the architects and developers can work on designing the other parts of the preliminary solution blueprint.

Designing the preliminary solution blueprint

Designing an end-to-end solution starts with understanding and solving shared requirements individually and as a whole. Solving the requirements individually without considering how they fit into the bigger picture would inevitably create gaps and broken experiences.

The ability to imagine, document, and communicate how the different functionalities complement each other to provide smooth journeys to the end user while maintaining high data quality standards is the core competency of a good software architect, and it is something that you can learn with rigorous practice and commitment.

The artifacts you learned about in this book are tools to help you design a performant, secure, and extendable end-to-end solution. At this stage, two key artifacts that can help you create the preliminary solution blueprint are the landscape architecture diagram and the data model diagram.

This application is planned to be a Salesforce native application where all its components are built on the Salesforce platform rather than built on an external system and then integrated with the Salesforce platform. However, this could change depending on the needed functionalities and the design decisions.

For example, requirement number 25 indicates that the application should automatically parse the uploaded resume and use it to create a detailed candidate profile. This can be achieved, to an extent, using the Salesforce platform and Apex code. However, there are certain limitations that you need to consider, such as the memory size available for your Salesforce native application and the maximum size of files you can parse in parallel. In most cases, you will shift memory-intense functionalities from the Salesforce platform to an infrastructure that gives you more control over memory management and processing power, such as **Heroku**, **AWS**, or **Microsoft Azure**.

The requirements shared by PSD and the extended set of requirements you derived from them are yet to be prioritized. The prioritization process can postpone the introduction of some functionalities to later stages due to their complexity or low value. Requirement 25 could be a good candidate for a later release. This means the application will not have this requirement's solution as part of its design for the first release. However, the application should be designed from day one to support this expected feature in the subsequent releases.

The architects should look at the complete known set of requirements and consider them all for the end-to-end solution, although only the prioritized requirements will be detailed.

Returning to requirement 25, you should design a solution that does not support this requirement in its first release but can still support it in later releases with minimal changes and effort. The following two approaches could be followed:

- You could design the solution to receive the resume as an attachment, then expect the recruiter to download and open this attachment every time they need to view something in it.

- Or you could design the solution to receive the resume as an attachment, then expect the recruiter to download it once and manually populate particular objects in the applications with data from the resume. Then use the data in the application from there onwards.

The first approach dodges requirement 25 completely and postpones any potential solution to the future. This means that once requirement 25 is developed and released, a significant change management activity will be required to help the end users adopt the new functionality.

The second approach adds more upfront workload to the end users but sets the foundations for a smooth and easy transition to the future desired functionality. The application's governance body must decide whether to go with the first approach or the second. There are several standard prioritization techniques, such as **ICE** and **RICE**. This book is not going to cover this topic, but you are encouraged to read more about these techniques from the following link:

https://en.wikipedia.org/wiki/Requirement_prioritization

In the case of the PSD's hypothetical scenario, assume that the second approach (where objects are created in Salesforce to store the job resume manually) is preferred.

The landscape architecture diagram would look like the following:

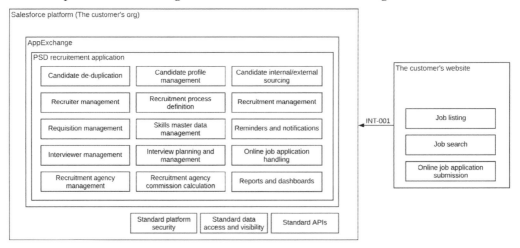

Figure 6.8: *The landscape architecture diagram for the application's first release*

While creating the landscape architecture diagram is also recommended to create another version with the expected future solution. The landscape architecture diagram could look like the following:

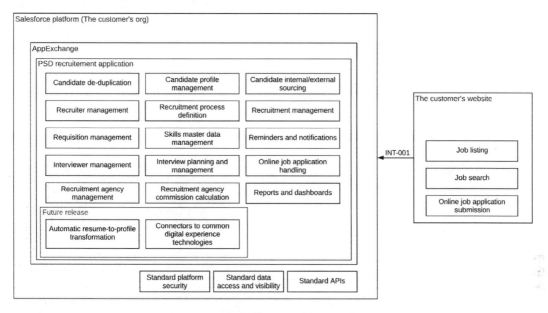

Figure 6.9: *The landscape architecture diagram*

You can include both versions in your solution blueprint for easy reading or simply use the second. Remember that this artifact, similar to all other artifacts of this solution, are live documents that are expected to change with time as you learn more about the application and the desired functionalities.

The role hierarchy diagram is one of the solution blueprint artifacts, and it has different importance and impact depending on the nature of the solution. The PSD recruitment application will be a managed application deployed via AppExchange. It is expected that the role hierarchy setup will be part of the installation process and will adapt to the role hierarchy used in the customer's Salesforce org. Therefore, you are not going to create a role hierarchy diagram for the application.

The data model diagram is the most crucial artifact at this stage. As you learned in *Chapter 1, Introduction to the Salesforce Platform*, the data model is the heart and soul of your application and a crucial factor in its success or failure. The data model diagram will help you design forward and avoid costly mistakes with your application's data structures.

The design of your data model is directly derived from the shared requirements. For example, requirement 1 indicates a need to define multiple departments in the system. This means you will need an object to store the departments and their definition. Requirement number 2 indicates a need to define a different recruitment process per department; this means you will need an object to store the recruitment process definition. What would be the relationship between these two objects? A department has a single recruitment process as per the requirement. You would probably think of designing your data model to look like the following:

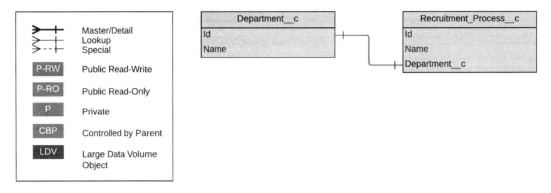

Figure 6.10: The data model diagram (first draft)

Notice that both objects are custom, as no standard object can be used to model a department or a recruitment process without significant modifications. Also, remember that standard objects might already be used by the customer planning to use your application.

The one-to-one relationship is interesting, however. You need to ask yourself, *how will that object be used within the recruitment process? What would make a recruitment process different? And how will that object help you provide a different recruitment process per department?*

A recruitment process consists of activities that take place at multiple *stages*. The stages are crucial to defining a process. You need to define a different set of recruitment stages per department. Each department could have one or more recruitment stages. The design of your data model could look different now. Something similar to the following:

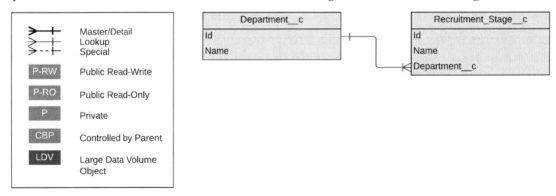

Figure 6.11: The data model diagram (second draft)

The relationship between the two objects is still a lookup. You should ask yourself, *can a recruitment stage record exist without a department? Will I ever have a use case where a user should be able to view a department but not its recruitment stages?* Assume that the answer is no for both of these questions for this scenario. You could then use a master/detail relationship instead of a lookup. The design of your data model could look like the following:

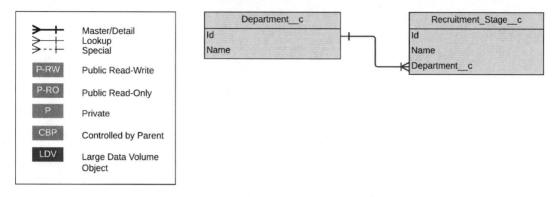

Figure 6.12: The data model diagram (third draft)

Next, you should ask yourself *what fields are relevant to both objects*? In some cases, you get these requirements straight from the business analysts. However, it would be best to consider what fields should logically exist in both objects. You can validate these assumptions with the business analysts and remove or update some of your assumed fields. However, you will also likely end up with additional fields they have yet to consider.

Do not expect all the fields to be shared by the business analyst, you are a technology specialist, and you should add value by thinking about what additional fields would make sense to add. You can compare with other existing applications in the market, use your experience, google for best practices, or validate with other architects.

For example, most companies have **Enterprise Resource Planning (ERP)** solutions in their landscape, where each department has a unique ID. It would be helpful if that ID could be imported into your application's data model for consistency. Having a sequence number for each recruitment stage makes sense; otherwise, there is no way to indicate their order.

Additional information about the department, such as the head of the department, the parent org structure (parent department), and a description (for both the department and the stage), could also be handy. Your data model could look like the following:

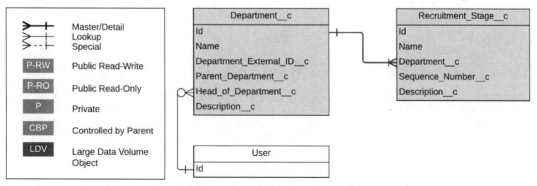

Figure 6.13: The data model diagram (fourth draft)

Remember that this is still a preliminary design, and it is very likely that your data model will look completely different in later stages.

Requirement 3 indicates a need for an object to hold the job post/job requisition and should have multiple statuses/stages. It happens that we have just created the **Recruitment_ Stage__c** object to keep recruitment statuses. The job requisition could be linked to the **Recruitment_Stage__c** object and use a lookup filter to show only those stages relevant to a particular department. You will also need a lookup to the department on the job requisition object to indicate which department owns it. Can a job requisition exist without a department? The answer is no. Will you ever have a use case where a user should be able to view a department but not its requisitions? Yes, that is very likely. This means a lookup relationship is more suitable here than a master/detail relationship. You can think of other relevant fields for the job requisition object, such as the start hiring data, desired end hiring data, actual end hiring date, hiring manager, and a few others that you can figure out after you go through the rest of the requirements. At this stage, your data model could look similar to the following:

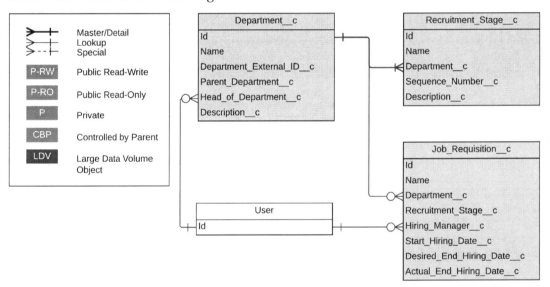

Figure 6.14: The data model diagram (fifth draft)

Continue going through the rest of the requirements and design your data model accordingly. Take your time and consider all aspects. For example, you will need an object to store the candidate's details. Would that be the standard **Contact** object, or is it better to use a custom object? As both options are theoretically valid with pros and cons, you must create a design decision and validate it with the application's design authority.

In *Chapter 4, Learn the Salesforce Application Development Lifecycle;* you came across a sample design decision template (*Figure 4.5: Design decision sample template*). You can use a similar template here to document your thoughts and recommendations, then bring that to the design authority for discussion and decision-making. Your design decision could look like the following:

- **Title**: Design decision DD-02817. The object used to model candidates.

- **Stakeholder**: Names of stakeholders, yourself included.

- **Dates and milestones**: Include relevant dates and milestones here, such as the deadline for decision-making.

- **Description**: The application needs to store the candidate's private details, such as first name, last name, email address, and mobile phone number, in the application so that it can be used during the resume creation and job application. A decision must be taken regarding the object used to model candidates in the system.

- **Option 1 title**: Use the standard **Contact** object.

- **Option 1 details**: Utilize the standard **Contact** object. The **Contact** object is included in all editions of the Salesforce platform and should be available to potential customers.

- **Option 1 pros**: The customer would likely have used the **Contact** object to store contacts relevant to their business. Using the same standard object ensures that all types of contacts are stored in a single location, enabling easy reporting and data-stewarding activities.

- **Option 1 cons**: There is a risk of cluttering the **Contact** object for the customer. The customer would likely need to introduce a new record type for candidates. This option also could force the customer to update existing validation and de-duplication rules they might have introduced to the **Contact** object.

- **Option 2 title**: Use a custom object (such as **Candidate__c**).

- **Option 2 details**: Introduce a custom **Candidate__c** object.

- **Option 2 pros**: Independent from any standard objects at the customer org, this avoids clashes with existing code and logic. Moreover, this approach gives PSD the ultimate control over the structure of this object.

- **Option 2 cons**: The data of the various business contacts in the customer org will be split over two objects, the standard **Contact** object and the custom **Candidate__c** object, which will introduce a challenge for data reporting and stewardship. Moreover, the customer might need to duplicate validations and custom logic that they introduced to their standard **Contact** object and is relevant to the **Candidate__c** object.

- **Recommendation**: Option 1 is recommended as the benefit of re-using existing logic outweighs the known risks.

- **Conclusion**: The design authority met on the given date and chose Option 1 as a solution.

Depending on the use case, you could have different pros and cons based on several internal and external factors (for example, you could have received clear guidance from a selected group of potential customers). For this scenario, assume the decision is to use the standard **Contact** object.

You might need similar design decisions for the job requisition object (is it better to use the standard Opportunity object or a custom object) and sometimes choose between standard objects (is it better to use the **Contact** or the **User** object to store the recruiter's detail?) Remember that some recruiters could belong to external agencies and do not have access to the Salesforce application).

Continue going through the requirements and creating design decisions when needed. Your created data model diagram could look like the following:

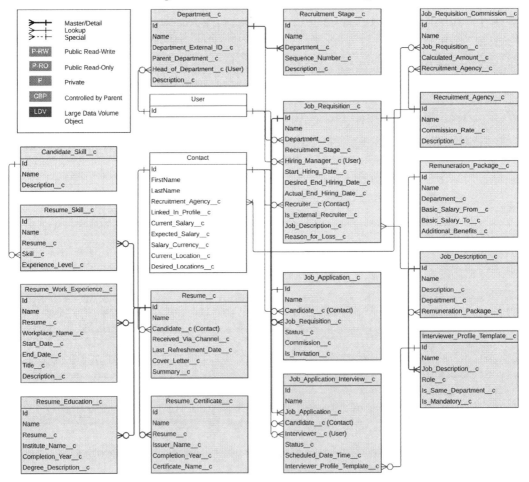

***Figure 6.15**: The data model diagram (sixth draft)*

Now, add your preliminary thoughts about the OWD for each object, and think of potential LDV objects (if any). Your data model diagram could look like the following:

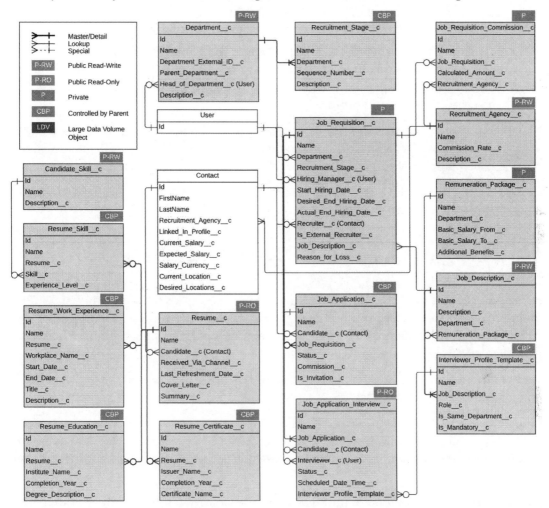

Figure 6.16: *The data model diagram (seventh draft)*

Some assumptions were made to come up with the OWD shown in the previous diagram. You have not received requirements about that, but you can make reasonable assumptions such as the following:

- A **Job_Requisition__c** can be confidential or publicly visible to the org's employees (partially or fully). You cannot control the record's visibility with the desired granularity if you set the object's OWD to anything but **Private**.

- The calculated agency commissions stored in **Job_Requisition_Commission__c** will likely be confidential and visible only to the record owner and whomever above that user in the role hierarchy, hence setting the OWD to **Private**.

- A **Job_Description__c** should be accessible to everyone but editable only to a subset of users. Setting the object to **Public Read-Only** allows you to have more granular control over the edit permission based on the user profiles, permission sets, and sharing rules.

- Lookup objects such as **Department__c** and **Candidate_Skill__c** should be accessible to all users. It is unlikely to require sophisticated access control for such objects, and you can set their OWD to **Public Read-Write** and control access to the object via profiles and permission sets only.

The data model will evolve and change as you progress in the application's lifecycle. You are very likely to add/change additional fields and objects at later stages, but you have to make the best possible efforts to identify as many as possible early on.

In parallel, the rest of the team will tirelessly work on formatting requirements into user stories validated with the different stakeholders.

Creating and validating the user stories

In *Chapter 4, Learn the Salesforce Application Development Lifecycle;* you learned the format of user stories and the value of using it. User stories are easier to understand and follow, giving a better view of the requirement and its value. Process flows and user stories combine to give the team a full view of the requirement and its position in the bigger picture.

Acceptance criteria should also accompany user stories. The acceptance criteria define when a story is considered done.

Look at the shared PSD requirements and try to format some of them as user stories. You will likely need input from the business/subject matter experts to create the acceptance criteria. Sometimes, you might be able to define the acceptance criteria and then get them validated/confirmed.

Start by formatting requirement number 1 as a user story. It could look like the following:

- User story US-001: As a *[superuser]*, I want *[to be able to define multiple departments in the application]* so that *[I can define a different recruitment process for each]*.

- *[Scenario]*: The superuser attempts to create a new record to define a department in the system.

- *[Given]* that the superuser provided the following information: department name (mandatory), department external id (optional, but unique if entered), parent department (optional), head of department (a user, mandatory), and a description (optional).

- *[When]* the data is entered, the superuser attempts to save the record.

- *[Then]* the record must be created with the given information.

You might have noticed that the user story complements the actors and licenses diagram by further defining what the actor is expected to do. This lays down the foundation to define personas for your application. Without this detail, you are likely to spend a lot of time and effort in the future trying to reverse engineer the solution to identify the targeted personas. You might have also noticed a unique name given to each user story. The format of this name is up to the team to decide. Still, using a consistent and easy-to-remember format is strongly recommended throughout the application lifecycle (and across the whole company, if possible).

Try formatting requirement number 2 as a user story. It could look like the following:

- User story US-002: As a *[superuser]*, I want *[to be able to define a different recruitment process per department]* so that *[I can give flexibility to each department to determine their process based on their needs]*.

- *[Scenario 1]*: The superuser attempts to create a new set of records to define the different stages a recruitment process can follow for a given department.

- *[Given]* that the superuser provided the following information: Stage name (mandatory), department id (mandatory, which should be the Salesforce id of the department), sequence number (mandatory), and a description (optional).

- *[When]* the data is entered, the superuser attempts to save the record.

- *[Then]* the record must be created with the given information. Each department's recruitment process should have at least one recruitment stage. The maximum number of expected stages is seven, but the system should be flexible to allow unlimited stages.

- *[Scenario 2]*: The superuser successfully creates a new department record.

- *[Given]* that the department does not already have recruitment stages defined.

- *[When]* the department record is created successfully.

- *[Then]* the system should automatically generate a recruitment stage record with the following information: stage name (draft), department id (the Salesforce id of the recently created department), sequence number (1), and description (empty).

The format of the user story is important, but what is even more important is the detail of the content. You should always strive to provide as much detail as possible in the story, as this will help the rest of the team build a high-quality solution and test it thoroughly using the correct test scenarios. If you do not provide detailed acceptance criteria, the testers will find determining what scenarios to test challenging. Clear and well-defined acceptance criteria can even help you create automated test scripts and increase the stability and quality of your solution without spending more time, money, and effort on regression tests.

You cannot build a safe and solid skyscraper without adequate foundations. Software development is very similar, and a successful application always has a solid foundation.

Try to format another requirement as a user story. You can choose requirement 7 this time. The created user story could look like the following:

- User story US-007: As a *[recruiter]*, I want *[to be able to view the complete history of a candidate's job applications]* so that *[I can get a better understanding of the candidates and their behavior and history]*.

- *[Scenario 1]*: The recruiter views a candidate's record to check if the candidate was previously shortlisted for a particular job.

- *[Given]* that the candidate applied previously to another non-confidential job.

- *[When]* the candidate record is displayed.

- *[Then]* the system should show all the application submission records of the given candidate for the past 10 years. The recruiter should be able to view any of these job applications by clicking on it.

- *[Scenario 2]*: The recruiter views a candidate's record to check if the candidate was previously shortlisted for a particular job.

- *[Given]* that the candidate applied previously to another confidential job that the recruiter has access to.

- *[When]* the candidate record is displayed.

- *[Then]* the system should show the application submission records belonging to confidential jobs/requisitions that the recruiter has access to and all other non-confidential job application submissions of the given candidate for the past 10 years. The recruiter should be able to view any of these job applications by clicking on it.

- *[Scenario 3]*: The recruiter views a candidate's record to check if the candidate was previously shortlisted for a particular job.

- *[Given]* that the candidate applied previously to another confidential job that the recruiter does not have access to.

- *[When]* the candidate record is displayed.

- *[Then]* the system should not show the application submission records that belong to confidential jobs/requisitions that the recruiter does not have access to and should show all other job application submissions of the given candidate for the past 10 years. The recruiter should be able to view any of these job applications by clicking on it.

Sharing and visibility requirements should also be included in the user story. Otherwise, you will risk unauthenticated data exposure due to misunderstanding the requirement.

Practice creating user stories for the remaining requirements. By the end of this activity, you will have a healthy list of detailed user stories that are ready to be further solutioned and implemented at later stages.

Summary

You started practicing creating a complete Salesforce application in this chapter using the RAD principles. You got introduced to a hypothetical scenario of a recruitment application targeted at small and medium companies. You learned the activities included in the *Requirement gathering and market benchmarking* phase and practiced some of these activities using the given hypothetical scenario.

You then moved on to the *blueprinting* phase and practiced activities such as identifying and spotting non-communicated requirements, creating process flows using BPMN diagrams, defining actors and licenses, creating a preliminary solution blueprint using artifacts such as the data model diagram and the landscape architecture diagram, and creating detailed user stories with well-defined acceptance criteria.

You learned by example that investing upfront in good software engineering practices always pays back. What may look like wasted time to detail the user stories and accompany them with solid artifacts such as BPMN diagrams is time well invested in avoiding spending much more time later to repair the application and fix gaps.

In the next chapter, you will continue developing PSD's recruitment application and step into the next phase of the RAD lifecycle, which is detailing, designing, and prototyping.

Join our book's Discord space

Join the book's Discord Workspace for Latest updates, Offers, Tech happenings around the world, New Release and Sessions with the Authors:

https://discord.bpbonline.com

Create a Sample Application: Solve and Build the Application - Part 1

Introduction

This chapter will continue building on the knowledge and practical experience you gained from the previous chapter as you solve the requirements shared by PSD. You will update the relevant artifact as you progress with the solution design and development. This chapter and the next will focus on the subsequent phases of the Salesforce **Rapid Application Development (RAD)** lifecycle, where you will pick up user requirements after the other, analyze, and solve.

In the previous chapter, you concluded the *blueprinting/pre-game* phase of the Salesforce RAD application lifecycle. In this chapter, you move to the *detailing, designing, and prototyping* phase and cover parts of the *developing/building and testing* phase. Similar to what you experienced in *Chapter 6, Create a Sample Application - Define and Refine the Requirements*, you will cover part of the activities included in these phases as it is impossible to list them all. Still, the actions you cover should give you enough knowledge and practical experience to develop Salesforce applications rapidly in your life.

Have a look next at the structure of this chapter.

Structure

The chapter covers the following topics:

- Introduction to the way the solution is created

- Designing, prototyping, and building: The job listing feature

- Designing, prototyping, and building: The internal/external candidate sourcing feature

Objectives

By the end of this chapter, you will gain knowledge and practical experience in Salesforce application design and building. You will learn when to create a wireframe and when that can be optional, and how to craft an end-to-end solution that offers flexibility and extendibility to allow your application to become future-embracing and enable you to quickly and rapidly introduce future enhancements. This chapter and the next will help you gain enough experience to start your journey of rapid SaaS application development using the Salesforce Platform.

Introduction to the way the solution is created

In *Chapter 6, Create a Sample Application - Define and Refine the Requirements*, you compiled a list of 33 requirements for the PSD recruitment application. You also managed to identify and document three distinct processes the application should cover. The three processes are:

1. Job listing

2. Internal/external candidate sourcing

3. Online job application submission

The 33 PSD requirements must be grouped to allow the team to work on related topics while maintaining a good understanding of the desired result. Requirements/user stories are usually grouped into *features* or *epics*. A *feature* can contain one or more business processes; some features may be a logical grouping of enhancement requirements. It is up to the project team to define how the requirements/user stories will be grouped. In this book, you will group the requirements based on their relevant business process. Each business process will be translated into an application *feature*. A release will contain multiple new and updated *features*; the release note should detail them to any external user.

You will continue using the same tools you used in the previous chapter. As a reminder, the tools you used were the following:

- A tool to capture user stories. Such as **Jira** (by **Atlassian**) or **MS Excel**.

- A tool to create various design artifacts. Such as **Lucidchart** (by **lucid**).

- At least one **Salesforce Developer Edition** org.

- A tool to document design decisions and host other artifacts. Such as **Confluence** (by **Atlassian** or **MS Word**.

In addition, you will need a tool to create wireframes. You can use tools such as **Figma**. In this chapter, the wireframes will be made using **Lucidchart**.

Starting designing, wireframing, and solutioning the first feature, the job listing.

Designing, prototyping, and building: The job listing feature

If you go through the shared requirements and compare them to the BPMN in *Figure 6.4*, you will find that the following can be included in the job listing feature:

- **Requirement number 3:** Ability to have multiple statuses/stages per job post to allow different activities to occur at each stage.

- **Requirement number 4:** Ability to create multiple job posts for each department.

- **Requirement number 9:** Ability to post the same job across multiple countries/ regions.

- **Requirement number 12:** Ability to define multiple interview processes and use one for each requisition.

- **Requirement number 13:** The application should help save time by suggesting a pay range based on the position's pay scale.

- **Requirement number 15:** The application must allow defining a set of interview types for each position. Suitable interviewers should get assigned to the interview sessions. For example, a developer should be interviewed by a peer developer, a senior developer, and an engineering director. In comparison, a senior developer should not be interviewed by someone more junior such as a developer. The application should allow defining a template of interviews for each position type.

- **Requirement number 16:** The application must allow defining a set of activities that need to be completed by the recruiter for each position type. For example, executive positions require far more preparation and market research than regular positions. The system should allow defining a template of activities that get assigned to the recruiter depending on the position type.

- **Requirement number 18:** The application should help remind agents and candidates of tasks expected to be completed.

- **Requirement number 20:** The application should support defining internal and external recruiters.

- **Requirement number 21:** The application should provide clarity on the recruitment agency each external recruiter works for and allow reporting on each of these agencies.

- **Requirement number 29:** The application should allow defining a set of skills that can be used to describe both the skills required for a position and the skills possessed by a candidate.

There are multiple ways to determine which requirements would fit under what feature. The team should use their best judgment and consider the relevancies and dependencies between the requirements. However, you might still end up with requirements that have dependencies over others in different features/epics.

Remember that you should work with user stories rather than requirements at this stage. In this book, requirements are still used for brevity, but user stories offer much more details to the development team. You created three user stories in the previous chapter, they are US-001, US002, and US007, they will be called out during the different stages of the application lifecycle, and you will learn how they form the foundation of crucial activities that will take place at later stages such as the creation of test scripts/test scenarios.

Start with the first requirement that belongs to the job listing feature, requirement number 3.

Ability to have multiple statuses/stages per job post

You already created a draft data model in the previous chapter (*Figure 6.16*). Based on that data model, the object **Job_Requisition__c** will represent a job post/job requisition. You also have other supporting objects, such as **Recruitment_Stage__c,** which represents a stage that a job post can go through. Each department can define different recruitment stages. Per your current data model diagram, there is a relationship between the **Job_Requisition__c** and the **Recruitment_Stage__c**. The relationship represents the recruitment stage that a job requisition is currently at. You can use lookup filters to restrict the available recruitment stages to the department that created the job requisition.

Do you need to communicate a specific UX behavior to the stakeholders for this requirement? Do you need to test a particular UX experience with a set of potential personas? Do you need to research the usage of the UX associated with this requirement with a set of users? If the answer to either of these questions is yes, you will need a prototype or a wireframe.

This requirement will rely on the standard Salesforce UI and behavior. Moreover, it is not an essential element in the job listing process but more of a building block. You can skip creating a prototype/wireframe for this requirement and proceed directly to developing it.

Start by creating the **Department__c**, **Job_Requisition__c**, and **Recruitment_Stage__c** objects based on the data model in *Figure 6.16*. While creating these objects, ensure you create a tab for the **Department__c** and **Job_Requisition__c** objects, as they need to be accessible directly by the users, while the **Recruitment_Stage__c** will be accessible through other objects.

The **Department__c** objects would look like the following in Salesforce:

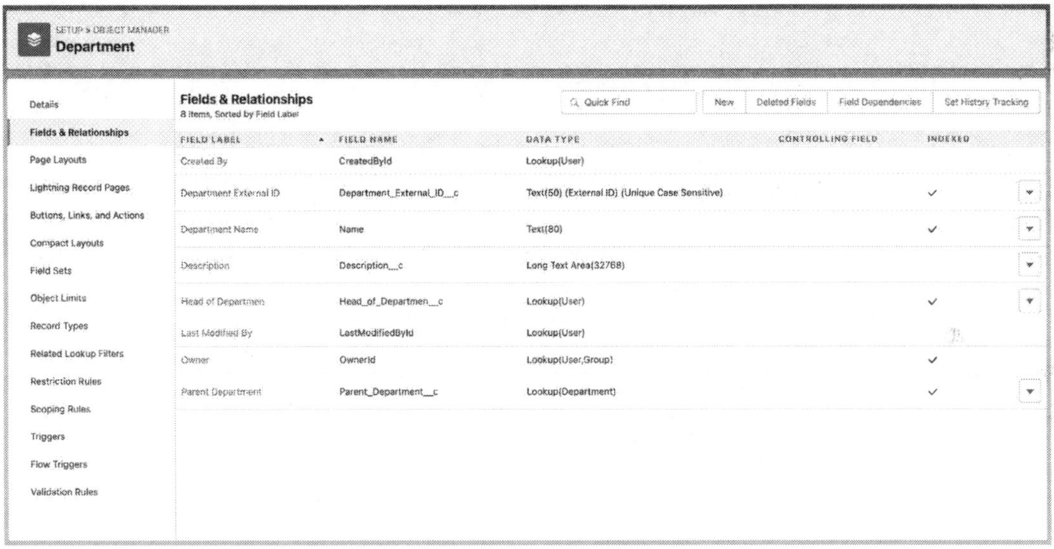

Figure 7.1: *The Department__c object in Salesforce*

The **Recruitment_Stage__c** objects would look like the following in Salesforce:

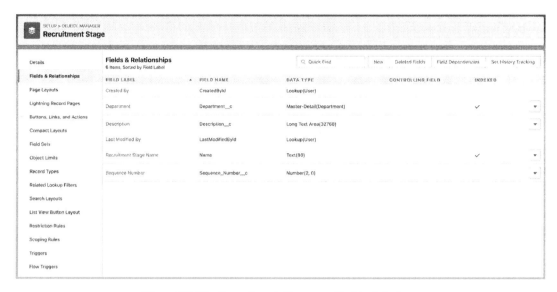

Figure 7.2: The Recruitment_Stage__c object in Salesforce

The **Job_Requisition__c** objects would look like the following in Salesforce:

Figure 7.3: The Job_Requisition__c object in Salesforce

Why the relationship between the **Department__c** and the **Job_Requisition__c** objects is a lookup relationship rather than master/detail? Can a requisition exist without a department? No. Then would it make more sense to use a master/detail relationship? This is where you need to think and rationally propose a solution, even if your requirement is unclear. There are confidential job requisitions that should not be seen by everyone. This is common in all companies, big or small. If you modeled the relationship between the two objects as master/detail, then any user with access to the **Department__c** object will automatically get access to all related. As a rapid Salesforce application developer, you need to think as a techno-functional professional, not just a classic developer. You need to think of all the aspects of the application and how its functionalities will be used. You will often propose the solution to the other stakeholders for validation rather than wait until a requirement is comprehensively detailed.

The Salesforce platform removes much of the complexities of classic software development. This should free you up to think of the functionalities and how they will be used by the users now that you do not need to worry about developing data access layers, APIs, and custom UIs.

The **Recruitment_Stage__c** field can be created similarly to the following using the lookup filters to restrict the allowed stages based on the relevant department:

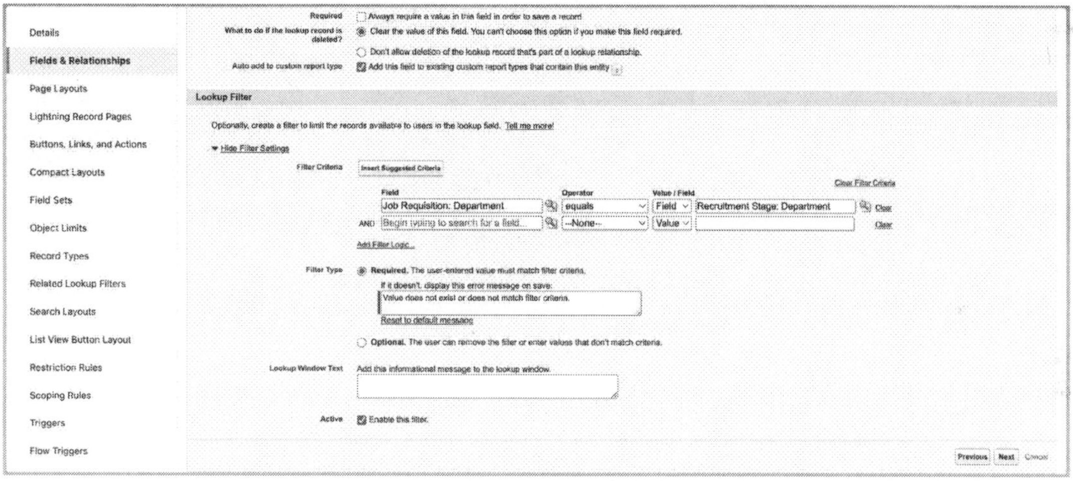

Figure 7.4: The Recruitment_Stage__c object in Salesforce

You will not be able to introduce the **Job_Description__c** and **Is_External_Recruiter__c** fields at this stage to the **Job_Requisition__c** as you have a dependency on some objects such as the **Remuneration_Package__c** and **Recruitment_Agency__c** objects. That should be fine; you can introduce the fields once the objects are created. It would have been a problem if you did not have a clear plan to introduce these objects to everyone on your team. But luckily, you have a good draft data model diagram that has been socialized with the rest of the team, and they all know what is expected to be built. It is a matter of planning and timing rather than an unaddressed gap.

The values of the field **Reason_for_Loss__c** is an example of information you need input from the business. As a RAD developer, you can use a temporary value so that you are not blocked from introducing the field and add a follow-up activity to replace this temporary value with actual values once you get that clarified by the business. There is no time to wait in RAD, be pragmatic and try to push things along in speed, then reiterate to adjust.

Adjust the page layout for the objects you created. In the Salesforce world, data is very close to the UI. You do not need explicit requirements to arrange the object's page layouts as per the best practice. Later, you can demo the UIs to your stakeholders and adjust them if needed. Always start by following the best UI practices you learned in this book (particularly in *Chapter 3, Develop a sample Salesforce application - PbP Phonebook. Figure 3.4*) in the absence of clear requirements and guidance.

Create a test record in the **Department__c** objects. You can access the object using the tab you created. You can search for the tab in the application launcher if it is not already visible to you, as shown in the following screenshot:

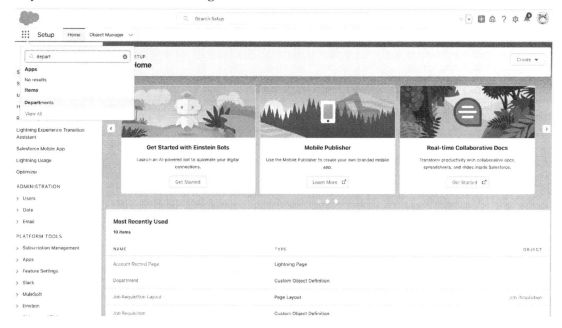

Figure 7.5: *Accessing the departments tab from the App Launcher*

The **Department__c** objects UI would look like the following in Salesforce:

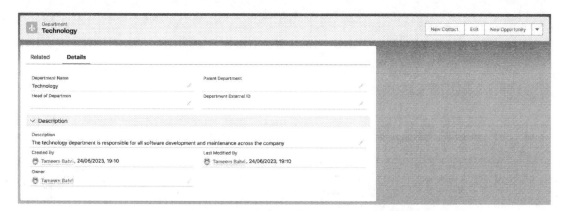

Figure 7.6: *The department object UI – first version*

As you can see, there is a space on the right side of the page, as the lightning pages use a *header and sidebar* layout for custom objects. You can change that using the **Lightning App Builder**. Click on the gear icon at the top right corner of the page and select **Edit Page**, as shown in the following screenshot:

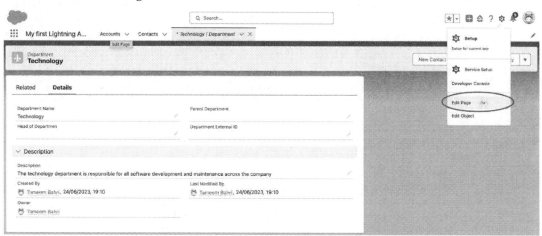

Figure 7.7: *Edit a lightning page in the Lightning App Builder*

In the Lightning App Builder, you can see a section showing the used template, as shown in the following screenshot:

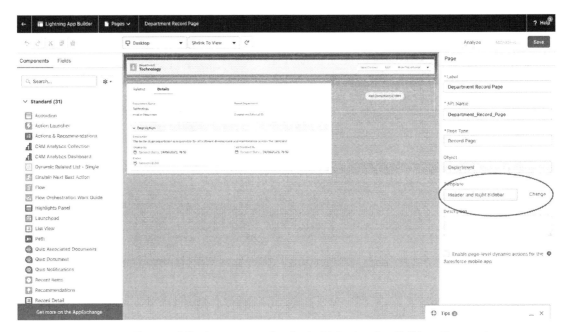

Figure 7.8: Change a lightning page template in the Lightning App Builder – first version

Click on the **Change** button to change the used template. A popup screen similar to the following will be displayed:

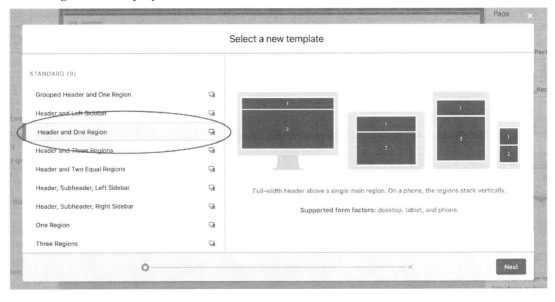

Figure 7.9: Change a lightning page template popup screen

Choose **Header and One Region** from the list as highlighted in the previous figure, then click **Next** to move to the next screen and accept the default values until you save your changes. Your **Department__c** object lightning page should look like the following screenshot:

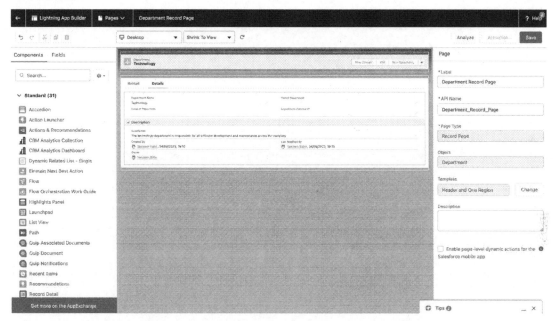

Figure 7.10*: Change a lightning page template in the Lightning App Builder – second version.png*

Click on the **Save** button at the top right corner to save your changes, and a popup such as the following will show up:

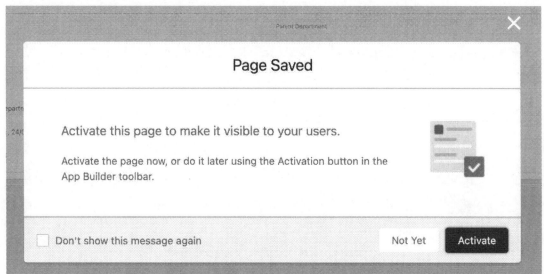

Figure 7.11*: Save changes to a lightning page*

Click on the **Activate** button to activate this page for the system users. Without this step, you will not be able to see the changes you have made in action. A screen similar to the following will be shown:

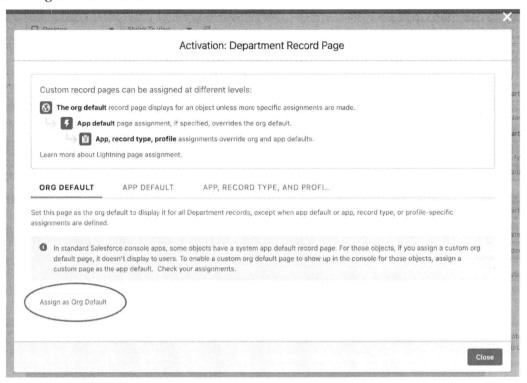

Figure 7.12: *Activate changes introduced to a lightning page*

Click on **Assign as Org Default** and accept the default settings on the following screens to complete the page activation. Once done, move back to the test department record that you created. It should now look like the following screenshot:

Figure 7.13: *The department object UI – second version*

You can see the impact of such small changes to the UI. It now looks much neater and user-friendly. Luckily, this is something easy to do in Salesforce applications. Switch to the **Related** section of your page and create some test recruitment stages. Your screen could look like the following screenshot:

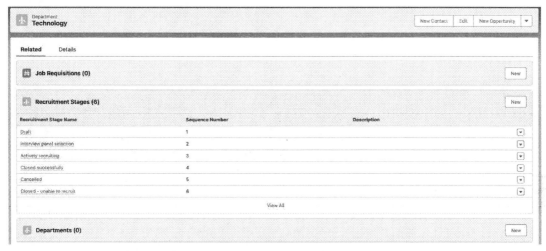

Figure 7.14: The department object UI with test recruitment stages

Following similar steps to adjust the lightning page template, the **Recruitment_Stage__c** objects UI would look like the following in Salesforce:

Figure 7.15: The recruitment stage object UI

The **Job_Requisition__c** objects UI would look like the following in Salesforce:

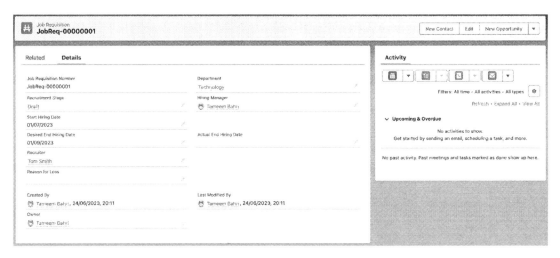

Figure 7.16: *The job requisition object UI*

You have now completed the design and build for the requirement. It might look like a lot of work in the book that spans multiple pages, but in reality, this is around one or two hours of work. There is hardly any other programming language available that allows you to build so many things in such a short time. Move on to the following requirement.

Ability to create multiple job posts for each department

This requirement is solved already, as the relationship type you have designed between the **Department__c** and **Job_Requisition__c** objects is one-to-many. If you look at the data model diagram again, you will notice that the relationship is one-to-none-or-many:

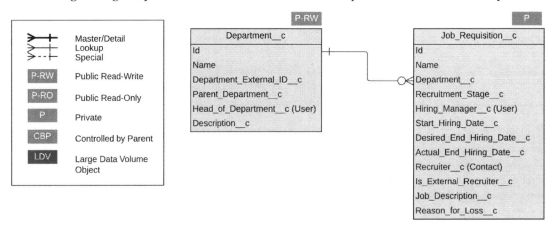

Figure 7.17: *The Department__c and Job_Requisition__c relationship*

This relationship means that a **Department__c** record may have none, one, or many **Job_Requisition__c** records. This is an accurate representation of the actual relationship between the custom objects you created in Salesforce. You can move to the next requirement.

Post the same job across multiple countries/ regions

The recruitment application offers several capabilities, but posting online or on other channels (such as social media) is not part of it. The requirement here might be misunderstood in its current shape, and this is why it is essential to format your requirements as user stories. The acceptance criteria in the user story, in particular, at very useful to understand the definition of *done*. Allowing each job to be tagged against a specific country should be enough in this case.

You can solve this requirement in different ways.

- You can introduce a **Country__c** picklist field to the **Job_Requisition__c** object. This means a **Job_Requisition__c** record is required per country.

- You can introduce a multi-select **Country__c** picklist field to the **Job_Requisition__c** object. This means a single **Job_Requisition__c** record will be enough for a multi-country job. However, this also means that only one recruiter can work on the job post across all countries and that the recruitment and interview processes are the same for all countries.

The latter solution negates one of the shared requirements in the job listing process shown in *Figure 6.4*. The process indicates that the recruiter should be auto-allocated to the job requisition based on the department, job type, and target location. This means the expectation is to have multiple recruiters working on the same job requisition for multiple countries; therefore, the first solution is more suitable.

Such a topic does not require a design decision as you only have one valid solution (the second option is invalid as it negates other shared requirements).

Introduce a **Country__c** picklist field to the **Job_Requisition__c** object. The hiring manager will need to create a job requisition per country in case of a multi-country job.

Move on to the next requirement.

Define multiple interview processes

This requirement indicates a need for different interview processes to be used with job requisitions. If you go through the other shared requirements, you will notice that requirement number 15 describes that also with more detail. When creating your user stories, you can combine relevant requirements into a single user story to make it easier to understand and solve.

Try to format these two requirements as a single user story. The created user story could look like the following:

- User story US-012: As a *[hiring manager]*, I want *[to be able to define multiple interview processes to be used with each job requisition]* so that *[the right interviewers can interview applicants for a particular job requisition]*.

- *[Scenario 1]*: The hiring manager creates a job requisition record for a specific job type.

- *[Given]* that there is a defined interviewer profile template for the given job type.

- *[When]* the recruiter updates the job requisition stage value to *interview panel selection*.

- *[Then]* the system should automatically create the right job interview sessions for the job requisition based on the job type/job description. The system is not expected to auto-assign the interview sessions or auto-schedule them; the recruiter will do both tasks manually. The system should automatically create job interview records with the right roles for the requisition.

A wireframe can help further clarify this requirement. The following wireframe can be used:

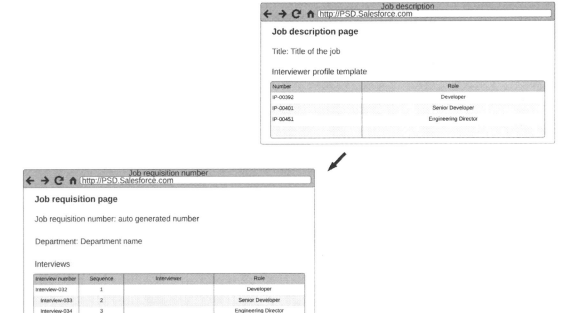

Figure 7.18: *Wireframe for US-012*

The wireframe shows how configurations on the interviewer profile template page have been used to create job interview records under the job requisition.

You still do not have an object in your data model that will allow you to define job interviews for each job requisition. This is a good example to show that the data model you created in the previous phase of your RAD application lifecycle could miss some objects and fields and that it is a living document that will keep changing throughout the lifetime of your application.

Your partial data model for US-012 could look like the following:

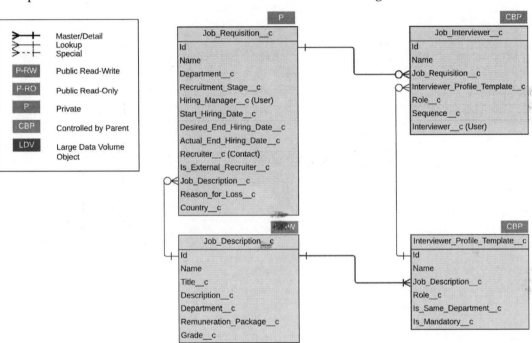

Figure 7.19: Partial data model for US-012

Including such artifacts with the user story will add immense value to the development team. The architects are expected to create and add the partial data model diagram, while the UX designers or the BAs are expected to add the wireframes.

If you have not created the **Remuneration_Package__c**, **Job_Description__c**, and **Interview_Profile_Template__c** objects, create them. The **Remuneration_Package__c** object would look like the following in Salesforce:

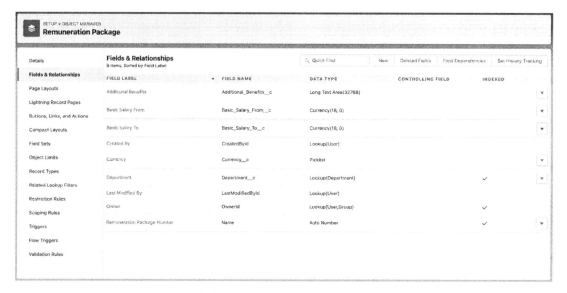

Figure 7.20: *The Remuneration_Package__c object in Salesforce*

The **Job_Description__c** object would look like the following in Salesforce:

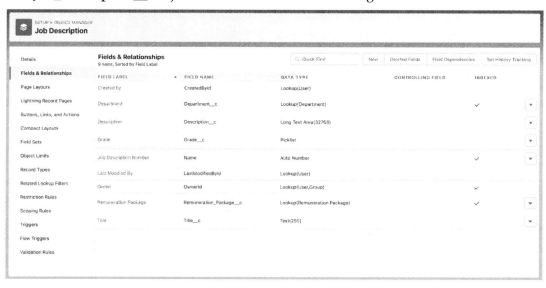

Figure 7.21: *The Job_Description__c object in Salesforce*

The **Interview_Profile_Template__c** object would look like the following in Salesforce:

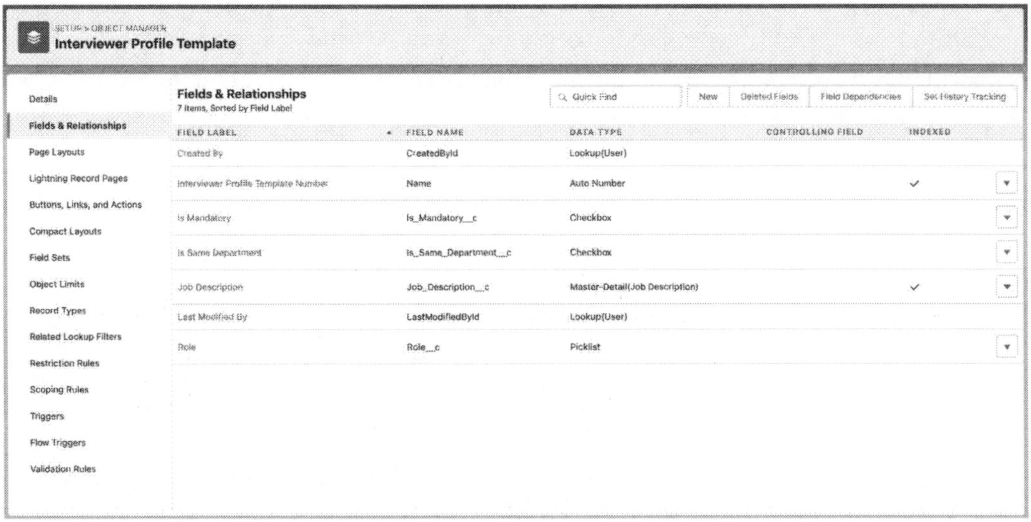

Figure 7.22: The Interview_Profile_Template__c object in Salesforce

The **Job_Interviewer__c** object would look like the following in Salesforce:

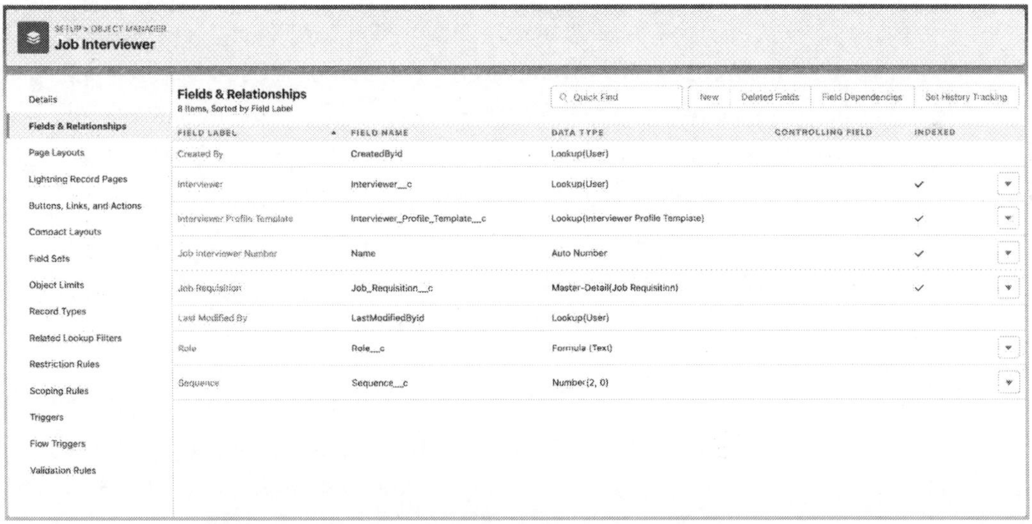

Figure 7.23: The Job_Interviewer__c object in Salesforce

You have not yet completed solving the user story. Your application still needs to create job interview records automatically with the right roles and link them to the relevant **Job_Requisition__c** record based on the job type/job description.

The trigger to this operation would be updating the **Job_Requisition__c Recruitment_Stage__c** field's value to *Interview panel selection*. You can achieve this automation using

Salesforce flows or using **Apex Triggers**. You would use the latter for sophisticated logic and the former for everything else. Assume that you will use an Apex trigger to create this automation. Your Apex trigger's code could look like the following.

```
trigger JobRequisitionTrigger on Job_Requisition__c (after update) {
    If (Trigger.IsAfter){
        If (Trigger.IsUpdate){
            JobRequisitionTriggerHandler.onAfterUpdate(Trigger.OldMap,
                                            Trigger.NewMap);
        }
    }
}
```

Please note that the code layout has been adjusted for the best fit in this book.

The trigger is calling logic from another class, **JobRequisitionTriggerHandler**. This is a best practice to keep your trigger code neat and tidy. The code for the **JobRequisitionTriggerHandler** class could look like the following:

```
public class JobRequisitionTriggerHandler {
    public static void onAfterUpdate(Map<ID,Job_Requisition__c> pOldMap,
                                    Map<ID,Job_Requisition__c> pNewMap){
        //Create Job_Application_Interview__c records based on the job type
        //Start by querying the extended values of the passed pNewMap.
        //This will ensure you have access to related record's values
        //such as Recruitment_Stage__r.Name
        Map<ID,Job_Requisition__c> pExtendedNewMap =
            new Map<ID, Job_Requisition__c>([SELECT Id, Department__c,
                                        Country__c, Recruiter__c,
                                        Job_Description__c,
                                        Recruitment_Stage__c,
                                        Recruitment_Stage__r.Name
                                        FROM Job_Requisition__c
                                        where ID in :pNewMap.
Keyset()]);

        //This map will be used to store the requisitions
        //that require creation of interview records
        Map<ID,Job_Requisition__c> pRequisitionsNeedInterviewRecords =
                                new Map<ID, Job_Requisition__c>();
```

```
//This set will be used to store the Job_Description__c ID
//that has requisitions that require creation of interview records
Set<ID> JDs = new Set<ID>();

//Start by detecting if the Recruitment_Stage__c field
//of the passed Job_Requisition__c records has been changed
for (Job_Requisition__c oNewReq: pExtendedNewMap.Values()) {
//Get the older version of the same record
//The older version will have the values of the object before the
update
Job_Requisition__c oOldReq = pOldMap.get(oNewReq.Id);
//Check if the value of the Recruitment_Stage__c has changed
if(oNewReq.Recruitment_Stage__c != oOldReq.Recruitment_Stage__c){
    //Check if the new value is equal to 'Interview panel
selection'.
    //Both if statements can be combined in a single line.
    //They were separated for easy reading
    //Please note the usage of a constants class to avoid hard
coding
    if(oNewReq.Recruitment_Stage__r.Name ==
        Constants.InterviewPanelSelectionStageName') {
        //Remember, you should not create a SOQL query within a
loop.
        //Capture the relevant Job_Requisition__c records
        //And add them to a map
        pRequisitionsNeedInterviewRecords.put(oNewReq.ID, oNewReq);
        //Also, capture a unique list of job descriptions
        JDs.add(oNewReq.Job_Description__c);
    }
}
}//End of loop

List<Job_Interviewer__c> JobInterviewerListToCreate =
                getJobInterviewerListToCreate(JDs,
pExtendedNewMap);

if(!JobInterviewerListToCreate.IsEmpty()){
```

```
                Insert JobInterviewerListToCreate;
        }
    }


    private static List<Job_Interviewer__c> getJobInterviewerListToCreate(
                        Set<ID> pJDs,Map<ID,Job_Requisition__c>
pJobReqsMap){
        List<Job_Interviewer__c> JobInterviewerListToCreate
                                        = new List<Job_Interviewer__
c>();


        //Query the interviewer profile templates that matches
        //the job description IDs captured in the previous loop
        List<Interviewer_Profile_Template__c> InterviewerTemplateList =
            new List<Interviewer_Profile_Template__c>(
                    [SELECT Id, Job_Description__c
                    From Interviewer_Profile_Template__c
                    where Job_Description__c in :pJDs]);
        for (Job_Requisition__c oReq: pJobReqsMap.Values()) {
            for (Interviewer_Profile_Template__c
                oInterviewerTemplate: InterviewerTemplateList){
                //Check if the job description matches.
                //Remember that triggers work in batches.
                //A mass update to job requisitions could have triggered
this code
                //You need to ensure you are picking the relevant records
only
                if(oReq.Job_Description__c ==
                    oInterviewerTemplate.Job_Description__c){
                    Job_Interviewer__c oNewJobInterview =
                        new Job_Interviewer__c();
                    oNewJobInterview.Job_Requisition__c =
                        oReq.Id;
                    oNewJobInterview.Interviewer_Profile_Template__c =
                        oInterviewerTemplate.Id;
                    //Do not auto fill the remaining Job_Interviewer__c
fields.
```

```
                    //The recruiter should fill them manually
                    JobInterviewerListToCreate.add(oNewJobInterview);
                }
            }
        }
        return JobInterviewerListToCreate;
    }
}
```

The code will create new **Job_Interview__c** records under the related **Job_Requisition__c**. The recruiter would then try to identify the right interviewer for each role and manually update the **Job_Interview__c** record.

Once an applicant is scheduled for interviews, the system can automatically copy the **Job_Interview__c** records to create **Job_Application_Interview__c** records for the given candidate. Move on to the following requirement.

Save time by suggesting a pay range

The data model already addresses this requirement, as each **Job_Requisition__c** record will be linked to a **Job_Description__c**. Each **Job_Description__c** will be linked to a **Remuneration_Package__c**, which should provide guidance on the pay range.

Requirement number 15 is the following, but you solved that already; you can move on to requirement 16.

Allow defining a set of activities that need to be completed

This requirement can be solved in multiple valid ways. You learned that such scenarios are precisely where a design decision can be handy. You can use a template similar to what you used in *Chapter 6, Create a Sample Application - Define and Refine the Requirements*. Your design decision could look like the following:

- **Title:** Design decision DD-02902. Auto creation of the recruiter's job requisition activities.

- **Stakeholder:** Names of stakeholders, yourself included.

- **Dates and milestones:** Include relevant dates and milestones here, such as the deadline for decision-making.

- **Description:** The application needs to auto-create activities that the recruiter should complete for each job requisition. The activities could differ based on the job type. A decision must be taken regarding the solution to this requirement.

- **Option 1 title:** Use **Salesforce flows** only.

- **Option 1 details:** Utilize standard **Salesforce flows** to create a configurable solution for generating tasks based on defined conditions. The administrator can update the *flow* to include all the different conditions and the actions for each (such as creating tasks with specific names and due dates).

- **Option 1 pros:** Less code required as the solution is mainly based on configurable Salesforce flows. This solution is also easy to track and test as the structure of the flows and the branching of the logic are easy to follow.

- **Option 1 cons:** The changes to the *flow* can only be made by an administrator or someone with high privilege. The standard end users will not be able to make the changes. The *flow* might get too crowded and difficult to read in complex scenarios.

- **Option 2 title:** Use **Salesforce flows** with a custom template object/configuration object.

- **Option 2 details:** Utilize standard **Salesforce flows** to read from a custom object that acts as a template and create tasks based on the values stored in the template object. The end users can update the template object to modify, add, or remove configurations. The logic of the *flow* itself will remain unchanged. The custom object will contain fields such as task name, due date, job type, and various other fields that can help find the records relevant to a specific scenario.

- **Option 2 pros:** The template object is maintained by end users, offering more flexibility for changing configurations.

- **Option 2 cons:** The solution is more difficult to test as it relies on the quality of the data stored in the template object. Moreover, the end users will need to be trained in using the template object.

- **Option 3 title:** Use **Salesforce Apex** with a custom template object/configuration object.

- **Option 3 details:** Similar to option 2, except for using Apex instead of Salesforce flows.

- **Option 3 pros:** Similar to option 2.

- **Option 3 cons:** Similar to option 2. In addition, this option requires coding.

- **Recommendation:** Option 1 is recommended as the design authority prefers using standard Salesforce out-of-the-box features as much as possible.

- **Conclusion:** The design authority met on the given date and chose Option 1 as a solution.

Remember that the selected/recommended approach could differ based on the factors impacting the application and the design authority. Do not consider the design decision recommendations in this book fit for all purposes. Move on to the following requirement.

Help remind agents and candidates of tasks

Your application is targeted for the **Salesforce Lightning Experience**. You plan to use standard activity objects such as Event and Task to define the activities the recruiter should complete. These objects come with built-in functionalities. In Lightning Experience, notification cards will appear to remind you of events and tasks. The user can personalize these reminders from their personal settings section.

This should suffice as a solution for this requirement. Move on to the next.

Support defining internal and external recruiters

You have already introduced a custom **Recruitment_Agency__c** to your data model and planned to use the standard Contact object to store the recruiter's details to support internal and external recruiters (the latter might not have access to your system). This requirement is addressed by your data model already. Another minor enhancement would be introducing a field on the Contact object to distinguish internal and external recruiters easily. This field could be a formula field such as the following:

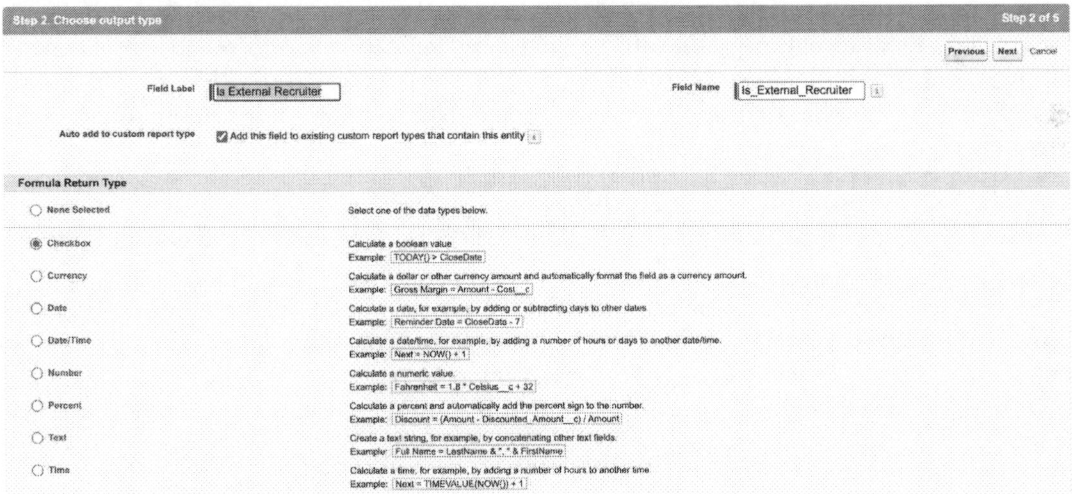

Figure 7.24: The creation of a formula field – part one

The formula could look like the following:

Simple Formula | Advanced Formula

Insert Field   Insert Operator ▼

Is External Recruiter (Checkbox) =

IF(ISNULL(Recruitment_Agency__c) , False, True)

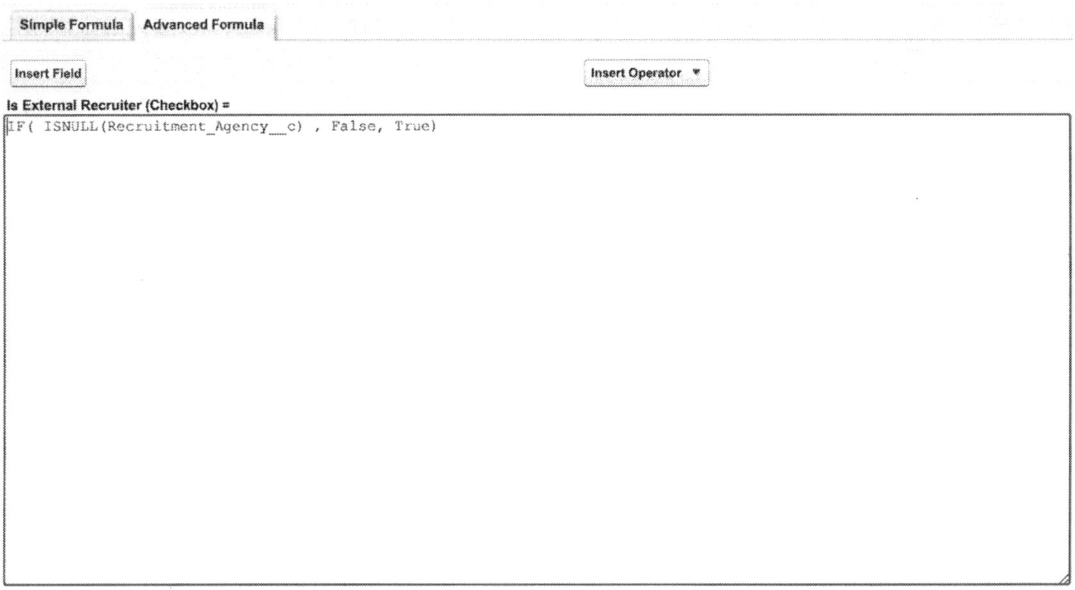

Figure 7.25: The creation of a formula field – part two

If you reviewed the job listing process diagram from *Chapter 6, Create a Sample Application – Define and Refine the Requirements (Figure 6.4)*, you would notice that the recruiter is expected to be automatically allocated to the job application based on the department, job type, and target location. You will need to add attributes to the **Contact** object that describes the locations covered by a recruiter, the departments the recruiter works with, and the job types they cover.

The locations can be a multi-select picklist as you do not have a dedicated locations object. You will need to introduce a junction/bridge object between the **Contact** and both the **Department__c** and **Job_Description__c** objects (as the relationship between these objects is going to be many-to-many, and you need to break such relationship using a junction/ bridge object). Your partial data model could look like the following:

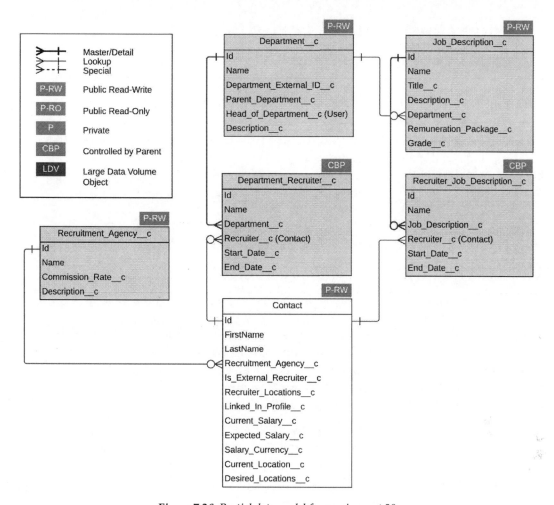

Figure 7.26: *Partial data model for requirement 20*

Notice that both newly introduced objects, **Recruiter_Job_Description__c** and **Department_Recruiter__c**, have **Start_Date__c** and **End_Date__c** fields. These objects represent a time-bound relationship (such as assigning a recruiter to a department); therefore, including start and end date fields in it is a best practice even if there is no explicit requirement. These fields can be made optional for the time being.

You need to introduce logic to query these objects and automatically determine and allocate a recruiter to a job requisition. You can use a **Salesforce flow** or a **Salesforce Trigger** with **Apex**. The details of that logic will be skipped here for brevity. Move on to the following requirement.

Provide clarity on the recruitment agency each external recruiter works for

Your data model already covers this requirement. Each external recruiter (Contact) is linked to a **Recruitment_Agency__c** record. You could have relied on the Account object to represent a recruitment agency. However, you are building an application that will be deployed to Salesforce customers via the **AppExchange**. Several factors can impact your decision, such as the desire to remove dependencies on standard objects that might have been utilized differently by the Salesforce customer.

Move on to the next requirement.

Allow defining a set of skills for a position and the candidate

During the previous phase of this application's lifecycle (covered in *Chapter 6, Create a Sample Application - Define and Refine the Requirements*), you planned to introduce the following custom objects **Candidate_Skill__c** and **Resume_Skill__c**. The first represents a skill a candidate can have, and the second represents a skill that a candidate includes in their resume. You have not planned to introduce an object to define the skills required for a particular job. This is another good example of how your data model is a living artifact that will change throughout the application lifecycle.

Introduce a new object, **Job_Requisition_Skill__c**, which will act as a bridge between the **Job_Requisition__c** and the **Candidate_Skill__c** objects (as the relationship between them is many-to-many. That is, a single requisition can have many skills associated and a single skill could be associated with many job requisitions).

Your partial data model diagram could look like the following:

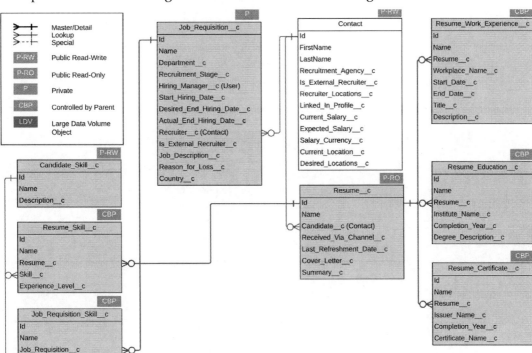

Figure 7.27: Partial data model for requirement 29

The expectation is that either the hiring manager or the recruiter would manually define the skills required for each job requisition. This is a good foundation for future enhancements where this activity can be automated.

Can you think of the required data structures and logic to fully automate the creation of job requisition skills based on the job description? This is something you can add to your application (it will not be covered in this book for brevity). You can draw inspiration from the data structures and logic introduced to automate creating interviewer records for each job requisition.

At this stage, your complete data model diagram could look like the following:

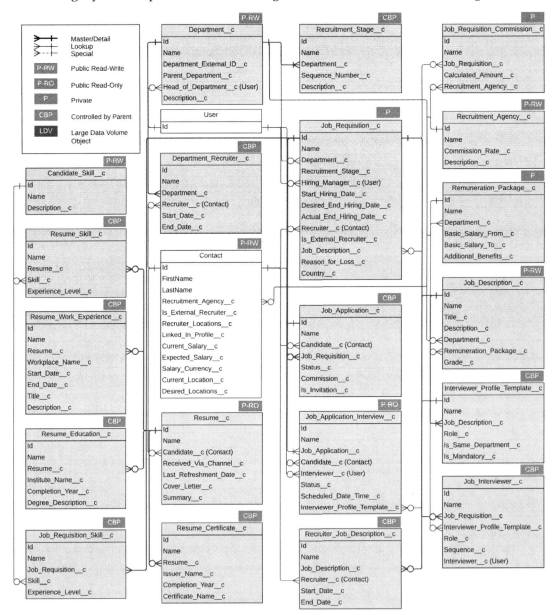

Figure 7.28: *The data model diagram (eighth draft)*

Congratulations, you have completed designing, prototyping, and building the internal/ external candidate sourcing feature. This feature is now ready to be tested and deployed. This will be something you cover in the next chapter. For the time being, proceed to the next feature.

Designing, prototyping, and building: The internal/external candidate sourcing feature

If you go through the shared requirements and compare them to the BPMN in *Figure 6.5*, you will find that the following can be included in the online job application submission feature:

- **Requirement number 7:** Ability to maintain a complete history of a candidate's application submissions.

- **Requirement number 8:** Ability to capture details about the candidates such as their personal details, resume, current and expected salary, and relevant currencies.

- **Requirement number 27:** The application should allow tracking of the history of each interviewer to show their participation in the past.

- **Requirement number 30:** The application should allow the creation of a profile of each candidate with their skills and level of expertise.

- **Requirement number 32:** The application should allow recruiters to search for internal candidates using multiple search parameters such as location, salary expectations, previous feedback, previously applied positions, skills, and last update date.

Start with the first requirement.

Maintain a complete history of a candidate's application submissions

You have already formatted this requirement as a user story in *Chapter 6, Create a Sample Application - Define and Refine the Requirements* (US-007). Your data model already supports this requirement, as all job applications for a particular candidate will appear under their **Contact** record.

Here is how it is illustrated in the partial data model:

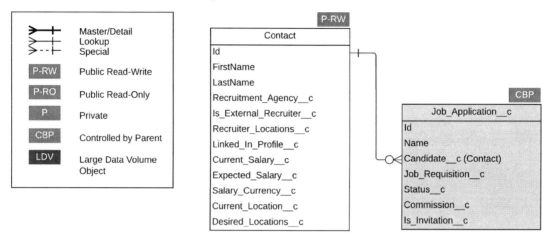

Figure 7.29: *Job applications for a specific candidate - data model*

Create the **Job_Application__c** object if you have not created it yet. It should look like the following in Salesforce:

Figure 7.30: *The Job_Application__c object in Salesforce*

A particular job application would look like the following in your Salesforce application:

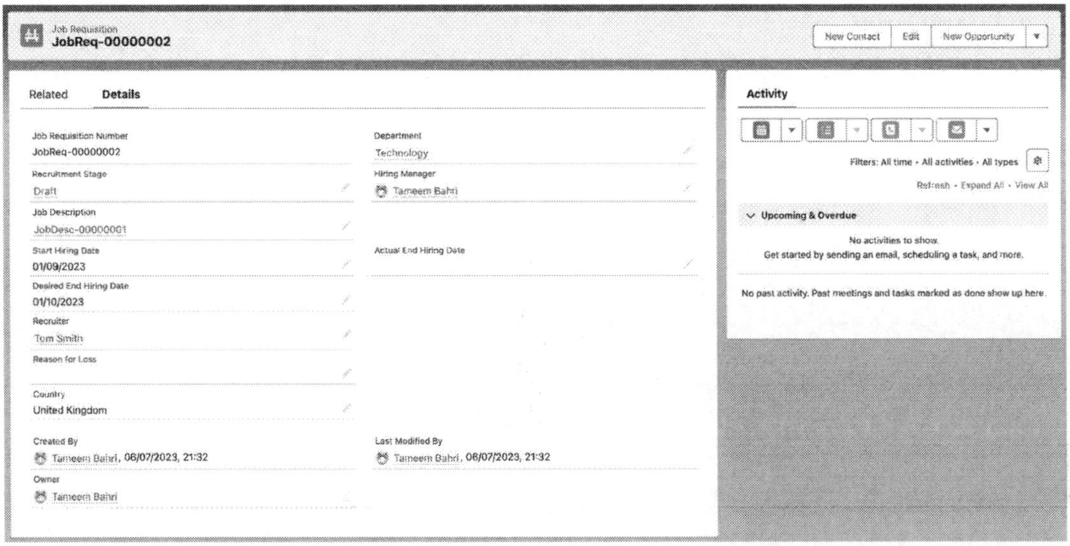

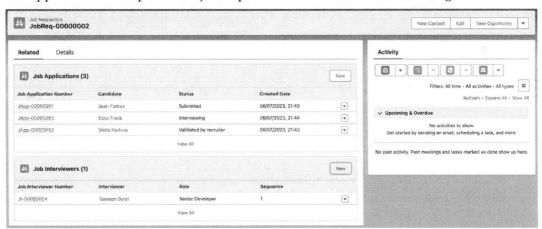

Figure 7.31: A sample job requisition displayed in the Salesforce application

The applications for a particular job requisition will look like the following:

Figure 7.32: Job applications submitted for a particular job requisition in the Salesforce application

If you click on one of those candidates, you will see the entire history of application submissions for that candidate. Your screen could look like the following:

Figure 7.33: Job applications for a specific candidate – screenshot

Move on to the next requirement.

Ability to capture details about the candidates

The requirement is about having fields and objects to capture candidate details such as their personal details, resume, current and expected salary, and relevant currencies. You have already introduced several custom fields to the Contact object, such as **Current_Salary__c** and **Expected_Salary__c**. You have also introduced several custom objects, such as the following:

- **Resume__c**: To capture details about the candidate's resume.

- **Resume_Education__c**: To capture details about the education of the candidate. This object is a child of the **Resume__c** object.

- **Resume_Work_Experience__c**: To capture details about the work experience of the candidate. This object is a child of the **Resume__c** object.

- **Resume_Certificate__c**: To capture details about any professional certificate that the candidate might possess. This object is a child of the **Resume__c** object.

- **Resume_Skill__c**: To capture the different skills a candidate has and experience level. This is a bridge/junction object between the **Resume__c** object and the **Candidate_Skill__c** object, which represents the master data of possible skills defined in the system.

You can always get some inspiration from other websites and tools that provides the capability of creating a resume, such as **LinkedIn** and **Glassdoor**. The objects and fields you introduced ensure that this requirement and requirement 30, which is very relevant to this requirement, are both fulfilled. You can move to the next requirement.

Allow tracking of the history of each interviewer

Salesforce makes application development easy in multiple ways. One of them is in establishing a UI representation of a relationship between both involved parties. For example, when you define a lookup relationship between two objects, both become aware of the other. Salesforce allows you to add a visual representation of that relationship automatically.

When you created a lookup between the `Job_Application_Interview__c` object and the interviewer record (`User`), you automatically enabled the ability to track and report the history of that interviewer's participation in job application interviews. You have already solved the next requirement (requirement 30). You can move directly to requirement 32.

Allow recruiters to search for internal candidates

As part of this requirement, the recruiter should be able to search using parameters such as location, salary expectations, previous feedback, previously applied positions, skills, and last update date.

The Salesforce global search (the search box at the top of the page in Salesforce) is a good tool for searching across objects and fields as it relies on the **Salesforce Object Search Language (SOSL)** rather than the **Salesforce Object Query Language (SOQL),** which you used in some code examples previously.

SOSL executes text-based queries across the searchable objects in your org. However, it is not a good fit for this requirement because of the user experience.

When you search using the Salesforce global search, the results are displayed using standard page results, which show all matches across the different objects. Imagine searching for candidates in a specific location, such as the United Kingdom. The show results will include all instances where the United Kingdom was mentioned in all searchable objects (assuming the word is stored as text rather than a reference). Searching for a candidate this way is very time-consuming. Moreover, Salesforce global search is limited and cannot deal with multi-parameter search (for example, search for candidates in a particular location who possess a specific skill and has been updated in less than six months).

Check the following example when you search for the word *United Kingdom* using the global search (results may vary depending on the data in your org, the show results are based on the default data in a Salesforce Developer org):

***Figure 7.34**: Search results using global search*

Moreover, previous feedbacks and skills are objects related to the candidate and job application objects. They are not values/fields that exist on the **Contact** directly. All these reasons and more indicate that you need a custom **Visualforce page/Lightning component** for this requirement. But what would this page/component look like? How will the user interact with it? How will you show back the results, and in what order? All these questions and more can be answered before writing a single line of code using a low-fidelity mockup or, in the simplest forms, a wireframe.

The wireframe can then be tested with the relevant stakeholders (usually includes a sample of end users), feedback is gathered, and the wireframe is adjusted accordingly. Once a consensus is reached about the wireframe, you can proceed with development:

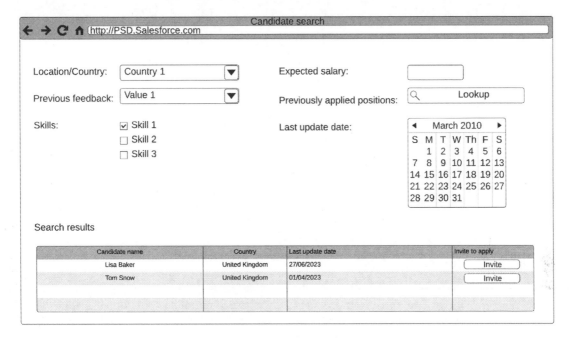

Figure 7.35: *Wireframe for the candidate search page*

The wireframe would evolve with time, and additional functionalities can be added, such as a link to the candidate page (the candidate name itself can be turned into that link) and a way to detect if an invite has already been sent for a particular job requisition or not. This functionality's evolution can occur as part of the first application release or in the future as part of other releases.

The code for that functionality will not be included in this book for brevity. Once a suitable candidate is found, an invitation should be sent.

In your data model, the object **Job_Application__c** has a flag **Is_Invitation__c;** this flag will be set to *true* if the job application is created out of an invitation.

When the recruiter finds a suitable candidate to invite for a job, the following code will be executed (the code is explained via inline comments):

```
public boolean inviteCandidate(ID pRequisitionID,
                                ID pCandidateID){
        //Invite an existing candidate
        //Create a Job_Application__c record with the flag
        //Is_Invitation__c set to true.
        Job_Application__c oJobApplicationToCreate = new Job_
Application__c();
        oJobApplicationToCreate.Candidate__c = pCandidateID;
```

```
oJobApplicationToCreate.Job_Requisition__c = pRequisitionID;
oJobApplicationToCreate.Is_Invitation__c = true;
//No need to set the value of the Status__c field
//As the default value should be good enough

//This time, the example will use the Database.insert method
//to insert records. This method gives better control
//over the insert transaction
Database.SaveResult oSaveResult = Database.insert(
                                oJobApplicationToCreate,
                    false);
if (oSaveResult.isSuccess()) {
    //Operation was successful
    //get the ID of the record that was processed
    System.debug('Successfully inserted record. Job Application ID:
'
            + oSaveResult.getId());
    Return true;
}
else {
    // Operation failed, get all errors
    for(Database.Error err : oSaveResult.getErrors()) {
        System.debug('The following error has occurred.');
        System.debug(err.getStatusCode() + ': ' + err.
getMessage());
        System.debug('Job Application fields that affected this
error: '
            + err.getFields());
    }
    Return false;
}
}
```

This code creates a **Job_Application__c** record and sets the **Is_Invitation__c** field/flag to true. Once the record is created, you can utilize a **Salesforce flow** or a **Salesforce Workflow rule** to send a notification email to the candidate with a link to apply for the job.

The same code logic can be fully accomplished using a Salesforce flow.

You might have noticed by now that RAD is more than just about utilizing point-and-click tools to develop functionalities quickly, as code creation can also be quick in the Salesforce world. RAD includes a set of principles and practices to help you develop your application rapidly but without leaving a trail of technical debt behind and risking your solution's scalability and extendibility.

Congratulations, you have completed designing, prototyping, and building your application's second feature. In the next chapter, you will continue tackling two more major features of your application before exploring methods to test your solution and ensure high-quality outcomes consistently.

Summary

This chapter was an intense practical experience building applications using the RAD lifecycle. You continued with the hypothetical application from the previous chapter. In this chapter, you started the *Detailing, designing, and prototyping* phase of the RAD lifecycle, tackled the requirements one by one, provided a detailed solution for each, and developed/built that solution as you go. You learned practically when and how to use design decisions and wireframes. You also experienced the continuously evolving nature of the design artifacts you created in the previous chapter and modified several on the go.

The practical experience you are gaining will turn into second nature with practice. And in a short time, you will notice that the time you spend generating, updating, and using the different artifacts throughout your application development lifecycle is significantly reduced. This will be the moment you start reaping all the benefits of RAD and experience the true power of the Salesforce platform.

In the next chapter, you will continue *Detailing, designing, prototyping,* and *building* your recruitment application.

Join our book's Discord space

Join the book's Discord Workspace for Latest updates, Offers, Tech happenings around the world, New Release and Sessions with the Authors:

https://discord.bpbonline.com

Create a Sample Application: Solve and Build the Application - Part 2

Introduction

This chapter will continue building on the knowledge and practical experience you gained from the previous chapter as you solve the requirements shared by PSD for building a recruitment application. Similar to what you did in *Chapter 7, Create a Sample Application - Solve and Build the Application - Part One*, you will update the relevant artifact as you progress with the solution design and development.

In the previous chapter, you started the Detailing, designing, and prototyping phase after concluding the blueprinting/pre-game phase in *Chapter 6, Create a Sample Application - Define and Refine the Requirements*. You solutioned and built two major features of PSD's recruitment application. In this chapter, you will tackle two other features, one that covers the online job application submission process, while the other acts as a container feature that includes several minor application enhancements. Container features are common in real life, although they lack the charm associated with process-related features.

Have a look next at the structure of this chapter.

Structure

The chapter covers the following topics:

- Recap and continue

- Designing, prototyping, and building - Online job application submission
- Designing, prototyping, and building - Other requirements
- Creating the PSD recruitment application

Objectives

By the end of this chapter, you will gain knowledge and practical experience in Salesforce application design and building. You will learn when to create a wireframe and when that can be optional, and how to craft an end-to-end solution that offers flexibility and extendibility to allow your application to become future embracing and enable you to quickly and rapidly introduce future enhancements. *Chapter 7, Create a Sample Application - Solve and Build the Application - Part One,* and this chapter will help you gain enough experience to start your journey of rapid SaaS application development using the Salesforce Platform.

Recap and continue

In *Chapter 6, Create a Sample Application - Define and Refine the Requirements,* you compiled a list of 33 requirements for the PSD recruitment application. You also managed to identify and document three distinct processes the application should cover. The three processes are:

1. Job listing.
2. Internal/external candidate sourcing.
3. Online job application submission.

You practiced formatting these requirements as user stories, then grouped the 33 requirements into *features* (also known as *epics*) to allow the team to work on related topics while maintaining a good understanding of the desired result. You learned that a *feature* could contain one or more business processes, while some features could act as *containers* to group a set of enhancements logically.

You learned that a *release* can contain multiple new and updated *features*; and that the release note should detail them to any external user. You will learn more about release notes in *Chapter 9, Create a Sample Application - Test and Deploy the Application.*

Toward the end of this chapter, you will group all the features you created into a **Lightning Application**.

You will continue using the same tools you used in the two previous chapters.

Next, you will start designing, wireframing, and solutioning the third application feature, the online job application submission.

Designing, prototyping, and building - Online job application submission

If you go through the shared requirements and compare them to the BPMN in *Figure 6.6*, you will find that the following can be included in the online job application submission:

- **Requirement number 11:** Ability to inform the candidate of updates happening to their application, at what stage it is, and the expected next steps.

- **Requirement number 24:** The application should allow candidates to apply using PSD's website. The candidate should be able to upload their resume and provide a cover letter.

- **Requirement number 25:** The application should automatically parse the uploaded resume and use it to create a detailed candidate profile in the system.

- **Requirement number 31:** The application should allow an internal candidate search to fill a position using a known candidate who initially applied for a different position. The application should also enable inviting the found candidate to apply for the new job.

You should work with user stories rather than requirements at this stage. To further solidify your skills with user story creation, you will format the requirements in this feature as user stories. This was not done for the other features in this book for brevity. You are encouraged to practice doing so for all other requirements that were not formatted as user stories in this book.

Formatting the requirements as user stories

Creating user stories is usually handled by **Business Analysts (BAs)** and **Product Owners (POs)**. While creating a software application, it is essential to think of *who* would use a specific feature and *how*. Building an application for a particular client/customer/consumer is one thing, and creating a generic application that would be liked and loved by many is another. Market intelligence and awareness of similar comparable products is an essential skill in software development as it allows you to look at broader capabilities than requested.

Take requirement 11 as an example. This requirement can be formatted as the following user story:

- User story US-011: As a *[job seeker]*, I want *[to be informed about the updates of my job application, at what stage it is, and the expected next steps]* so that *[I can give prepare for the next steps and be assured that someone has picked up my application and working on it]*.

- *[Scenario 1]*: The job application record is updated to any stage.

- *[Given]* that the job requisition the candidate applied to is still open.

- *[When]* the **Status__c** field of the job application is updated to any value different than its current value.

- *[Then]* the candidate/job seeker must receive an email notification with a message indicating the new status value the application has moved to and a description of the activities included/expected at that step.

That sounds good, right?

It depends. Suppose you are building an application for a known client/customer (such as an application that a particular company will exclusively use). In that case, you can build to the shared requirement and scope only, although that is not recommended.

If you are building an application that is supposed to be sold/used by several potential clients/customers with different backgrounds, then building an application that *delivers more* is a recipe for success.

But what *more* could be delivered? It is a simple email notification. This is where market intelligence and acumen add much value. You might have experienced submitting different types of applications on several platforms. Many of them would send you email updates upon status change; some would even send you a push notification on your mobile or show a notification indicator on a customer portal upon logging in. But your application does not currently have a planned integration with a mobile application or a customer portal. Actually, it is part of the company's short-term strategy to build this as a headless recruitment application where the customer can integrate their portal regardless of its technology.

A good software design includes open ends that welcome expansions and integrations without restricting the consumer to a particular way or channel. In this case, your application can also emit a Salesforce Platform Event that the customer can subscribe to and consume to do further expansions (such as sending a mobile push notification).

You may deprioritize the additional functionality for a few releases or include it with the first release. This will be a decision that needs to be made by the application governance body. Sometimes, you may need to split this into two or more user stories. In this case, assume the plan is to include this functionality in the first release. Your user story will be updated to have the following additional acceptance criteria.

- *[Scenario 2]*: The job application record is updated to any stage.

- *[Given]* that the job requisition the candidate applied to is still open.

- *[When]* the **Status__c** field of the job application is updated to any value different than its current value.

- *[Then]* the application must emit an event compatible with the **Bayeux** protocol that includes a message indicating the candidate id, job requisition number, new application status, and a description of the activities included/expected at that step.

Bayeux is a protocol for asynchronous message transportation. It is used primarily over **HTTP** and **WebSockets** transportation protocols. **Bayeux** is a performant protocol with low latency. **CometD** is an event-routing bus that implements the **Bayeux** protocol. **Salesforce Platform Events** can be subscribed to using **CometD** clients.

The requirement indicates the need to emit an event that is compatible with a particular standard but does not specify a solution. Keeping the requirement definition separate from the suggested solution is essential to avoid biased solutions.

Move on to requirement 24. This requirement can be formatted as the following user story:

- User story US-024: As a *[job seeker]*, I want *[to be able to apply to a job online via a website by uploading my resume and cover letter]* so that *[I can easily apply to the job using my existing resume]*.

- *[Scenario 1]*: The candidate applies via the website using an uploaded resume.

- *[Given]* that the job requisition the candidate applied to is available/visible online and the candidate uses a resume file of less than 5 MB and the following file types (*.PDF, *.DOC, *.DOCX).

- *[When]* the candidate chooses to apply by uploading a resume. Fill in the required details (email, first name, last name), and provide a file that meets the given criteria.

- *[Then]* the website should create a job application in the recruitment application, link it with the correct job requisition and candidate record, and attach the resume to it. The status of the newly created job application should be *"submitted."*

Is that enough? In most cases, that should be good enough. However, explicitly calling out negative scenarios leaves nothing for the imagination, making testing the functionality much easier. The user story can be updated to have the following additional acceptance criteria.

- *[Scenario 2]*: The candidate applies via the website but fails to upload a resume.

- *[Given]* that the job requisition the candidate applied to is available/visible online.

- *[When]* the candidate chose to apply by uploading a resume. Fill in the required details (email, first name, last name), but fail/forget to provide a file.

- *[Then]* the application should return an error message that the website should display to the user to indicate that a file with the specified size and type is required.

- *[Scenario 3]*: The candidate applies via the website but provides a resume file that does not meet one or more file requirements.

- *[Given]* that the job requisition the candidate applied to is available/visible online and the candidate is using a resume file that exceeds the size of 5 MB or is not one of the following file types (*.PDF, *.DOC, *.DOCX).

- *[When]* the candidate chooses to apply by uploading a resume file. Fill in the required details (email, first name, last name), and provide a file that does not meet the required specifications.

- *[Then]* the application should return an error message that the website should display to the user to indicate that a file with the specified size and type is required.

A good user story does not leave any part of the requirement unclear. Assumptions are risks in disguise.

Move on to requirement 25. This requirement may look simple, but it is pretty complex. The system is expected to parse the uploaded file, detect its different sections, understand its purpose, then map it to specific data elements within the application's data model.

The uploaded resumes could be in any format, tabular, unobstructed text, horizontal sections, vertical sections, and a mix of all that. There is no existing software that mastered this transformation with 100% accuracy. This indicates that the requirement is complex and might require a compromise from the application's governance body.

This type of requirement is a good example of good-to-have functionalities that can be included in later releases. AI technologies can add much value to such use cases. Such solutions require intensive testing and fine-tuning. It is fair to assume that this requirement will be deprioritized for the first release.

Move on to requirement 31. You solved part of this requirement as part of the *internal/external candidate sourcing feature*. The experience of the job seeker is covered by the *online job application submission feature*. The requirement can be formatted as the following user story:

- User story US-031: As a *[job seeker]* that has been invited to apply for a job, I want *[to be able to apply to the job online via a website either by uploading my updated resume or using my existing profile held by the application]* so that *[I can have the option to apply using a current or previous version of the resume]*.

- *[Scenario 1]*: The candidate applies for a job after receiving an invitation using the invitation link.

- *[Given]* that the job requisition the candidate applied to is available/visible online, and the candidate follows a link in the invitation email received to apply for a job.

- *[When]* the candidate clicks on the link in the invitation email.

- *[Then]* the website should allow the user to apply using the existing/known profile/resume or upload a new resume. The application should create a job application, link it with the correct job requisition and candidate record, and attach the resume to it (if a new resume is provided). The status of the newly created job application should be *"submitted."*

- *[Scenario 2]*: The candidate applies for a job after receiving an invitation without using the invitation link.

- *[Given]* that the job requisition the candidate applied to is available/visible online, and the candidate receives an invitation email to apply to the job with a link.

- *[When]* the candidate navigates to the job requisition without using the link (such as accessing it directly via the website or search engine results).

- *[Then]* the website should give users the standard option to apply as per US-024.

The user stories can be further groomed and fine-tuned. You are encouraged to practice the creation of user stories more.

Now that you formatted the requirements as user stories, resume solving, and building the application, starting with US-011.

Solving and building US-011

You can choose between two main Salesforce platform features to send an email to external recipients. You can use **Salesforce Flows** (via the **Salesforce Flow Builder**) or **Apex** code. In the past, this was possible via other features, such as **Salesforce Process Builder** and **Workflow Rules**. However, both features are set to retire as the **Salesforce Flow Builder** is considered the future for low-code development.

So you have two valid solutions for this requirement. Do you need to create and validate a design decision with the design authority? Answering this question depends on the development team's maturity and the requirement's sensitivity. When you establish a design authority for the first time in a team, you might need to cast a wider net to catch more (and possibly all) design-related topics. You can even introduce a rule that requires every user story's solution to go through the design authority. This will introduce more stress to the team and turn the design authority into a bottleneck. This might sound bad, but remember that bottlenecks have been used for thousands of years to regulate the water flow. They are still relevant and probably will continue to be for thousands of years to come. Bottlenecks are not all bad and are very useful if you need a strictly controlled process.

A mature team would likely need less control, especially if the team is familiar with the process of using design decisions and particularly when champions are supporting this from within the team itself. Mature teams tend to have specific regulations that automatically govern minor design decisions. Some teams might even use tools to ensure overall team adherence.

In this case, there is no explicit value for using Apex; Salesforce Flow Builder can create performant flows quicker. The functionality is not critical and unlikely to interfere with other functionalities. Moreover, it is unlikely to grow more complex over time. All of these reasons would qualify a solution based on Salesforce Flows automatically.

Do you need to communicate a specific UX behavior to the stakeholders for this requirement? Do you need to test a particular UX experience with a set of potential personas? Do you need to research the usage of the UX associated with this requirement with a set of users? The answer to all these questions is no, which means you do not need a prototype or a wireframe for this requirement.

You can proceed with creating the Salesforce Flow that will solve this requirement. Navigate to the **Flows** menu item from the setup section, then click the **New Flow** button. You will see the familiar page to select the new flow type. An update to the **Job_Application__c** record triggers your flow, so you should choose to create a **Record-Triggered Flow**. As shown in the following screenshot:

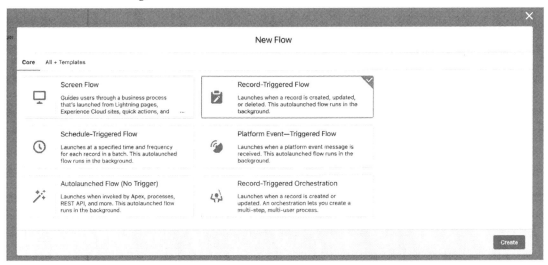

Figure 8.1: Developing a Salesforce flow for US-011, choosing the flow type

Proceed with setting up the flow to be triggered by a record update, as shown in the following screenshot:

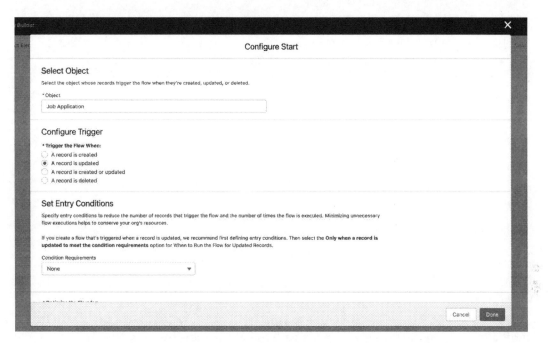

Figure 8.2: *Developing a Salesforce flow for US-011, setting the flow values*

Next, you need to define the conditions/criteria that trigger this flow upon record update. In this case, it is a change in the **Status__c** field, as shown in the following screenshot:

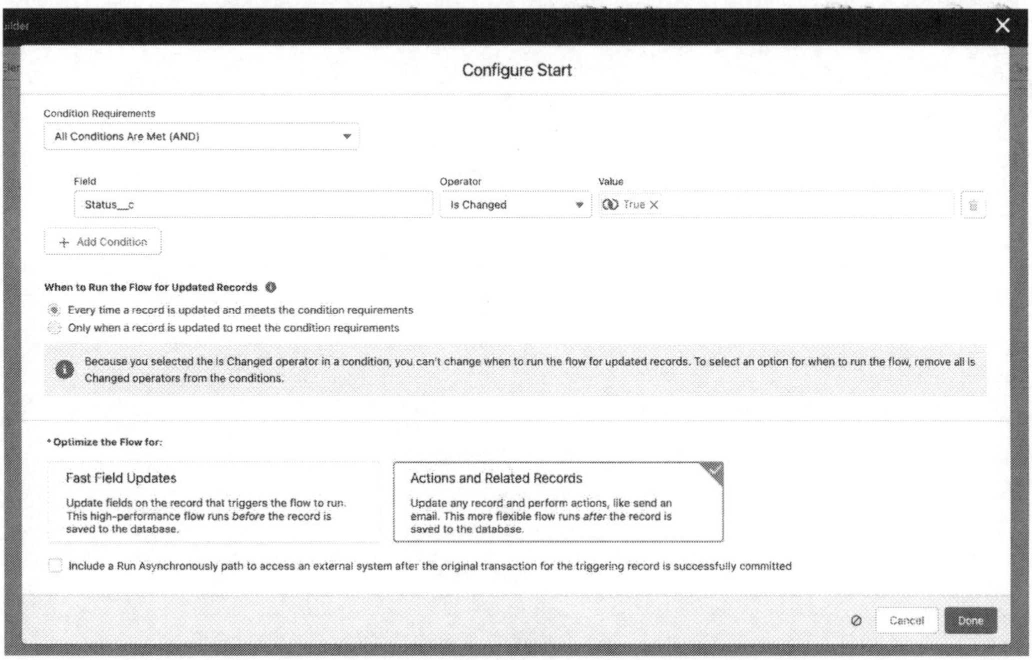

Figure 8.3: *Developing a Salesforce flow for US-011, defining conditions*

Once you click the **Done** button, you will be redirected to a page summarizing your flow. Your page could look like the following:

Figure 8.4: *Developing a Salesforce flow for US-011, the created flow*

You now need to create an action that runs immediately and sends an email to the candidate. Click on the plus sign underneath the word **Run Immediately**, as shown in the following screenshot:

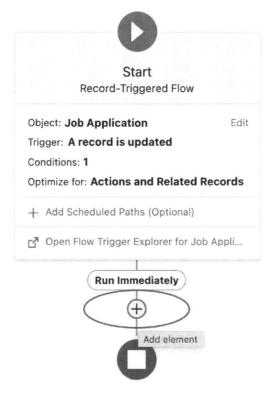

Figure 8.5: *Developing a Salesforce flow for US-011, choosing the flow type*

Select **Send Email Alert** from the **Add Element screen**; your screen will look similar to the following screenshot:

Figure 8.6: *Developing a Salesforce flow for US-011, configuring the immediate action*

Set up the email alert parameters. You can use an email template or a static email body. Look at the other parameters and hover over the help sign next to each to learn more about it. You can set values similar to those shown in the screenshot below:

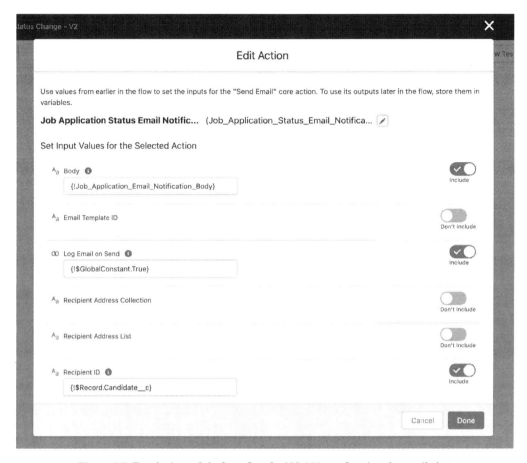

Figure 8.7: Developing a Salesforce flow for US-011, configuring the email alert

Finally, save and activate your flow as shown in the following screenshot:

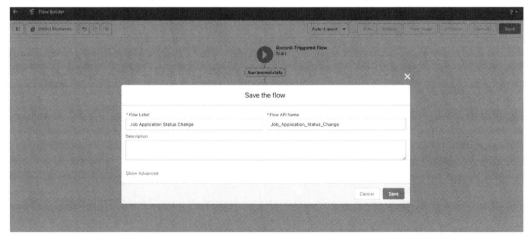

Figure 8.8: Developing a Salesforce flow for US-011, choosing the flow type

You can now test your flow. Update the status of a job application record; an email should be sent to the associated candidate's email address.

You still need to emit a platform event. Platform events can be easily defined in the Salesforce Platform. Navigate to the **Platform Events** menu from the setup screen, as shown in the following screenshot:

Figure 8.9: *Developing a Salesforce flow for US-011, navigating to the platform events section*

Create a new platform event; you will notice the similarity between the UI and the one you experienced while creating custom objects. Your screen could look like the following:

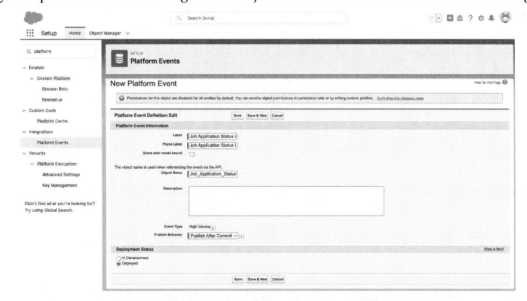

Figure 8.10: *Developing a Salesforce flow for US-011, creating a platform event*

Next, create the four needed fields. You will notice that you have fewer field types to choose from for platform events. Your platform event could look like the following after creating the fields:

Figure 8.11: *Developing a Salesforce flow for US-011, the created platform event*

You need to add another immediate action to your flow to publish a **Job_Application_ Status_Update__e** platform event. You might need to refresh the Flow Builder screen (by hitting the browser's refresh button). Then select the plus sign under the email notification action that you created before and choose the **Create Records** option from the **Add Element** screen, as shown in the following screenshot:

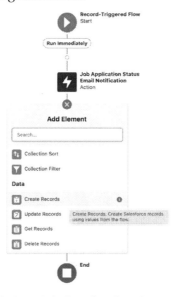

Figure 8.12: *Developing a Salesforce flow for US-011, updating the flow*

Next, set up the values of the **Create Records** element as shown in the following screenshot:

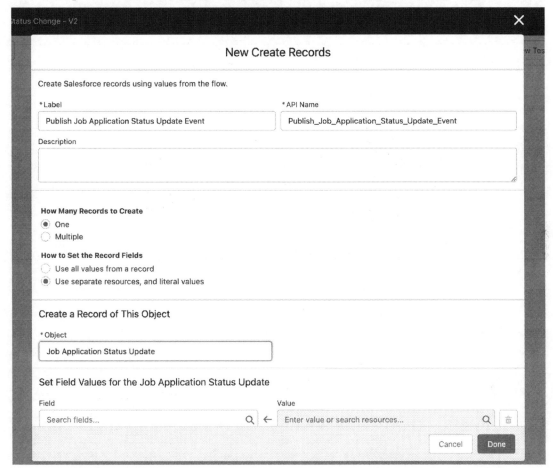

Figure 8.13: *Developing a Salesforce flow for US-011, configuring the flow to publish the event*

Complete setting up the values of the **Job_Application_Status_Update__e** platform event that will be published. You might notice that you do not have a value to enter for the **Description_of_Activities__c** field. This is an example of a missing feature that will be missed in the first release but can be introduced in later releases because you designed your solution with extensibility in mind. Your screen could look like the following screenshot:

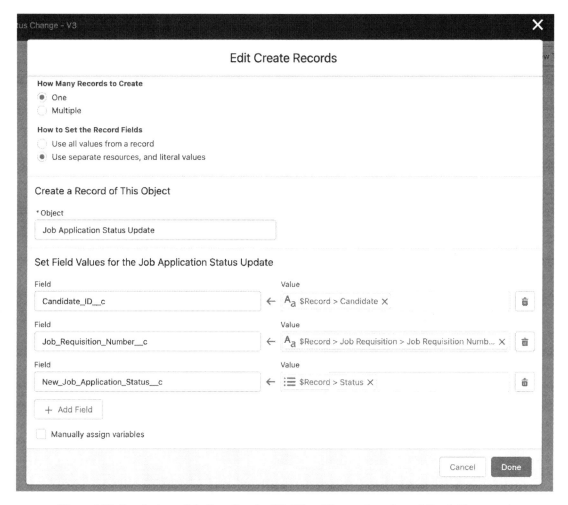

Figure 8.14: Developing a Salesforce flow for US-011, setting up the values of the platform event

Save and activate the new version of your flow. You have now completed building the solution for this user story. You can now move on to the next user story.

Solving and building US-024

This user story includes a complex requirement that is divided mainly into two parts:

- A screen/page that displays the job requisition details publicly online and allows users to apply by providing a predefined set of information and attaching a file.

- An API (or a set of APIs) that accepts the input from the online screen/page and creates a candidate record (if it does not exist already) and job application record linked with it, and the job requisition record. The API is also expected to attach the file to the job application.

There are also a set of questions that you will encounter while solving the requirement, such as:

- There is a need to validate the uploaded file type and size. Which part of the solution should handle this? The front end or the back end?

- Should the screen/page required in the first part of this requirement be part of the application?

- Should the API (or set of APIs) required in the second part of this requirement be part of the application?

Several other considerations might cross your mind and were skipped here for brevity. To solve a complex requirement, though, you always need to break it into smaller parts and solve each progressively. You eat the elephant one bite at a time.

Start with the first part of the problem and ask yourself the common questions you learned about UX. Do you need to communicate a specific UX behavior? Do you need to test a particular UX experience? Do you need to research the usage of a particular UX?

The required screen/page can be built in multiple ways. And can have different functionalities built within it. But is it going to be part of your application? According to the application's strategy, the answer is *no*. The website and its pages are not part of the application, not for the foreseeable future, at least. The application is planned to be headless (where different UIs/heads can be connected to it via APIs). You can skip this requirement, indicating that such functionality is not part of the application; this part of the requirement can go into the backlog.

The second part of the requirement is about designing an API to allow the described behavior. You can either rely on the standard Salesforce APIs for this (such as the REST API) or build a custom API and ship it as part of the solution. The first approach requires no development and shifts the responsibility of validating file size and type to your application's consumer (as they will need to introduce these functionalities). The second approach requires more development but provides your customers with a pre-defined functionality that you can design to be configurable and extendable.

Developing a custom API is a complex topic that this book will not cover. Therefore, this requirement will be solved using the standard Salesforce APIs.

You will likely need to introduce validations on both ends when you design a solution with a loosely coupled front and back end (such as headless solutions). For example, validating the file size and type for this requirement will be a functionality that you need to introduce on the front end (to ensure optimal performance, where all possible validations are done on the client machine/browser rather than on the backend server) and the backend (to ensure that the validation logic is consistently executed regardless of the source. This is particularly useful if your logic can be called from different UIs and devices).

This requirement is related to an integration interface. Therefore, you must also document that interface as part of your solution. You will not develop the external screen/page that will invoke the APIs. However, you still need to document the integration interface, particularly if you plan to wrap its logic in a custom-developed API. You learned how to document integration interfaces in *Chapter 5, Understand the Supporting Tools and Artifacts* under the section *Define the Integration Interfaces*. You can use the same approach to document the integration interface for the US-024 user story. The documented interface could look like the following:

Interface name	Source/ destination	Layer	Pattern	Description	Security and authentication
INT-001	External system -> Salesforce	Business Logic	Remote Process Invocation— Request and Reply	The external system will invoke a custom developed Salesforce API (exposed as a REST web service) to create or update a candidate record, a job application record (linked to a particular job requisition), and a file attached to the job application which contains the candidate's resume. This whole transaction is atomic and if any part of it fails, the whole transaction is rolled back.	OAuth 2.0 web-server flow (then refresh token flow) for web and mobile applications, OAuth 2.0 User-agent flow for JavaScript Single page applications, secured using HTTPS

Table 8.1: The application's list of integration interfaces

This should wrap up the solution for this requirement/user story. However, this requirement is ideal to practice more UX concepts. Assume that the required screen/page is actually part of the application. In this case, you will need to design the UX associated with it. The screen/page can be built in several ways, with different associated UX.

For example, the screen could look like the following:

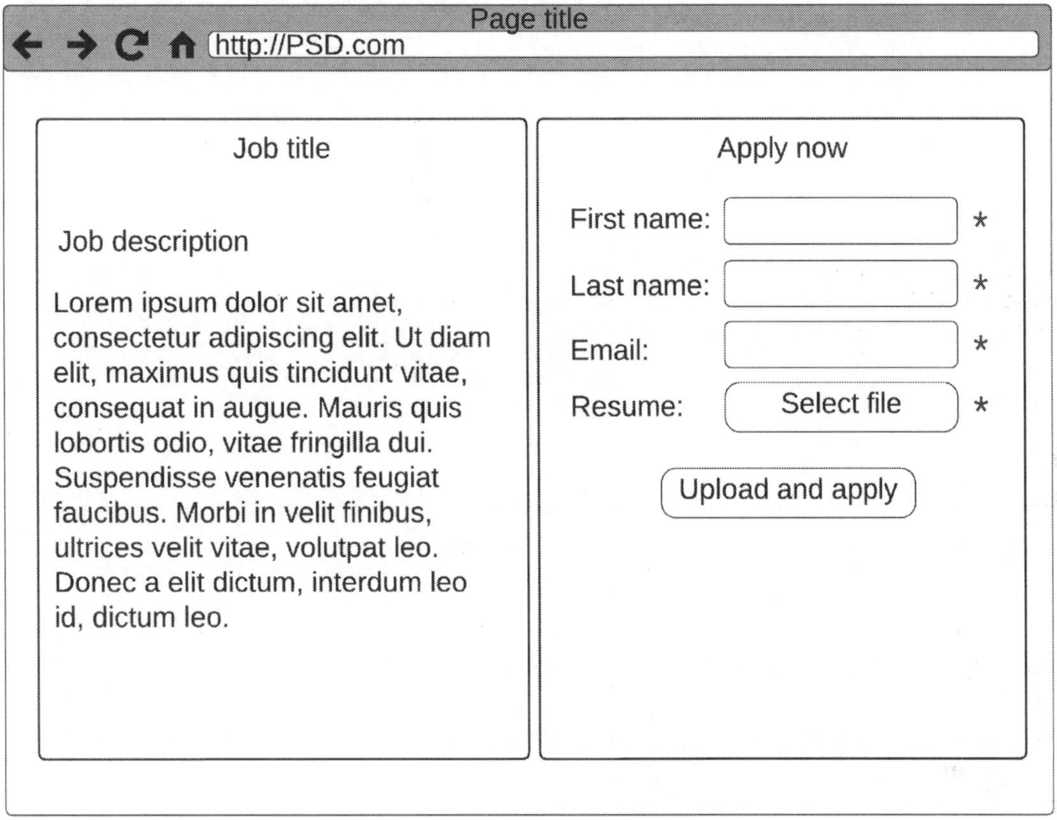

Figure 8.15: Solving US-024, the first wireframe

In this example, you notice that the description of the job requisition is presented on the left side of the page, while the right side is reserved for capturing the candidate's details and uploading the file. The informative part of the page is mixed with the part that enables submitting an application. This approach minimizes the number of steps required to apply but overloads the page with data that belongs to two different contexts.

The same screen/page can be designed differently where the job description information is separate from the screen that gathers the candidate details. The screen could be designed to look like a multi-step wizard focusing on a particular set of the journey each time.

The screen can be presented using the following wireframes:

Figure 8.16: Solving US-024, the second wireframe

The second wireframe represents the second step, which is the screen that enables submitting an application:

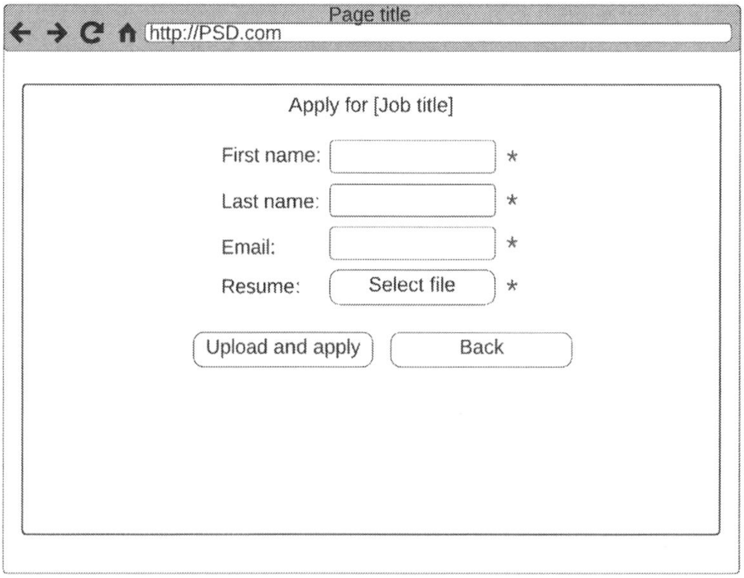

Figure 8.17: Solving US-024, the third wireframe

Both approaches are valid, and there are dozens of other approaches that you can consider. But which one is optimal?

Moreover, notice that in both cases, no information is communicated to the user to indicate the expected file type and size.

You need to run experiments and test different UX experiences with your audience to determine the optimal for your case. But before that, you need to narrow down the approaches to a testable set, as it is not feasible to test fifty different approaches even if you have many users to experiment with. Learning from comparable products in the market can help you narrow your tested UX to a handful of options.

However, regardless of the UX you test, some basics must be maintained, such as providing information to the user about the expected file type and size. This universal experience has become a fundamental part of every similar solution. You should not aim at reinventing the wheel but instead, build on top of the standards the market has introduced throughout the past years.

You can create multiple interactive low-fidelity prototypes and test each with a set of users to determine the suitable UX for your application. Each prototype should have the minimal standard expected behaviors in the software industry. Keep in mind that the standard expected behavior evolves over time. For example, twenty years ago, no website had a mechanism that allowed logging into it via another website. Today, social sign-on (where you can log into a website using credentials from a social media provider, such as Facebook) is standard across all modern websites.

Your hypothetically approved wireframe (which represents the selected UX) could look like the following:

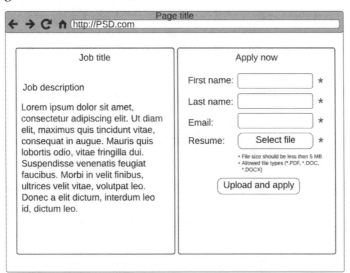

Figure 8.18: Solving US-024, the hypothetically selected wireframe

Please remember that tools such as **Figma** allow the development of richer and more interactive prototypes than we can show in a book.

Now that you learned more about UX design, you can move on to the next user story.

Solving and building US-031

This requirement extends US-024 as it describes a different scenario for using the same functionality. In this use case, the job seeker has been invited to apply for the job. Therefore, the UX is slightly different as the system should recognize the invitation, identify the candidate, and show a slightly different UI based on that. Moreover, the backend API should also recognize the difference and, instead of creating a new candidate record, link the existing candidate record to the job application and update the invitation record to indicate that it has been accepted.

Out of these needs, two particular questions will require your attention:

1. How will the system recognize the invitation and automatically identify the candidate?

2. How will the UI/UX differ for this use case?

Start with the first question. Depending on your experience, you might have an answer already, but if you do not, try to observe what other similar systems are doing.

You might have already received several emails with links that redirect you to some websites upon clicking. The websites usually recognize the link and, depending on what these websites know about you, show personalized screens (can contain information such as your name, email address, and so on). You should ask yourself, how do they do that? Curiosity and tech savviness are critical skills for the software specialist. Even if you did not manage to get an answer by googling it, you could still observe a few interesting aspects that may become handy one day.

For example, you could notice that many of the links in the promotional emails you receive have an *ID* as part of its **Uniform Resource Locator (URL)**, such as:

**http://www.somedomein.com/pagename.
jsp?id=NUAhr39wjned21ksmn9jnHSAY3nak72n**

Kindly note that this URL is an example and is not expected to be used.

You can notice that part of the URL contains an ID, which is the following part:

id=NUAhr39wjned21ksmn9jnHSAY3nak72n

This is simply a parameter being passed to the target page (in this example, it is **pagename. jsp**). This ID is unique per each email sent. This means that each recipient has a different ID associated with their link. When the target page receives this ID, it can query the information stored in the system against this unique ID. This concept is one of the cornerstones of modern-day digital marketing. Such links are usually called **Call to Action (CTA)** links.

Some CTAs are designed to be used once and only. Such as the CTAs you get when you request a *forgotten password* link. Time-sensitive CTAs can also be time-bound, meaning they are only valid for a particular period. Such CTAs are common in the world of *digital signature* applications and many other fields.

In your application, the invitation sent to the candidate should include a unique ID; this ID can be used to recognize the candidate and the invitation, then use both information during the job application submission process.

You will need to introduce some changes to your data model, plus a mechanism to create and populate the unique ID for each sent invitation (this can be accomplished using an **Apex** trigger).

Your update **Job_Application__c** object would look like the following:

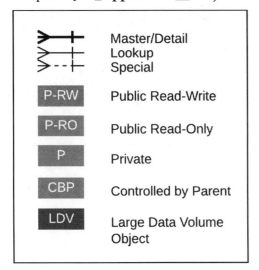
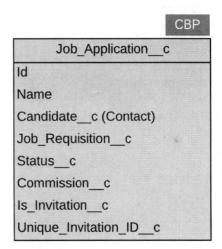

Figure 8.19: Solving US-031, The updated Job_Application__c object

The **Unique_Invitation_ID__c** field should be hidden from all page layouts and users to avoid confusion and potential manipulation.

Next, create a trigger for the **Job_Application__c** object. The trigger should call the **onBeforeUpdate** method of the following class before updating a **Job_Application__c** record. The *before* trigger is used to optimize the transaction as you add the newly generated GUID (Globally Unique Identifier) to the updated record without needing to update it twice. Your trigger could look like the following:

```
trigger JobApplicationTrigger on Job_Application__c (before update) {
    If (Trigger.IsBefore){
```

```
        If (Trigger.IsUpdate){
            JobApplicationTriggerHandler.onBeforeUpdate(Trigger.OldMap,
                                                    Trigger.NewMap);
        }
    }
}
```

The code for the **JobApplicationTriggerHandler** class could look like the following:

```
public class JobApplicationTriggerHandler {
    public static void onBeforeUpdate(Map<ID,Job_Application__c> pOldMap,
                                    Map<ID,Job_Application__c> pNewMap){
        //Check if the Is_Invitation__c check box has been updated
        //and the new value is true, then generate a new unique ID (GUID)
        //for the invitation.
        for (Job_Application__c oUpdatedJobAppRecord: pNewMap.Values()) {
            if((oUpdatedJobAppRecord.Is_Invitation__c !=
                pOldMap.get(oUpdatedJobAppRecord.Id).Is_Invitation__c) &&
                (oUpdatedJobAppRecord.Is_Invitation__c)){
                oUpdatedJobAppRecord.Unique_Invitation_ID__c =
generateGUID();
            }
        }
    }
    private static String generateGUID(){
        //This is a reusable code that can generate GUIDs
        //There are also other ways to generate GUID.
        Blob oAESKey = Crypto.GenerateAESKey(128);
        String oHexAESKey = EncodingUtil.ConvertTohex(oAESKey);
        String GUID = oHexAESKey.SubString(0,8)+ '-' +
                    oHexAESKey.SubString(8,12) + '-' +
                    oHexAESKey.SubString(12,16) + '-' +
                    oHexAESKey.SubString(16,20) + '-' +
                    oHexAESKey.substring(20);
        return GUID;
    }
}
```

The generated GUID could look like the following:

9b8e418e-c70b-13cd-a381-d3afa160eede

Please note that the GUID is unique; you should get a different value every time you try the code. None of them will match the value in the book. The uniqueness of the GUIDs makes them ideal for the use case we have in this user story, which requires a unique, unpredictable link to be sent to the invited candidate. The uniquely generated CTA link (including the unique GUID) can be included in the body of an email sent using a Salesforce Flow.

Next, you need to tackle the other challenge in this requirement; how will the UI/UX look like for the invited candidate?

To illustrate that, you will need a new set of wireframes/prototypes. The new wireframe could look like the following:

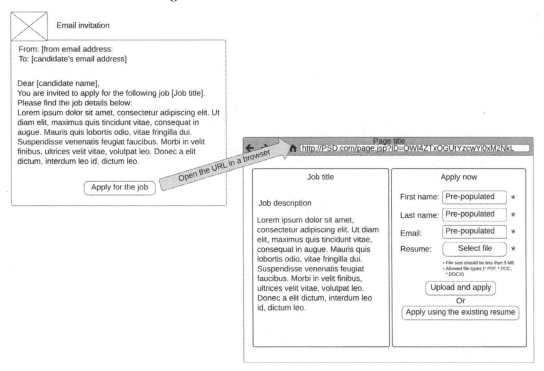

Figure 8.20: *Solving US-031, the wireframe for the invited candidates' job application submission page*

The invited candidate can apply using a fresh resume or their existing resume (which should be saved in your application already, considering that this is a known candidate).

This user story concludes your application's third major feature. Next, you will solve a selected set of requirements as part of a *container* feature.

Designing, prototyping, and building - Other requirements

The project team can select the requirements that will be addressed in each *container* feature based on many factors, including relativity, ease of introduction, external factors (such as a demand from a key customer), or other factors. In this book, the following requirements will be included in this *container* feature:

- **Requirement number 22:** The application should allow defining a specific commission rate for each recruitment agency.

- **Requirement number 23:** The application should calculate the commission of external recruiters if used.

- **Requirement number 26:** The application should allow tracking of the history of each recruiter and show key indicators such as the total number of successfully recruited candidates vs. the number of lost candidates.

- **Requirement number 28:** The application should show indicators such as the positions that take the longest to recruit and in which countries.

- **Requirement number 33:** The application should have a configurable data refreshing exercise to allow a specific team to update the candidate details.

Practice formatting these requirements as user stories, then proceed with solving the requirements, starting with the following.

Allow defining a specific commission rate

You have already fulfilled this requirement by introducing the **Commission_Rate__c** field on the **Recruitment_Agency__c** object. Each external recruiter (represented using the standard **Contact** object with a specific **record type**) is linked to a **Recruitment_Agency__c** object. The following partial data model is a reminder:

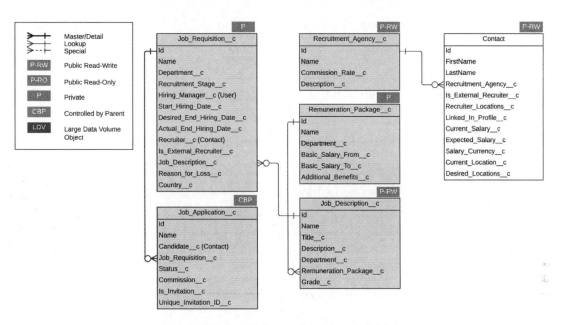

Figure 8.21: Partial data model, agency definition

The recruitment agency commission is usually calculated based on multiple factors that are part of the signed agreement between the recruitment agency and the company using their services. These factors could be the final agreed candidate salary, pre-agreed flat rate, pre-agreed allocation/quota, and so on. This requirement might look easy, but it is an example of a sub-optimally gathered requirement where oversimplification impacted its completeness.

This requirement is also related to requirement number 23, which is all about the commission calculation. Solving requirement 22 without considering requirement 23 is a common mistake that you might encounter during your professional life. As a software specialist, you should question the requirements and validate how they fit within the bigger picture. Oversimplification is a common mistake, particularly in the absence of good **product management** practices and the usage of **comparator products**.

Move on to the following requirement to reveal more about the extended scope of this requirement.

Calculate the commission of external recruiters

There are several ways to calculate a commission. Such details are usually captured as part of an agreed contract. The module that calculates commissions can be a whole separate application. There are several examples of such applications in the market already.

For example, to solve this requirement, you can introduce a new field under the **Job_ Requisition__c** object to hold the agreed salary. Still, you will need to capture details about the selected candidate on the same **Job_Requisition__c** record. Otherwise, you could risk a data discrepancy challenge. Your data should always be stored in high quality and with the least possible errors. Storing the agreed salary on one record and a flag indicating the selected candidate on another could pose a risk if the data on the candidate record gets updated. Solid knowledge of **Relational Database Management Systems (RDBMS)** design practices is essential for the software specialist.

Alternatively, you might want to avoid storing salary information in Salesforce. In this case, you could keep this value in an external system that will use the **Commission_Rate__c** value on the **Recruitment_Agency__c** object to calculate the commission. You might also want to allow your application to calculate a flat-rate commission.

This requirement is much more sophisticated than it initially sounds. The requirement can be excluded from the application's scope, pushed to a future release, or released incrementally via multiple releases using what is known in the **product management** world as a **Minimum Viable Product (MVP)**.

An MVP is a product with minimal features that are good enough for a specific set of customers (called early adopters). An MVP is usually used to validate a product (or a feature of a product) early with minimal impact and the shortest possible time-to-market.

Defining the scope of MVP and the order of features to be included is a crucial skill, as you could lose the faith of your customers if you launch an MVP product that feels unfinished or half-baked. Moreover, the order of incrementally building an MVP is essential, as a lousy order could result in a dramatic increase in the cost due to rework activities.

You are encouraged to read more about defining MVP scope for software products (which has slightly different concepts than other types of products) in other books and sources, as this is outside this book's scope.

In this book, requirements 22 and 23 will be considered out of scope. Move on to the next requirement.

Allow tracking of the history of each recruiter

To address this requirement and report indicators such as successfully recruited candidates vs. the number of lost candidates, you need to count the number of job applications lost or withdrawn by the candidate for each job application. You can do that in many ways, but considering that the relationship between the **Job_Application__c** object and the **Job_Requisition__c** object is a master/detail, the easiest way would be to utilize **roll-up summary** fields; you can then use these fields in standard reports and dashboards.

You will need two roll-up summary fields at least, one to count the total number of job applications/candidates per job requisition and the other to count the number of lost job applications.

Navigate to the object manager for the **Job_Requisition__c** object, and create the first roll-up summary field similar to the following screenshot:

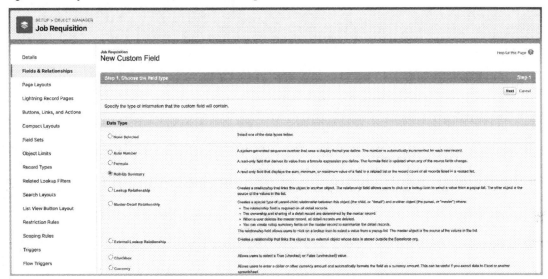

Figure 8.22: *The creation of the first roll-up summary field – step one*

Name the field **Total_Number_of_Candidates __c** and proceed to the next step to define the used roll-up summary formula. Select the **Job Applications** as the summarized object and choose **Count** as a roll-up type. Keep the default selection of the **Filter Criteria** to **All records should be included in the calculation** similar to what is shown in the following screenshot:

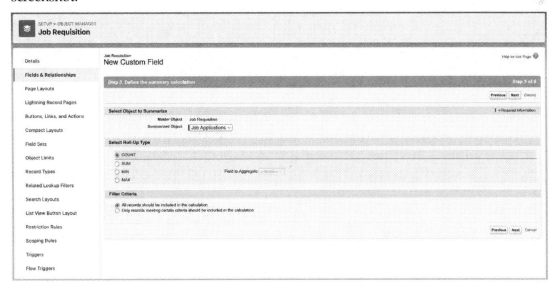

Figure 8.23: *The creation of the first roll-up summary field – step two*

Continue with the next steps as usual. Once done, create another roll-up summary field, name it **Number_of_Lost_Candidates__c** as shown in the following screenshot:

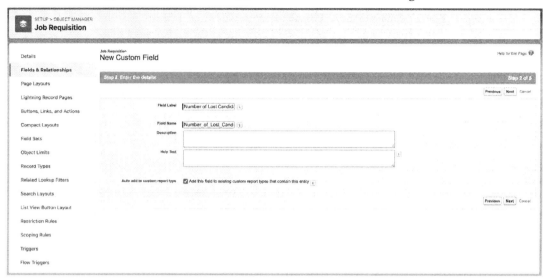

Figure 8.24: *The creation of the second roll-up summary field – step one*

Next, configure the field as shown in the following screenshot. This time, you will define filter criteria for the roll-up function:

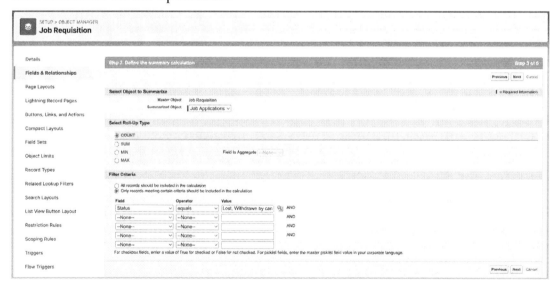

Figure 8.25: *The creation of the second roll-up summary field – step two*

In the previous screenshot, the following **Status** values were selected:

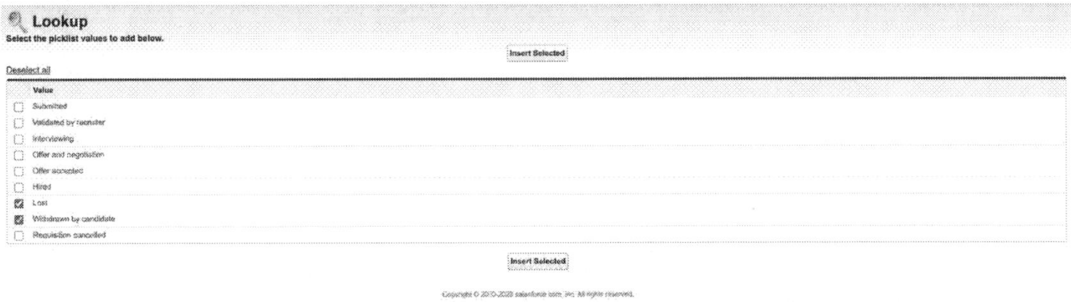

Figure 8.26: The creation of the second roll-up summary field - configuring the filter criteria

Continue with the remaining steps as usual. Now you have the two roll-up summary fields and can create a report that utilizes them. You already learned how to create reports, so this chapter will not cover this step.

Roll-up summary fields are a strong point-and-click configurable feature that can save you much time and effort, but only if the underlying data model is designed to support it. This is another example of the importance of your data model for your overall application design.

Move on to the next requirement.

Show indicators such as longest-to-recruit positions

You can address this straightforward requirement using standard reports and dashboards. Keep in mind that you are building an application that will be used by another company / customer. You do not necessarily know the data volumes in their org. Are they publishing 5 jobs every month or 500? (although you expect the customer to be a small / medium size company). Standard reports and dashboards have known limitations. You can learn more about that at the following link.

https://help.salesforce.com/s/articleView?id=sf.rd_reports_dashboards_limits_overview.htm&type=5

You should include a detailed description of the expected data volumes your application's pre-created reports and dashboards are tested with (for example, less than 1 million job requisitions at any time). If customers need to report on larger data volumes, they can use other tools such as Salesforce CRM Analytics, Power BI, Tableau, or others. The important thing to remember while building a software application (including Salesforce platform applications) is that you need to document the conditions under which your software has been tested. This sets the expectations from your end and reduces the chances of conflicts with your future customers. You can move to the next requirement.

Configurable data refreshing exercise

You came across a similar requirement in *Chapter 3, Develop a sample Salesforce application - PbP Phonebook*. It would be nice if you could simply copy the settings you introduced there and use them straight away in the PSD recruitment application. The good news is that this is doable as the Salesforce platform is Metadata-driven, meaning that most of its settings and configurations are stored as meta-data that can be copied from one Salesforce org to another. In *Chapter 9, Create a Sample Application - Test and Deploy the Application*, you will learn more about deploying your application.

There are two other prerequisites for re-using modules in different applications:

- The module has to be designed with re-use in mind.

- The module has to be well documented.

Both topics should be adequately addressed using the RAAD lifecycle principles and artifacts.

You have now created all the main features of your applications. The next step is to wrap those features together and create a *Salesforce Application* that enables your potential users to use the functionalities you created easily and intuitively.

Creating the PSD recruitment application

Follow the following steps to create a Salesforce Lightning Application for the PSD recruitment app.

First, from the setup menu, navigate to the **App Manager,** as shown in the following screenshot:

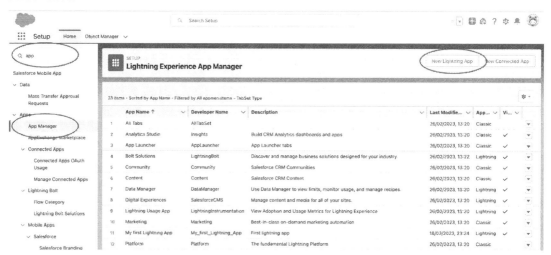

Figure 8.27: Creating a Salesforce Lightning Application - step one

Enter the application details and select the color theme. You can also upload an image of your choice to be used with the application. Your screen could look like the following:

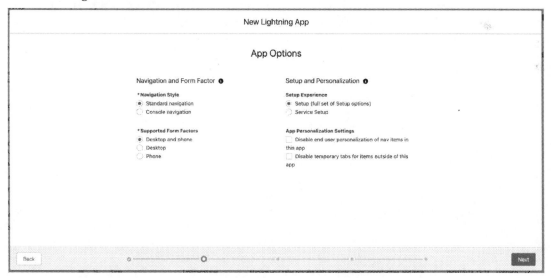

Figure 8.28: Creating a Salesforce Lightning Application - step two

Next, configure the application options; you can accept the default settings as shown in the following screenshot:

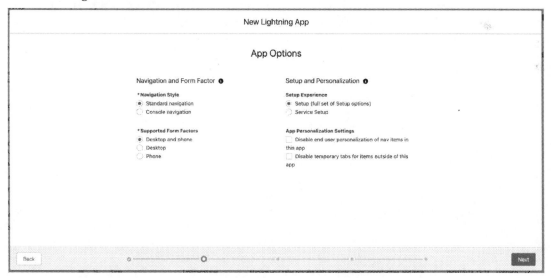

Figure 8.29: Creating a Salesforce Lightning Application - step three

The next step is used to add a utility item to your application in desktop view, as shown in the following screenshot. You can skip this step and click **Next**:

Figure 8.30: Creating a Salesforce Lightning Application - step four

The next step is critical, as you need to choose the tabs shown in your application. You can also control the order of these tabs. Keep in mind that the best applications are those that have the simplest UIs. Try to keep the number of tabs as limited as possible. If needed, you can create multiple applications with different tabs (such as creating an application for the end users and another for the administrators). In this book, one application will be used for both. Your screen could look like the following screenshot:

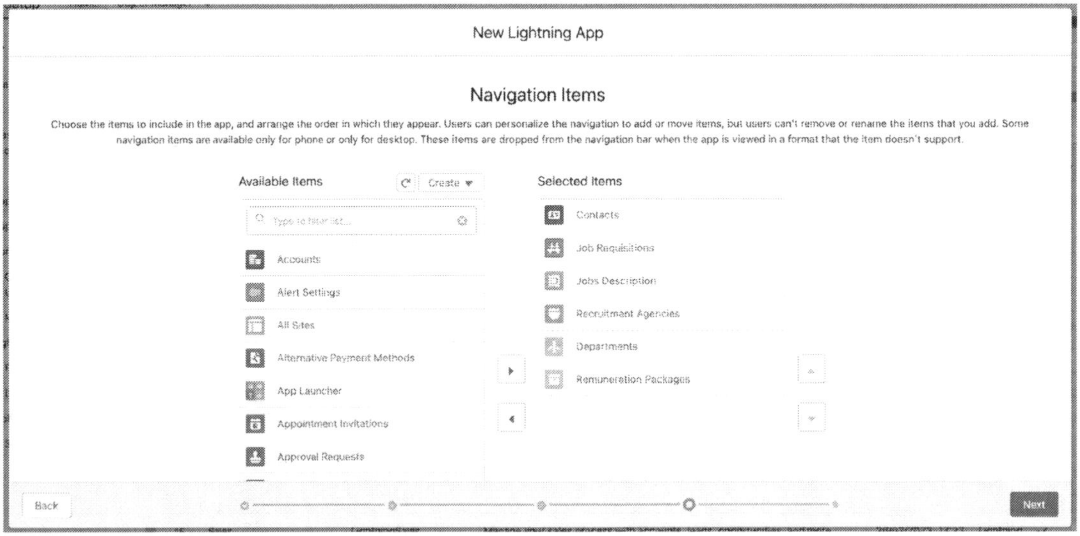

Figure 8.31: Creating a Salesforce Lightning Application - step five

The last step is to configure the user profiles who will have access to this application. This step is not crucial in your case, considering that you are building an application that should be shipped and installed to other Salesforce orgs. Such configuration is essential, though, for the target orgs. Your screen could look like the following:

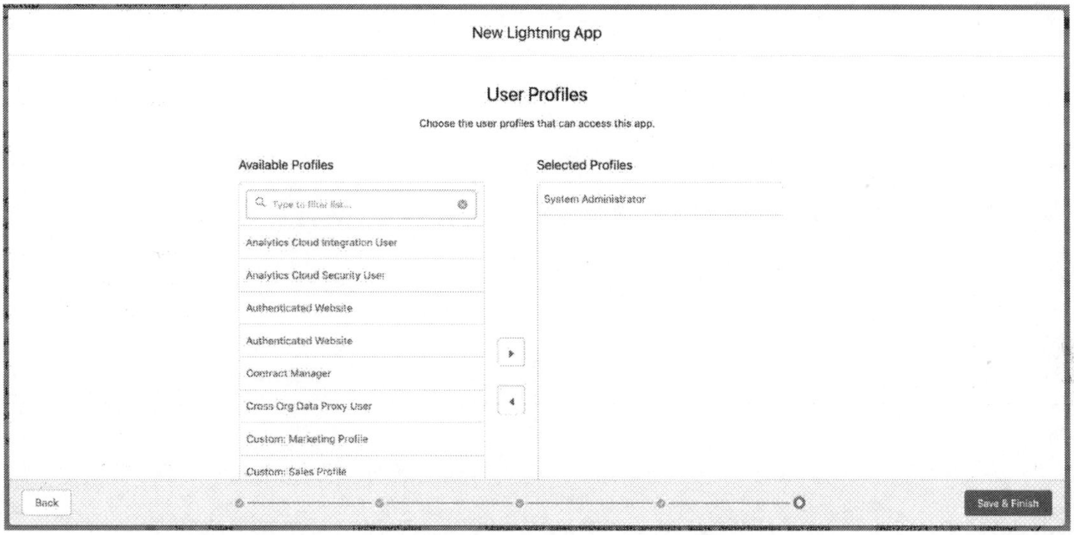

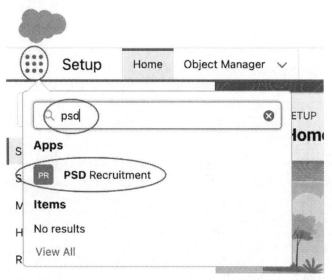

Figure 8.32: Creating a Salesforce Lightning Application - step six

Congratulations! You now have a ready-to-use recruitment application. You can view your application from the app launcher, as shown in the following screenshot:

Figure 8.33: Creating a Salesforce Lightning Application - step six

Your application could look similar to the following screenshot:

Figure 8.34: *Creating a Salesforce Lightning Application - step six*

This concludes the *Detailing, designing, and prototyping* phase. You technically combined that with building activities from the next phase (*developing/building and testing*) in an agile manner, as the boundary between the two phases is loosely defined. The next chapter will teach you more about testing and deploying your application.

Summary

This chapter was an intense practical experience building applications using the RAD lifecycle. You continued with the hypothetical application from the previous chapter. In this chapter, you continued the *Detailing, designing, and prototyping* phase of the RAD lifecycle. You continued solving the requirements one by one, provided a detailed solution for each, and developed/built that solution as you go. You learned practically some key concepts such as MVP, re-use, and de-scoping.

The practical experience you are gaining will turn into second nature with practice. And in a short time, you will notice that the time you spend generating, updating, and using the different artifacts throughout your application development lifecycle is significantly reduced. This will be the moment you start reaping all the benefits of RAD and experience the true power of the Salesforce platform.

You have built the first version of the PSD recruitment application, which is now ready to be tested and deployed. In the next chapter, you will learn about essential testing practices and activities to help you efficiently test your solution. You will also wrap the application and set it up for deployment into another Salesforce org.

CHAPTER 9

Create a Sample Application: Test and Deploy

Introduction

In the previous two chapters, you analyzed, designed, and built a Salesforce recruitment application for PSD, a hypothetical application development company. You practiced using the Salesforce **Rapid Application Development (RAD)** lifecycle.

In the previous chapter, you concluded the *Detailing, designing, and prototyping* phase and covered parts of the *Developing/Building and Testing* phase. In this chapter, you will conclude the *Developing/Building and Testing* phase and venture into the *Deploying/Releasing* phase.

You will learn about the importance of testing your application. You will come across the test case format, types, and management. You will learn about potential tools for each test type and dive deeper into one of the major tools in your toolbox, the Apex test classes.

You will then learn more about **managed** and **unmanaged Salesforce Packages** and practice creating an unmanaged package to deploy your application to a different org. You will also learn some fundamental concepts about **Continues Integration/Continuous Delivery (CI/CD)** that have not been covered so far.

Have a look next at the structure of this chapter.

Structure

The chapter covers the following topics:

- The importance of a comprehensive test suite

- Deeper dive into test types and tools

- Writing test cases

- Deploying your application

Objectives

By the end of this chapter, you will gain knowledge and practical experience in designing, writing, and creating test cases for your Salesforce application. You will learn how to create a robust test suite that can act as your first and most formidable line of defense to detect bugs earlier. And you will learn how to execute it regularly as part of your release cycle. Finally, you will practice wrapping your application and deploying it to other Salesforce orgs.

The importance of a comprehensive test suite

Many software professionals recognize the importance of software testing. Some applications prioritize bug-free software due to the industry's needs. But generally, all applications aim at customer satisfaction and therefore desire bug-free applications. The question is, how to achieve that?

Building comprehensive testing suits that are executed more frequently and efficiently is a crucial success factor. Such test suits require creating test cases that cover all or most of the application functionalities, including positive and negative usage of these functionalities. Creating robust test suits starts by writing a good test case. A poorly written test case can be more harmful than helpful.

Start with a few foundational definitions:

- **Positive tests:** a form of software testing that involves using valid data sets as input and evaluating if the application behaves as expected. Positive testing is performed to ensure that the software application performs the tasks that it is intended to do.

- **Negative tests:** a form of software testing that involves using invalid/improper data sets as input and evaluating if the application behaves as expected in handling such input. Negative testing is performed to ensure that the software application is handling errors and exceptions the way it is intended to do without crashing or becoming unstable.

- **Test case:** a description of how to test software. A test case includes instructions for the executor (tester/automated tester) to validate one or more functionalities. Test cases can consist of positive and negative tests. In both types of tests, input date, actions to perform, and outputs are included and considered.

- **Test suite:** A group of test cases organized in one or more segments (such as by feature or module)

Test cases are foundational building blocks in software testing. They are sometimes confused with other terms, such as test scenarios, scripts, plans, and use cases. Here is a brief comparison of each:

- **Test scenario:** outlines a functionality to test, such as verifying customer registration functionality. Test scenarios usually have their unique identifiers and are used to derive test cases from them. A test scenario describes the high-level actions, while the test cases cover the low-level actions.

- **Test script:** An interchangeable term with test cases. Both describe a set of actions that verifies software functionality. However, the term test script is more often used in test automation (where an automated robot/application handles executing the test actions).

- **Test plan:** A document that covers all software testing aspects, such as project scope, deliverables, stakeholders and their responsibilities, key dates and milestones, and defect mitigation strategy. The purpose of this document is to set the expectations for all relevant parties and communicate what will happen during testing.

- **Use case:** Describe how the system should perform under specific conditions. The business requirements usually outline use cases (in user stories, this is represented as scenarios). This outline describes how the user would interact with the application and what input/output to expect. Use cases further explain how the functionality should work, while test cases describe how it should be tested. Test cases are derived from use cases.

You briefly learned about different types of tests in *Chapter 4, Learn the Salesforce Application Development Lifecycle, Table 4.1*. Next, you will dive deeper into a specific set of these test types and learn more about them.

Deeper dive into test types and tools

There are multiple ways to group the different types of tests. This book grouped them under three main categories to help you memorize them. These categories are:

1. **Functional tests:** This category includes test types to verify the behavior of specific system functionalities.

2. **Non-functional tests:** This category includes test types to verify the system's behavior concerning particular system functionalities.

3. **Cross-functional tests:** This category includes test types that combine functional and non-functional tests.

Have a closer look at these different test categories next.

Functional tests

This category focuses on testing specific software functionalities and verifying whether they work as intended. Several types of tests can be considered part of functional tests, such as the following:

- **Functionality test:** this is the most common type of functional test. The QA team creates functionality tests associated with one or more functionality. The QA team executes functionality tests after the developers finish developing a particular feature. Functionality tests form part of the regression test suite (which you will learn more about in the cross-functional tests section), as they are usually related to software functionalities. In a well-structured environment, any change in a particular functionality should trigger all related test cases to ensure that the newly introduced change has not accidentally impacted any of the functionality's behaviors. You might also need to invoke the regression test suits for related functionalities. Functionality tests can include test cases that are executed manually or test scripts that are executed automatically. Applications with high demands should aim at automating most, if not all, of their functionality tests, as this, ensures execution consistency and the ability to trigger these tests more frequently. Manually executed functional tests do not require specific tools to execute (apart from the tool used to write the test case and the tested software itself). There is no shortage of automated testing tools; some rely on simple scripting languages to write the test automation, while others rely on point-and-click capabilities. **Provar, OpKey, Tricentis, Cigniti, Selenium**, and **Leapwork** are all examples of such tools. Some of these tools are more specialized in the Salesforce ecosystem. You might want to consider these, particularly if you are building a native Salesforce application. A test case that performs a successful portal login and then validates specific values and flags (such as cookies, session ID, tokens and so on.) to verify that the user has logged in is an example of functionality testing.

- **Usability test:** This type of test case assesses the opinions of potential end users on a particular functionality. These test cases are usually designed and executed by UX researchers. Usability testing can be conducted in various ways, such as moderated or unmoderated, and it can involve different facilitating tools such as **UXArmy, Maze, Userbrain, Hotjar,** and many more. It can also be executed in person or remotely. The tester would gather an end user's viewpoint and utilize it to pinpoint sub-optimal experiences that could impact the application's usability.

Depending on the aim and technique of UX research, usability tests can be either formal (known inputs and outputs) or informal (Unknown inputs or outputs. Tests are executed to discover the outcome). An example of such a test case would be assigning participants (primarily customers) a task to locate a product on your website, buy it, and then request an order cancellation. The test will validate whether they can successfully complete the task and if the system is intuitive enough.

- **UI test:** This test ensures that the user interface functions as intended. These tests are conducted to examine the visual elements of software and focus on items such as component alignment, menus, sub-menus, tables, coolers, and buttons to confirm that all these items are displayed how they are expected to be displayed. UI tests might also include videos, voices, and other types of multimedia. These tests are usually executed by the QA team and can be executed manually or using a test automation tool. Worth mentioning that automating UI tests could get tricky as changes to the UI is more frequent.

  You should attempt to use the **Salesforce Lightning Design System** whenever developing a custom **Lightning Component** or **Visualforce** page to reduce the risk of creating something requiring intensive UI testing.

  An example of such a test case is navigating to the home page and validating that the website navigation menu is displayed correctly on desktop and mobile browsers.

- **User acceptance test (UAT):** This type of test case ensures that the product is validated by the end user. The QA team helps the user/customer to conduct user acceptance tests in a testing environment and verify that the product flows seamlessly from start to finish. In most cases, UAT is done with users who represent the customer rather than the customers themselves, but this depends on the nature of the application and its intended customers (internal users vs. external users).

  User acceptance tests are especially useful when business requirements change during the development process, as Stakeholders do not always communicate these changes effectively with the development team. UAT scripts are prepared by the QA team, who also share the feedback with the development team and other stakeholders. An example of such a test case is verifying if a user can sign up online for a new account and log in afterward to execute a particular functionality.

- **Exploratory test:** This is an informal test where the tester examines the system on an ad-hoc basis to uncover defects that may have been missed during structured testing. Although exploratory tests do not follow a specific set of actions, they still require some structure, particularly in terms of time-boxing and results documentation. Exploratory tests can support validating requirements as they test the system using methods and ways different than those in scripted tests. The QA team would then learn from the gaps found and aim at enhancing their existing test cases and scripts.

An example of such a test case is to check how using the browser's Back button multiple times affects a particular functionality.

- **Unit test:** By definition, this type of test case aims at verifying the behavior of the smallest and isolated possible set of functionalities. Unit tests are a powerful tool that allows developers to systematically test their code (and sometimes configurations) before handing it over to the QA team. Unit tests are automated by nature and, therefore, naturally incorporated into the regression test suite. Automated tests are much cheaper and faster to execute, which allows the execution of many test cases frequently (such as upon the release of any new/updated functionality). In the Salesforce world, unit tests are even more powerful as they can be used to test some point-and-click developments, such as testing the outcome of Salesforce flows. As a Salesforce professional, you should consider unit tests as a first line of defense against bugs and a first contributor to your regression test suite. You should use them not only to cover any code you create (Salesforce mandates covering at least 75% of your Apex code with unit tests) but to automate functionality test cases whenever possible. Unit tests are also crucial in **Test Driven Development (TDD)**, which is a software development practice that aims at creating tests before code (unlike the classic behavior of creating tests after the code is created). Many have praised TDD for producing some of the most robust and bug-free software. Salesforce applications can utilize TDD techniques whenever a custom code is created. TDD is recommended when you are creating highly complicated logic in your code. In this chapter, you will learn how to create a test case and then create a unit test to cover it.

More types of tests can fit under the functional testing category. But this book aims to introduce you to the most common types rather than provide an exhaustive list. You are encouraged to read more about functional testing using other resources.

Non-functional tests

Non-functional tests validate the behavior of the software under different types of workloads. Several types of tests can be considered part of functional tests, such as the following:

- **Security test cases:** These tests are designed to detect software security weaknesses. This type of testing seeks to enhance the protection of software and evaluate the system's ability to withstand common types of cyber-attacks while also determining the associated risk level of the product. Security tests can include activities such as vulnerability and configuration scanning and penetration testing (also known as pen-testing or intrusive testing). The primary objective of security testing is to provide practical insights into software vulnerabilities and their severity and risk level.

Penetration tests validate your application's security by simulating a cyber-attack. A good example is to attempt logging into your portal without valid credentials or verifying if your publicly exposed APIs are adequately secure and can withstand a **Distributed Denial of Service (DDoS)** attack. Penetration tests are executed using specific tools and techniques (usually performed by a third party) such as **Kali Linux**, **Wireshark**, **Metasploit**, **Hashcat**, **Hydra**, and many more.

Salesforce vulnerability scanners can provide valuable information about potential risks. There are specialized tools in the market, such as **Dynatrace** and **DigitSec**. Remember that vulnerability scanners are good for detecting security flaws that have already been well-identified and included in the scanner. Vulnerability scanners should not be relied on to detect vulnerabilities that have not been made public yet. **zero-day vulnerability** is a name given to disclosed cyber security vulnerabilities that have not been patched yet.

- **Integration test (for distributed and non-distributed systems):** These tests aim at validating the behavior of multiple elements when merged together or connected to each other. In the context of standard non-distributed applications, the integration test would refer to testing a set of functionalities when merged into the application. An example of this use case would be merging code developed in a low-level environment (such as a developer sandbox) into a higher-level environment (such as pre-production or production). The functionality (or set of functionalities) could work well while isolated in the low-level environment but could fail when integrated with other application functionalities. The failure would likely be caused by the fact that the low-level environment did not receive the latest code updates from other development environments that might have introduced changes to the higher-level environment. In the context of distributed applications (applications that consist of more than one part integrated and communicating over a network), the concept of integration tests could be extended to testing the behavior of the entire integrated distributed application. For example, you could have an application that captures input from the user, passes it to another remote system for validation, and upon successful validation, create a record in a database. In this case, the test would be extended to validate whether the integration works as expected. If the integration is happening using APIs, then this type of testing is sometimes referred to as **API testing**.

- **Performance test:** This test validates the application performance under usual and unusual conditions. As you learned in *Chapter 4, Learn the Salesforce Application Development Lifecycle, Table 4.1,* you should measure and document the conditions and results of your application's performance and load tests and include them in your overall application documentation. One additional point a Salesforce professional must be aware of is that sandbox environments are hosted on a different infrastructure than production environments. Performance and performance plus load tests should occur in product or production-like environments. You should contact Salesforce if you are planning to execute a performance test over a production environment.

There are several types of performance testing, such as stress, spike, and load testing.

- **Load test:** One of the performance testing types. This test validates a functionality's behavior (or the entire application's behavior) while fully loaded (or overloaded) with data. It is worth mentioning that outside the Salesforce ecosystem, the same term is sometimes used to refer to testing the system's behavior upon overloading it with requests.

- **Database test:** Databases are not usually considered an application functionality. Yet this type of test case validates key database-related functionalities such as data quality and consistency. Database tests ensure that the application's data is stored in the expected format, location, quality and according to the business requirements and regulations. Database testing can also include verifying if the users accessing the database can only see and do what they are expected to see and do. Database tests can be extended to validate the device that the data is stored on. An example of database testing is to validate if the customer's confidential data is stored at the right location and format (for example, encrypted).

The last category of test types combines elements from both functional and non-functional tests.

Cross-functional tests

This test category includes a set of tests that utilize one or more of the previously mentioned functional and non-functional tests. You will classically find the cross-functional test listed as another type of functional test. However, modern software is more sophisticated by nature, and therefore it is important to include non-functional tests in these test types. Two types of cross-functional tests will be listed in this book; they are the following:

- **Regression test:** A suite of tests, functional and non-functional, that aims at covering most, if not all, the system functionalities. Regression tests validate if the system is still behaving as expected after introducing a new / modified feature. This type of test is extremely important as it ensures that your entire system behaves as expected. A common mistake is to test only the changing feature (or the new feature and related features), omitting other features that are deemed *unchanged*. Just to discover that an unknown dependency is causing one of the software functionalities to misbehave or completely break down.

- You should automate as much as possible of your regression tests so that you can efficiently and consistently invoke the entire suite upon releasing any new functionality. Highly sophisticated applications could have automated regression test suits that run for days to complete. A regression test suite can be broken down into independent modules with clearly defined boundaries and dependencies in these edge cases.

An example of a regression test suite is a comprehensive set of unit tests, manually executed functionality tests, automated functionality tests, performance tests, and integration tests.

- **Smoke test:** This test ensures the software is stable and performing as expected in production at any given time. This test is not necessarily performed as part of a release cycle, as it could be periodically invoked to validate the system's status. Smoke tests can include a suite of selected functional (and rarely, non-functional) tests. Smoke tests have to be lightweight so that they do not impact the overall performance of the production environment. Therefore, they usually include tests for only the most common or business-crucial functionalities. The result of an abnormal behavior should be reported immediately to the right stakeholders.

  Smoke tests are usually fully automated and scheduled to run at a specific interval (such as every 10 minutes). Smoke tests act as early warning signals for the technology team that something abnormal is happening. Several tools available in the market can detect a platform's availability from an infrastructure perspective; smoke tests, however, aim to detect abnormalities in the business logic and key application functionalities early. As mentioned earlier, no specific tools are used for smoke tests as they are a combination of functional tests.

- Salesforce applications would rarely have a smoke test suite as part of them. But you might want to include that as a post-installation activity. For example, you could build a Salesforce application and publish it to AppExchange. Then offer installation/implementation services to your customers, which includes configuring and customizing your application. You can create a smoke test suite that fits the business needs of that particular customer as part of your installation/implementation services.

That concludes the three main categories of tests. Next, you will learn to write test cases.

Writing test cases

Test cases can be written any time before development work starts on a given user story. However, it is recommended that testers write test cases in the early stages of the software development lifecycle and straight after the requirements are formatted as user stories. Testers would rely on the user stories (particularly their acceptance criteria) and the overall test plan to create different use cases, scenarios, and, eventually, test cases.

While writing the test cases, it is important to consider the application flows, as the user's path to functionality is crucial and must be appropriately validated. For example, account settings changes must be tested on both mobile apps and web browsers to ensure functionality across all platforms.

Next, you will be introduced to the commonly used test case format.

Formatting test cases

Test cases should be written clearly and concisely, ensuring accuracy and simplicity for anyone who reads and executes the tests. Like any other software documentation, test cases should be readable and understandable by any audience, not just the application's development team. While some details are essential, it is best to keep test cases economical and easy to execute on a high level, to reduce maintenance when the application changes. Well-written test cases should be repeatable and reusable, as few tests run only once, and reusable tests can save time when developing additional functionality. Each test case should be traceable, allowing for easy documentation and results analysis by the team.

When creating test case documentation, it is important to include all relevant information needed to run the test and collect data. The exact format for test cases may vary from one software development company to the other but typically includes the following details:

- **Feature/module name:** The name of the feature or module that this test belongs to.

- **Test case ID and/or name:** A unique identifier of the test case which follows a specific naming convention. Such as TC-03823.

- **Tester name:** The name of the person who conducted the test. In a few cases, the person's name will also be known even before performing the test. This is relevant only to manually executed tests.

- **Test data:** Describes the test data set, such as the database name where the data used during the tests is stored. For Salesforce applications, this value usually includes the relevant objects for this test.

- **Preconditions/assumptions:** Details of all prerequisite steps expected to be accomplished before executing the given test. This can also be an assumed situation, such as "after a successful email validation." The successful execution of other test cases could be listed here as prerequisites.

- **Test priority:** Highlights the importance of the test, usually using predefined values such as low, medium, and high.

- **Test scenario:** A description or reference to the high-level action that needs to be validated. In most cases, the test case will simply refer to the unique name/ID of the test scenario. Remember that test cases are derived from the test scenarios.

- **Testing environment:** This value describes the environment(s) where this test case will be executed. For example, *Pre-Prod*. Any additional details relating to the characteristics of that environment can also be added here. For example, a *Pre-Prod environment that has been refreshed no longer than one week.*

- **Testing steps:** The ordered and detailed steps the tester should follow while executing the test case. It is important to keep these steps up to date and easy to follow to allow any QA professional/tester to execute the use case.

- **Expected results:** The expected output or behavior from the system. Similar to the testing steps, this value has to be detailed and up to date to get the maximum value of your test case. The expected result could be a positive or a negative value. For example, the expected value could be a specific type of exception.

- **Actual results:** The actual output or behavior received after conducting the test.

- **Test result:** This is where you capture whether the test successfully verified the expected behavior. The typical values used are *pass, fail, not executed,* and *blocked.*

Several other values can be captured for specific test types. For example, a performance test would include much more details about the expected time for completing a transaction or a particular step in a transaction.

To help solidify the knowledge, try to write a test case next.

Practicing creating a test case

The following practical example will help you understand the following:

1. How to create and format a test case.

2. How to build a unit test to validate the test case. Remember that unit tests are a very powerful way to ensure your Salesforce code meets high-quality standards. But in this example, you will see that unit tests are excellent tools to test point-and-click configured functionalities.

In *Chapter 8, Create a Sample Application - Solve and Build the Application - Part Two,* and in the section *Formatting the requirements as user stories,* you formatted requirement 11 as a user story. The user story was called US-011. Here is a reminder of that user story:

- User story US-011: As a *[job seeker],* I want *[to be informed about the updates of my job application, at what stage it is, and the expected next steps]* so that *[I can give prepare for the next steps and be assured that someone has picked up my application and working on it].*

- *[Scenario 1]:* The job application record is updated to any stage.

- *[Given]* that the job requisition the candidate applied to is still open.

- *[When]* the **Status__c** field of the job application is updated to any value different than its current value.

- *[Then]* the candidate/job seeker must receive an email notification with a message indicating the new status value the application has moved to and a description of the activities included/expected at that step.

- *[Scenario 2]*: The job application record is updated to any stage.

- *[Given]* that the job requisition the candidate applied to is still open.

- *[When]* the **Status__c** field of the job application is updated to any value different than its current value.

- *[Then]* the application must emit an event compatible with the **Bayeux** protocol that includes a message indicating the candidate id, job requisition number, new application status, and a description of the activities included/expected at that step.

First, use the provided requirements and scenarios to format the test case. Your test case could look like the following:

- **Feature/module name:** The online job application submission feature.

- **Test case ID and/or name:** TC-0001.

- **Tester name:** You can use the name of the developer who will create the Apex unit test.

- **Test data:** The test will use records from the **Job_Application__c** object. Several other objects are required as prerequisites, such as **Job_Requisition__c** and **Contact**.

- **Preconditions/assumptions:** A **Job_Requisition__c** record is created and linked with the right **Department__c** and **Job_Description__c** records. Tow **Contact** records are required, one for the applicant and the other for the recruiter.

- **Test priority:** Medium.

- **Test scenario: US-011, scenario 2**.

- **Testing environment:** All environments.

- **Testing steps:** After creating the records listed in the preconditions, locate the **Job_Application__c** record and change the value of the **Status__c** field from its current value to any other value, then save the record.

- **Expected results: A single Salesforce Platform Event from the type Job_Application_Status_Update__e is emitted** as per the scenario for each updated **Job_Application__c** record.

- **Actual results:** This value will be populated each time the test is executed.

- **Test result:** This value will be populated each time the test is executed.

Note that the test case is not written as a unit test from the beginning. It is simply written as a test case; it can be executed manually or automatically via any suitable tool, such as Apex unit tests.

The QA team should aim at fulfilling test cases using an automated-first mentality. Anything that can be automated must be automated; the sooner, the better. For example, the time required to execute this use case manually would probably be similar to half the time required to write an Apex unit test. The advantage of unit tests, though, is that you do not need to invest time to execute them again in every targeted environment. You invest once in building these automated unit tests and use them many times. The saved cost is immense, and you are encouraged to calculate that for every project you participate in.

Next, practice creating an Apex unit test that fulfills this test case.

Creating an Apex unit test

Creating unit tests have the following three main steps:

1. Set up the test by creating any required data or so. You are strongly encouraged to use test data generated for testing purposes only. You should avoid using real data that exists in the target test environments unless necessary. Setting up the test data might be a time-consuming activity. Therefore, you are encouraged to use *test data factory classes* (sometimes also called *test utility classes*) to turn the methods you create to generate test data into reusable methods that can save you significant time in the future. You can read more about *test data factory classes* at the following link:

   https://developer.salesforce.com/docs/atlas.en-us.apexcode.meta/apexcode/apex_testing_utility_classes.htm

   Worth mentioning that there are 3rd party data factories available in the market that you can use to save time. This book will not list any, but you are encouraged to experiment with some.

2. Execute the test; one test case is usually mapped to a single test method in your Apex class. You are encouraged to write *bulkified* tests that test multiple records simultaneously.

3. Validate the results. Salesforce provides the **Assert** class that has many useful methods, such as **Assert.areEqual**. You can read more about the **Assert** class at the following link:

   https://developer.salesforce.com/docs/atlas.en-us.apexref.meta/apexref/apex_class_System_Assert.htm

Start with the first step. The following class is an example of a *test data factory class*. You do not have to abide by its format, as this should suit your application. You can use the following code as an example to learn from and tweak to fit your application's needs.

```
@isTest
public class TestDataFactory {
    public static List<Contact> createContacts(Integer pContactCount) {
        List<Contact> oNewContacts = new List<Contact>();
        for(Integer i=0;i<pContactCount;i++) {
            Contact oContact = new Contact(FirstName='TestFirst' + i,
                                           LastName='TestLast' + i,
                                           email='TestEmail'+i+'@Domain.com');
            oNewContacts.add(oContact);
        }

        return oNewContacts;
    }

    public static List<Job_Requisition__c> createJobRequisitions(
                                            Integer pReqCount,
                                            Department__c pDep,
                                            Contact pContact,
                                            Recruitment_Stage__c pRecS)
{
        List<Job_Requisition__c> oNewReqs = new List<Job_Requisition__c>();
        for(Integer i=0;i<pReqCount;i++) {
            Job_Requisition__c oReq = new Job_Requisition__c();
            oReq.Department__c = pDep.ID;
            oReq.Recruiter__c = pContact.ID;
            oReq.Recruitment_Stage__c = pRecS.ID;

            oNewReqs.add(oReq);
        }

        return oNewReqs;
    }

    public static List<Department__c> createDepartments(Integer pCount) {
        List<Department__c> oNewRecords = new List<Department__c>();
        for(Integer i=0;i<pCount;i++) {
```

```
        Department__c oDept = new Department__c(Name='TestDepartment' +
i);

        oNewRecords.add(oDept);
    }

    return oNewRecords;
}


public static List<Recruitment_Stage__c> createRecStage(
                                    Integer pCount,
                                    Department__c pDepartment)
{
    List<Recruitment_Stage__c> oNewRecords =
                        new List<Recruitment_Stage__c>();
    for(Integer i=0;i<pCount;i++) {
        Recruitment_Stage__c oRecStage =
            new Recruitment_Stage__c(Name='TestDepartment' + i,
                            Department__c = pDepartment.Id,
                            Sequence_Number__c = i);
        oNewRecords.add(oRecStage);
    }

    return oNewRecords;
}
}
```

The second and third steps are clarified in the following code, which represents the Apex unit test that you can use to validate the test case TC-0001:

```
@isTest
private class JobApplicationStatusChangeFLTest {
    public static List<Job_Requisition__c> oTestRequisitions;
    public static List<Recruitment_Stage__c> oRecStages;
    @TestSetup static void setupTestData() {
        //Create 2 contacts, one to be used for the recruiter
        //The other to be used for the candidate
        List<Contact> oTestContacts = TestDataFactory.createContacts(2);
        insert oTestContacts;
        //Create a department
```

```
        List<Department__c> oTestDepartments =
                                TestDataFactory.createDepartments(1);
        insert oTestDepartments;
        //Create a recruitment stage linked to the department
        oRecStages = TestDataFactory.createRecStage(2,oTestDepartments[0]);
        insert oRecStages;
        //Create a job requisition
        oTestRequisitions = TestDataFactory.createJobRequisitions(1,

oTestDepartments[0],

oTestContacts[0],

                                                            oRecStages[0]);

        //Set the recruiter__c value for the job requisition to the first
contact
        oTestRequisitions[0].Recruiter__c = oTestContacts[0].Id;
        insert oTestRequisitions;
        //Create a job application
        Job_Application__c oNewJobApp = new Job_Application__c();
        oNewJobApp.Candidate__c = oTestContacts[1].Id;
        oNewJobApp.Job_Requisition__c = oTestRequisitions[0].Id;
        //Hardcoded Status__c value for simplicity, avoid in real life
        oNewJobApp.Status__c = 'Submitted';

        Insert oNewJobApp;
    }

    @IsTest
    static void validatePublishingJobApplicationStatusEvent() {
        Job_Application__c oJob = [select ID, Status__c
                                    from Job_Application__c];
        //Hardcoded Status__c value for simplicity, avoid in real life
        oJob.Status__c = 'Offer accepted';
        oJob.Is_Invitation__c = true;

        //Start the test
```

```
        Test.startTest();
        Update oJob;
        //Stop the test
        //This ensures that Apex code and Flow executions have all complete
        Test.stopTest();

        //Assess the test results using the System class
        //As the test here is updating a single Job application, the
expected
        //result is to have a single Job_Application_Status_Update__e event
in the
        //JobApplicationStatusUpdateTriggerHandler.ListOfReceivedEvents
list
        //Note that the
        //JobApplicationStatusUpdateTriggerHandler.ListOfReceivedEvents
        //list has been created just to facilitate this test as currently
there is
        //no direct mechanism to validate if a platform event has been
        //published by a flow or not from within an Apex unit test
        Assert.areEqual(1,
            JobApplicationStatusUpdateTriggerHandler.ListOfReceivedEvents.
size());
    }
}
```

To validate if the Salesforce flow created a platform event, the following trigger was created to subscribe to the **Job_Application_Status_Update__e** event:

```
trigger JobApplicationStatusUpdateTrigger on Job_Application_Status_
Update__e (after insert) {
    If (Trigger.IsAfter){
        If (Trigger.IsInsert){
            JobApplicationStatusUpdateTriggerHandler.onAfterInsert(Trigger.
NewMap);
        }
    }
}
```

Here is the trigger handler for that trigger:

```
public class JobApplicationStatusUpdateTriggerHandler {
```

```
//The following static field will only be used in Apex tests
public static List<Job_Application_Status_Update__e>
ListOfReceivedEvents
    = new List<Job_Application_Status_Update__e>();


public static void onAfterInsert(
        Map<ID,Job_Application_Status_Update__e> pNewMap){
    //Trigger.NewMap is only available in before update,
    //after insert, after update, and after undelete triggers


    //Execute the following statement only during tests
    if(Test.isRunningTest()){
        //Add the received events to the static field (a list)
        ListOfReceivedEvents.add(pNewMap.values());
    }
}
}
}
```

Congratulations, you have created your first Apex unit test. To run that test, locate the **JobApplicationStatusChangeFLTest** class and click the **Run Test** button as shown in the following screenshot:

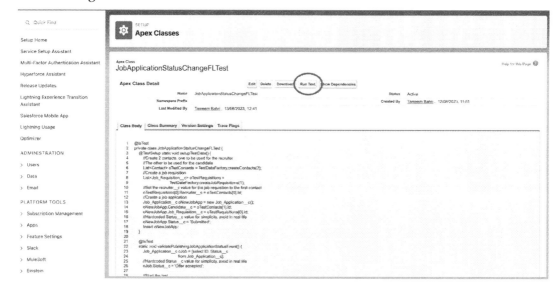

Figure 9.1: *Running a test class*

You should receive a screen similar to the following for a short period, which shows that your test is running. Note that your test might not run immediately and might be queued for a short period before it gets executed. Salesforce managed this process automatically:

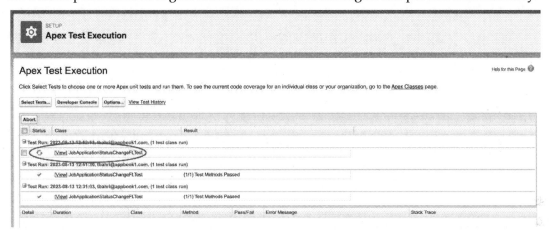

Figure 9.2: The execution of a test class

Once the test completes successfully, you should see a screen similar to the following:

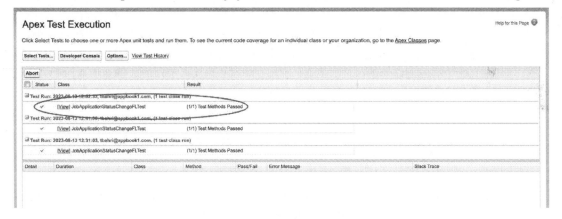

Figure 9.3: Execution results of a test class

You can automatically trigger Apex unit tests when promoting this code from one low environment to a higher one. This ensures that all your Apex unit tests that form part of your regression test suite are consistently and efficiently executed at the right stage of your development lifecycle.

Deploying your application

It is time to package your application and prepare it for deployment. Suppose you are building an application that will be used exclusively by the same company that made the application. In that case, you are likely to require a **Continuous Integration/Continuous Delivery (CI/CD)** setup where your functionalities are promoted from your low-level environments (such as developer sandboxes) to production, going through several other environments such as a QA environment, staging environment, and pre-prod.

You learned about the typical environment setup in such cases in *Chapter 3, Develop a sample Salesforce application - PbP Phonebook, Figure 3.7.*

Suppose you are building an application that will be sold to multiple customers (and deployed to their orgs). In that case, you are likely to have a CI/CD setup up to the developer org that will contain the final metadata of your application (this org is sometimes called *packaging org*). If you plan to deploy the application via AppExchange (the most likely case), you will need a **Salesforce Partner Community** account. After logging into that account, you can connect the **Partner Console** to your developer org. You can list your applications to AppExchange as **managed** or **unmanaged packages**.

You can learn more about the process of publishing your application to AppExchange from the following link:

https://developer.salesforce.com/docs/atlas.en-us.packagingGuide.meta/ packagingGuide/appexchange_publish_organizations.htm

The following is a short description of **managed** and **unmanaged packages**:

- **Managed packages:** Salesforce partners use managed packages to sell and distribute their applications to customers. Developers can manage user-based licenses for their published apps using the **License Management Application (LMA)** and the AppExchange platform.

  Managed packages combine configuration elements and code into one entity, such as a logical functional module, reusable code libraries, or entire sub-systems. Managed packages can be upgraded (with some limitations, such as the inability to remove particular objects or fields).

  Once a managed package is listed on AppExchange, it becomes available to end-users, who can buy and install it in their Salesforce org.

  The AppExchange's managed packages come with robust safeguards to prevent any interference with the customizations on the customer's org or other managed packages that the customer might have installed to the same org. Additionally, managed package-defined dependencies enable one managed package to be extended by another.

  The AppExchange packages have strong safeguards against interfering with a company's customizations or other managed packages. Managed package-defined dependencies also allow one managed package to be extended by another.

- **Unmanaged packages:** Salesforce's unmanaged packages allow publishers to provide an installation link that the customers can use to deploy the application to their orgs. Customers can modify the installed code (similar to what you do to an open-source code). The customer's copy of the components of an unmanaged package is editable after installation. The application developer cannot control the installed components and cannot make changes or upgrades.

  Unmanaged packages are free and provide code visibility. They allow the transportation of unrelated components from one organization to another. However, once a new version is released, it cannot be upgraded and may require reinstallation in the new organization.

Here are six major differences between managed and unmanaged packages:

- **Customization:** When using unmanaged packages, you can customize both the metadata and code. However, managed packages restrict code access and metadata access (such as triggers, lightning components, and Apex classes).

- **Installation:** Unmanaged packages can be installed using direct links. Managed packages are installed only via AppExchange (after passing specific security reviews by Salesforce).

- **Updates:** To install a new version of an Unmanaged package, users must first uninstall the previous version and then re-install the latest version. The unmanaged package provider can only use Push upgrades if the managed package is not free and provided via AppExchange. Providing an updated version of a managed package is straightforward via AppExchange.

- **Security:** Unmanaged packages are not reviewed by the Security Review team, which can be risky. On the other hand, managed packages undergo a thorough review before being made available on the Salesforce AppExchange, making them highly secure.

- **Purpose and usage:** Salesforce Partners utilize managed packages to sell their applications. Conversely, Unmanaged packages are used to distribute applications as a template in an open-source style.

- **Org Limits:** When using an unmanaged package in Salesforce, the overall limits of your organization are consumed and impacted (such as the number of tabs, custom objects, and so on). Managed packages, on the other hand, do not consume many of the target org's limits (such as the number of tabs and custom objects) which gives the consuming org more freedom.

As you learned from previous chapters, this book will not cover the process of publishing to AppExchange. However, you will learn to package your application as an unmanaged package and deploy it to another org using a direct link.

Before creating your first unmanaged package, go through the following section to learn fundamental knowledge about CI/CD.

Understanding CI/CD concepts in release management

You were introduced to CI/CD in *Chapter 4, Learn the Salesforce Application Development Lifecycle*, under the *Understanding CI/CD* section. Here are more details to further solidify your knowledge. Here are the main concepts of CI:

- When a team of developers works on the same codebase, they frequently need to merge their work and resolve conflicts. One of the CI concepts is the regular and continuous merge (in most cases, automated) of the developers' work into a shared build environment. This concept helps avoid conflicts at later stages of the development lifecycle and helps detect such conflicts early on. There is less chance of conflicts if the developers know each other's changes. By frequently merging their work, developers can identify and resolve conflicts early.

- CI also promotes the concept of working with the most up-to-date code base to avoid conflicts. There are more chances of conflicts if the developers are using old code bases. The older the code base, the higher the risk of encountering difficult-to-solve conflicts. If the code base is only a few hours old, the chances of conflicts are much lower. To achieve this, developers are expected to refresh their code base from the latest version in the build environment; this whole activity can be automated. **Source Code Management (SCM)** applications are essential for the CI/CD setup.

Here are the main concepts of CD:

- Automating the testing and deployment process can help close the communication gap between development and operations teams. Moreover, CD enables a rapid process of releasing functionalities and bug fixes. To achieve this, it is important to establish a well-rounded development environment strategy, choose appropriate release management automation tools (such as **Copado, Flosum**, or other similar tools), and create a comprehensive automated testing plan. By doing so, you can ensure that you have a solid foundation for successful CD implementation.

Now that you expanded your knowledge about the foundations of CI/CD move on to create your application's package.

Packaging your application as an unmanaged package

Before packaging your application, you must ensure that the average test coverage for all Apex classes included in your package is 75% or above. This is a mandatory requirement to upload the package. The best practice is getting all your Apex classes to over 90% of test coverage.

To package your application, log in to the developer org where the application has been built, and go to the setup page. Then search for **Package Manager** or **Packaging** as shown in the following screenshot (you will find the desired menu even before you complete writing the whole word):

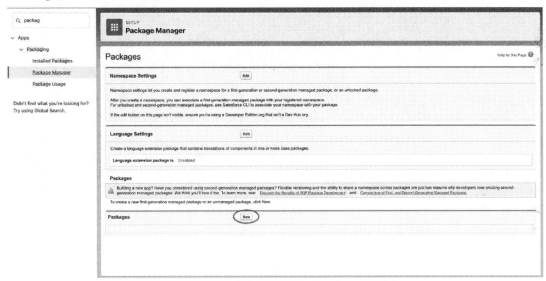

Figure 9.4: Creating an unmanaged package - step one

Click on the **New** button in the **Package Manager** screen, as shown in the figure. This will open a page to enter the name of the package. Use a meaningful name such as **PSD Recruitment;** this will be the package name your customers will see:

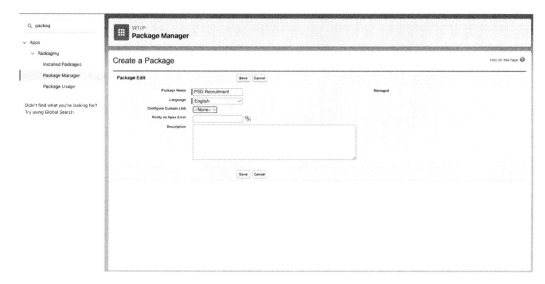

Figure 9.5: Creating an unmanaged package - step two

Once saved, you will be redirected to a page where you can specify the components included in your package, as shown in the following screenshot:

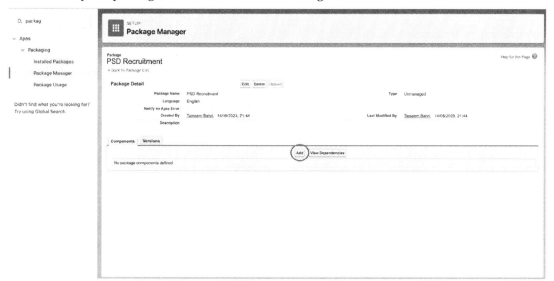

Figure 9.6: Creating an unmanaged package - step three

Click the **Add** button; this will allow you to select the components to add. The term *component* here refers to all types of metadata included in your application, such as objects, fields, applications, flows, and so on. You can filter the components based on their types to simplify finding the right components for your package. Salesforce will detect and add some of the dependent components (for example, if you add a custom object, all of its custom fields will be automatically added). However, you need to ensure that all your application components are included. The screen will look similar to the following screenshot:

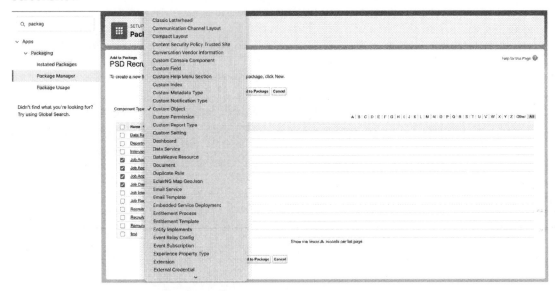

Figure 9.7: *Creating an unmanaged package - step four*

Use the **Add to Package** button to add the selected components to the package. You might need to repeat this activity multiple times until all your application components are added.

Once you finish adding all relevant components, click the **Upload** button, as shown in the following screenshot:

Figure 9.8: *Creating an unmanaged package - step five*

In the next screen, you can specify the version's name and number. Try to stick to a standard versioning strategy, such as the one you learned about in *Chapter 4, Learn the Salesforce Application Development Lifecycle,* under the *Understanding CI/CD* section. You can also use a password to protect the package from being installed by unauthorized individuals. Your screen would look similar to the following screenshot:

Figure 9.9: Creating an unmanaged package - step six

If you scroll down, you will find that you can specify **Package Requirements**. Package requirements allow you to specify particular features at the target org, such as **B2B Commerce**. If the customer does not have the specified feature in their org, they will not be able to install your package. Your screen would look similar to the following screenshot:

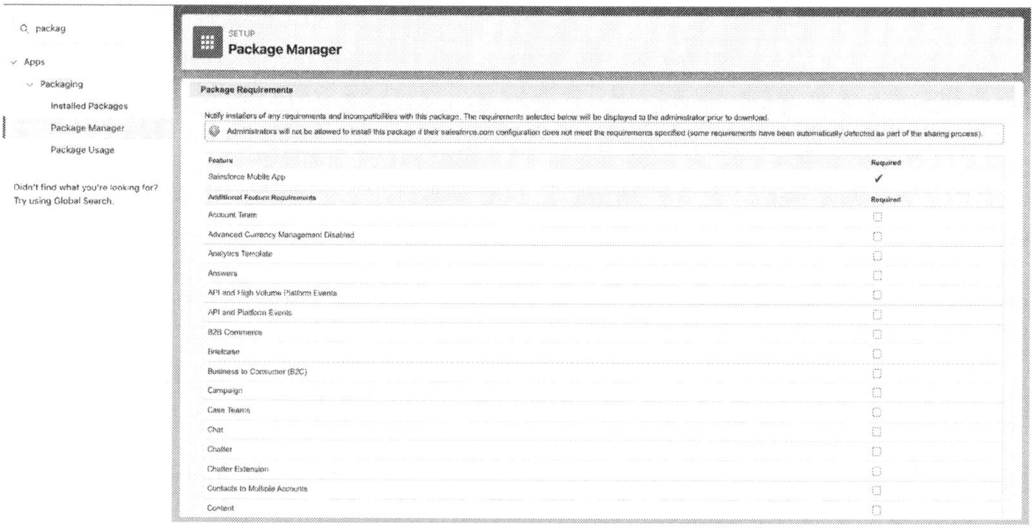

Figure 9.10: Creating an unmanaged package - step seven

If you keep scrolling down, you will notice that you can even specify **Object Requirements** for your package. You can add more requirements to your package here, such as enabling **Field History Tracking** for a particular object. Your screen would look similar to the following screenshot:

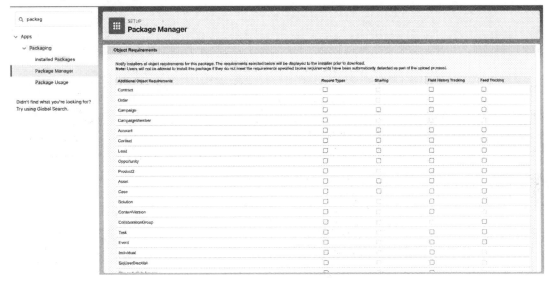

Figure 9.11: *Creating an unmanaged package - step eight*

Once you complete specifying the package requirements (none in the case of the PSD recruitment application), click on the **Upload** button to start uploading your package. Your screen will look like the following:

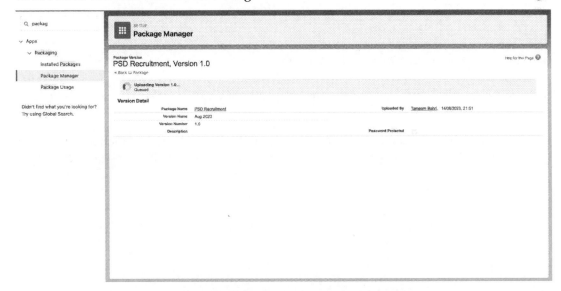

Figure 9.12: *Creating an unmanaged package - step nine*

The uploading process could last for several minutes (or more, depending on its size). By the end of the uploading process, you will be redirected to a screen similar to the following:

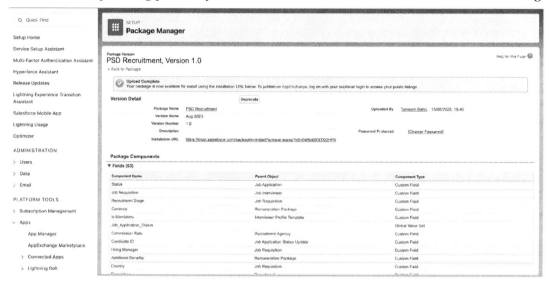

Figure 9.13: *Creating an unmanaged package - step ten*

Copy the value in the **Installation URL** field. Note that the URL will differ from what you see in this book, as Salesforce will generate a unique URL for every newly uploaded package. You will use the **Installation URL** next to install your packaged application into another Salesforce org.

Deploying your unmanaged package to a new org

Sign up for a new developer org using the steps you followed in *Chapter 1, Introduction to the Salesforce Platform*, under the *Benefits for Developers* section. It is recommended to use a different browser than the one you use to log in to the org where the application has been developed. You can also use the private mode of your browser, but using a separate browser is simpler.

Once you complete signing up for the new org, paste the package installation URL to the new browser. You will be asked to log in to the new org (even if you have already logged into it in the same browser). Once you log in, you will see a screen similar to the following:

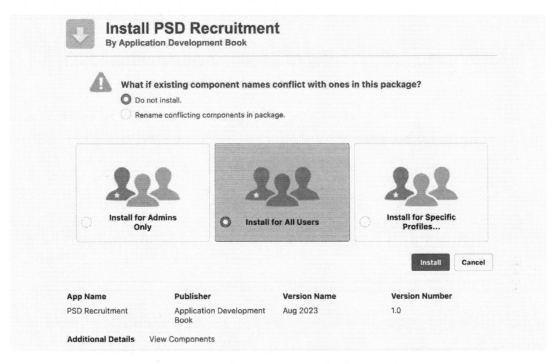

Figure 9.14: Installing the unmanaged package - step one

Select **Install for All Users**, then click the **Install** button. Package installation may take several minutes depending on the package's size and the target organization's complexity. You will get a screen similar to the following screenshot once the package has been successfully installed:

Figure 9.15: Installing the unmanaged package - step two

If you login to the new org and go to the **Installed packages** page, you will see the newly installed package listed there, similar to the following screenshot:

Figure 9.16: *Verifying the installed package*

You can start using the PSD recruitment application. The application will be accessible via the **App Launcher** menu, similar to any other Salesforce application in that org. You can configure accessibility to the application and the custom objects installed with it using the standard Salesforce capabilities you learned and practices using throughout this book.

Congratulations! You now have a working Salesforce application that can be deployed and used by others.

Summary

You learned the importance of tests in high-availability and high-reliability applications. You learned key testing concepts such as test cases, test scenarios, and test scrip. You looked deeper into the different types of tests you might need for your Salesforce application and practices creating Apex unit tests that can cover both code and configurations.

You then learned how to package your application as an unmanaged package and deploy it into other Salesforce orgs. Your rapidly developed application is now ready to be used by customers. More importantly, you created detailed documentation for your solution while designing and building it. You utilized the concept of designing forward to design and develop a scalable and extendable solution rapidly and efficiently.

The last phase of the RAD application lifecycle is the *Application maintenance and live feedback gathering*. In the next chapter, you will learn how to create and publish a release note with every new application version. And you will be introduced to best practices in gathering customer feedback and turning them into a valuable source for your application backlog. In the next and final chapter, you will also be introduced to some advanced application development topics and concepts.

CHAPTER 10

Tips and Tricks and the Way Forward

Introduction

In the previous three chapters, you used the **Rapid Application Development (RAD)** lifecycle to analyze, design, build, and deploy a Salesforce recruitment application for PSD, a hypothetical application development company.

The final phase of the RAD application lifecycle is the *Application maintenance and live feedback gathering*. In this chapter, you will learn about the value of release notes, how to create useful and impactful release notes, and how to efficiently publish and share them with the right audience. You will also learn how to enrich your application backlog using ideas and feedback gathered from your customers directly. You will learn some best practices and anti-patterns to avoid. You will also get introduced to some advanced application development topics that you might find handy as you progress your career in Salesforce application development, such as highly customizable and AI-powered applications.

Finally, you will be introduced to further learning materials and resources you can continue learning from.

Have a look next at the structure of this chapter.

Structure

The chapter covers the following topics:

- Creating and publishing release notes
- Introducing a feedback-gathering loop
- Developing highly customized applications
- Creating AI-powered applications
- Continue learning
- Summary

Objectives

By the end of this chapter, you will gain knowledge and practical experience in creating and communicating impactful release notes. You will learn the best practices in creating customer feedback loops and learn advanced Salesforce application development topics and techniques. Finally, you will be introduced to additional learning materials to continue your journey.

Creating and publishing release notes

In the software industry, product managers and developers use release notes to inform users about product improvements, bug fixes, and new features. Release notes are usually organized as pages, blogs, and feeds to make it simple and convenient for readers to learn about the latest updates.

Including release notes in the release cycle is not a choice; it is mandatory for any software. This is because release notes offer a plethora of value to current and potential users as well as other external and internal stakeholders, including, but not limited to, market analysts, industry professionals, investors, and even the internal application team itself.

The importance of release notes

The value of release notes is immense and covers a broad and diverse audience. It is not easy to list all the benefits of release notes, but here are some:

- **Increase product utilization:** By informing users of new releases, they become aware of the latest features to explore and experiment with. As a result, they are likely to log into the app, embrace novel functionalities, and ultimately increase usage frequency.

- **Avoid losing customers:** To prevent customers/users from leaving due to a lack of product knowledge and updates, inform them promptly when a new feature is released. Even if users are not actively anticipating a specific improvement, keeping them informed through release notes can reassure them that your company is constantly working to meet their needs. Furthermore, linking release notes to ideas and feedback your customers provide can support the impression that you value their input and have a solid idea-taking process, which is a massive advantage for any modern software company. You will learn about that later in this chapter under the section *Introducing a feedback-gathering loop*.

- **Gain new customers:** Prospective customers prefer constantly evolving and innovative products, ensuring longevity and avoiding the need for rework/reimplementation and data migrations. Regularly posting high-quality release notes in a prominent public location (preferably combined with solid **Search Engine Optimization (SEO)** demonstrates the reliability of your development team and the maturity of your company in the software industry.

- **Reduce support requests:** If more users are aware of your new releases, you will receive fewer support requests about the release date or fixing specific issues and bugs.

- **Reduce training cost:** The more your application users are aware of your product, the less you need to spend to train them on updates. Modern software companies tend to be as open and transparent about their product as possible, promoting self-learning for current and potential users. Salesforce is a great example, as they provide comprehensive release notes, updated Trailhead modules, and updated developer orgs for every major release. There are many other examples in the market. Reducing the training cost will be particularly appreciated by your partners (think of all the Salesforce partners who benefit from the Salesforce release notes for their internal training and knowledge sharing).

- **Increase internal knowledge:** You will be surprised to learn how little internal teams could know about their own application. The more sophisticated the application is, the larger the team that develops and maintains it becomes. Larger teams come with their challenges, and one of them is ensuring that all team members have a decent level of knowledge of what each other is doing. Release notes are known to be an out-facing knowledge-sharing tool, but it is also a very powerful channel for internal knowledge-sharing.

One of the common questions (and challenges) around release notes is about the responsibility of creating and maintaining them.

Who owns the creation of release notes

The responsibility of writing and publishing release notes will depend on the size and complexity of the application and/or the company that built the application.

- In startups with only one or two individuals, the principal developer should be responsible for composing release notes.

- In medium-sized companies, the product manager/product owner is the main responsible person. When the application provides functionalities covered by a handful of product owners, each becomes responsible for their product, and the principal product owner assumes the responsibility of ensuring that all the release notes are streamlined.

- In large companies, particularly with sophisticated applications that offer dozens of functionalities owned by a large group of product managers/product owners, the product owners act as the primary source of information for their respective areas under the supervision of a chief product officer and support from professional editors and technical writers.

While the team arrangements and responsibilities could vary from one company to the other, there is a known best practice for impactful release notes that can be followed.

Best practices for impactful release notes

An impactful release note delivers all the value highlighted earlier in this chapter and more. While creating your release notes, you should avoid these three common mistakes:

- **Avoid technical language and jargon:** Release notes provide information about technical updates made to a product. However, it is crucial to avoid using jargon and terms that are only known (or presumably known) by the known audience. Avoid using technical terms only known to developers and business terms not known enough to existing or potential release note readers.

  For instance, it's not helpful to see a release note that says, *"Salesforce instance trouble ticket #42351 failover issue resolved"*. This message will not benefit anyone except the user/customer who raised ticket #42351. Another example is *"Sales users will be able to use the customer address APIs for better data quality."* This message seems to be directed to a particular audience who are fully aware of the referred data quality issues; other readers will not be able to understand what the problem was and how it is now addressed.

- **Avoid vague messages:** Release notes that do not share detailed enough information can frustrate readers. Statements such as *"Several improvements and performance enhancements were introduced"* and *"Several security issues were addressed"* do not share enough details to make them valuable for any reader.

- **Avoid lengthy release notes:** Even when the application is complex and contains hundreds of updates and new features, the release notes must be structured so as not to take too long to read. Remember that you are trying to make it simpler for your readers to understand what has been released; going through dozens of pages is not very helpful. Salesforce's three annual major releases include hundreds of updated and new features; this is why Salesforce ensures they are grouped and structured to enable you to drill down to a particular knowledge article and even search for it.

Now that you learned about these three common mistakes, check out the best practices to follow for an impactful release note:

- **Tailor the content to match the technical understanding of your existing and potential audience:** Keep your language simple and descriptive. Avoid jargon and expand terms when used for the first time in an article. For example, a statement such as "We updated our SSO policy" might be straightforward to several of your existing audience. However, remember that an impactful release note goes beyond informing the existing audience about an update. Tailor your messages to be easily understandable for existing and potential readers, such as *"We updated our Single Sign On (SSO) policy."*

- **Provide the right level of details:** Aim for short and concise messages without losing the required details. Try to include graphics and short videos when relevant, as they provide an alternate and quick way to communicate your message. Use hyperlinks to provide additional details when needed.

- **Group the relevant notes together:** Organizing and grouping relevant notes can help your readers go through the content quickly. For example, you could group the notes under headings such as *Bug Fixes*, *Improvements*, and *New features*. You could also introduce these headings as subgroups under bigger categories such as *Service Cloud updates*, *Sales Cloud updates*, and *App Cloud updates*.

- **Link the released feature to the customer's ideas:** If the released feature/update is derived from an idea shared by your customers, give them back the credit and provide a link to the original idea they submitted. You will learn more about working with the feedback/ideas provided by your customers later in this chapter under the section *Introducing a feedback-gathering loop*.

- **Consider using a release note tool:** With release notes software, you can expedite the process of publishing release notes without adding significantly more effort. Specialized release note software provides a streamlined process for publishing content across multiple channels, including web, social media, email, and others, with powerful capabilities to manage the look and feel of your note. Your content will always look professional on all devices. Remember that release notes can reflect an image of your company.

Some release note tools can offer advanced capabilities, such as restricting some content for specific users or supporting multiple languages. You can check some well-known release note products such as **ReleaseNotes**, **AnnounceKit**, and **LaunchNotes**.

- **Consider having a dedicated release note site:** Creating a dedicated website (it can also be a subdomain from your full website) makes it easier for your readers to learn about the latest updates about your product. A dedicated website adds value even for an internal audience, providing an easier and more predictable place to find knowledge. Some release note software offers the ability to launch and manage a dedicated release notes website.

- **Announce via multi-channels, particularly email:** You can share your release notes via multiple channels and techniques such as in-app widgets, website banners, company social media, or directly via Customer success managers. Readers might have different preferences and should aim to support as many channels as possible. The email channel, in particular, must be one of them. Emails are still one of the most popular digital channels around; it is simple, easy to use and consume, and helps you engage with active and inactive readers.

Next, you will learn more about creating a release note by going through a general release note template.

Sample template

Dedicated release note software provides multiple templates to choose from. In general, the simplest form of a release note template should contain the following:

- **The application name:** The name of your application. It is best to include this information in some channels (such as email and website) as the same channel might be used for other applications.

- **The release name/number:** This is the unique release name, which can be a unique name, a version number, or a combination of both. The best practice for software applications is to use a version number that follows a standard versioning strategy, such as the one you learned about in *Chapter 4, Learn the Salesforce Application Development Lifecycle,* under the *Understanding CI/CD* section, optionally combined with a release name.

- **The release date:** The date of the release should be clearly visible to the reader

- **Table of contents:** The table of contents can take multiple shapes and forms depending on the used channel. If you are circulating a PDF attached to an email, the table of contents would likely follow the classic structure used in books and Word documents. You can use the same approach on a website or opt for something more innovative, such as thumbnails explaining each new/updated feature. Check the following websites for some creative examples: **https://www.productplan.com/release-notes/** and **https://www.intercom.com/changes/en**

- **New features:** You need to group the new features somehow. One way to do this is by grouping them into *new* and *updated* features. It is essential to ensure that your features are listed with a clear reference (such as a number). The simplest way to achieve that is by using a numbered list.

- **New features:** As explained before, this is one way of grouping your features. The application's principal release note owner should decide the correct grouping that suits the company's strategy. When describing the updates for existing features, ensure you provide enough details to remind the users of the original feature behavior and why it has been updated.

- **Bug fixes:** This is another grouping of the updates. You can gain more customer trust by acknowledging bugs and transparently communicating the introduced bug fixes.

- **Retired features:** When a feature is retired, it is best to call it out clearly and explicitly. You can include features that have been retired in this release and features planned to retire in the upcoming known releases.

- **Reference to ideas:** This is not a section on its own but rather an area that you need to add under each relevant feature update. This way, you link the feature to the related ideas reported by your customers and show that you value their opinions, which encourages them (and other customers) to engage and provide more ideas.

There are endless ways to communicate your release notes, including infographics, interactive diagrams, animated images, videos, and even short videos used by popular social media such as **TikTok**. You are encouraged to look for an innovative way of communicating your release notes as long as it respects the best practices you learned in this chapter.

Next, you will learn more about creating a lively feedback-gathering loop for your application.

Introducing a feedback-gathering loop

The software industry has gone far in the past thirty years, and it continues to evolve and change with innovations that are changing the shape of the industry. What used to be acceptable in the past might not be in today's modern standards, and some of the application features that used to be considered optional at its time are now regarded as essential and must-haves.

In today's modern software world, the customer is the center of attention of all modern-thinking companies. Therefore, the feedback you receive from your customers is precious. You need to encourage your customers to provide their input and gather more than just a **Net Promoter Score (NPS),** which gauges how satisfied the customers are with your product. You should open the floor for them to provide suggestions and ideas to enhance your product.

In the past, the product management team managed the application roadmap internally. The ideas for enhancements were solicited from internal stakeholders, business experts, and market researchers. In some cases, the requests from major customers were used to enrich the application's roadmap. Smaller customers did not get a vote, meaning their side of the story and their ideas on enhancing the product were lost.

The more innovative software companies used to send regular communications to their customers, gathering their feedback on a predefined set of enhancements. This feedback request mostly asked the customers to prioritize a list of enhancements and new features and plan the product's next set of enhancements accordingly. This approach is undoubtedly an improvement from the first, but this is not considered enough in today's modern software standards.

The customer is expecting a free form of feedback gathering where they can provide suggestions for enhancements that might not have been already on the potential list of enhancements or have not been requested by any other customers yet. The customer is expecting a much more engaging and communicative way of handling their suggestions; they would like to know the status of their ideas, do other customers share the interest in these ideas, how many customers find this idea useful, whether the idea has been included in any planned releases, and if so then what release. Moreover, in today's digital social media world, feedback providers are rightfully looking for more recognition for themselves rather than the companies they represent.

Some of the more innovative companies put the received ideas for voting. If an idea is voted by many, then it gets prioritized and finds its way into the applications' roadmap. Salesforce is one of the leading software providers that offers such experience with their **IdeaExchange** website. You are encouraged to visit that website and be inspired by it:

https://ideas.salesforce.com

There are specialized software products used to gather and manage customer ideas, such as **UserVoice**, **Brightidea**, **Aha!**, and **Planbox**. Leading multi-billion software vendors across the globe use some of these products. This reflects the importance of customer feedback gathering and handling in today's modern software world.

The lifecycle of a modern idea-gathering activity includes the following steps:

- Ideas are received from customers. Several channels, such as email, web, and dedicated applications, could be used. Some modern software provides easy ways to give an idea from within the application itself. The customers should be encouraged to provide their ideas and feedback; therefore, gathering the input should be as simple and intuitive as possible. Avoid long forms and details at this stage, as they might simply deter your customers from providing feedback. You can enrich a gathered idea with more details later if it is deemed attractive.

- After the ideas are gathered centrally (single system, single source of truth), they are deduplicated. Similar ideas are merged together. Some modern idea management software deduplicates the ideas automatically upon creation. For example, your customer could be using the web channel to provide their idea, and while they are typing their suggestions, the system would automatically and incrementally surface similar ideas. The customer can then decide to proceed with a new idea or vote for one of the existing ideas. The idea management software would likely provide further deduplication capability for the system administrators (or idea curators) to deduplicate on demand and ensure no data redundancies.

- The gathered ideas are exposed to the community and stakeholders based on predefined logic (some ideas might be kept private or accessible to a limited set of users). Modern idea management software provides a configurable way to determine what ideas to show to the wider community and at what stage.

- The community members voluntarily vote for ideas. Votes could be treated equally, or more weight could be given to specific individuals based on predefined criteria (for example, based on their role within the company). Some ideas might be deemed mandatory enhancements or high-priority due to pre-defined internal logic (for example, features prioritized based on the company's strategic intent). Some idea management software provides more than one mechanism for voting. For example, each community member could get a predefined number of votes each month; they can vote multiple times for the same idea as long as they do not exceed their monthly vote allowance. Other more common mechanisms restrict voting to one vote per community member. The company can decide which strategy/voting mechanism works best for them.

- The application's product management team shortlists ideas based on votes and/or pre-defined criteria. The product management team might request more details from the idea creator or the community members who voted for the idea. The status of shortlisted ideas is updated and reflected in the community portal.

- The company's stakeholder board votes on the shortlisted ideas. Several factors could play a role here, including the company strategy, the importance of the feature to specific customers, the value expected out of the feature, the short and long-term impact of introducing or not introducing the feature, and several more.

- The selected ideas are confirmed. Once confirmed, the status of the confirmed ideas is updated and reflected in the community portal.

- The product management team promotes the idea into a feature or multiple features. Detailed requirements are created and added as necessary. Establishing a link between the feature and the relevant ideas is crucial, as the aggregated progress in developing the feature should be reflected in the idea; this will ensure that your customers are aware of the progress in developing and releasing their ideas.

- The features (derived out of ideas) are associated with upcoming releases. Ideally, The company should have a transparent roadmap showing the key features planned for the upcoming three releases.

- The requirements are introduced to the application backlog and handled as per the delivery process.

- Once a feature is deployed to production, its status should be updated immediately (ideally, automatically) to reflect its delivery. A release note can then be associated with the idea to tie all elements of your release together: the idea, the idea's status, and the relevant release note.

The process has to be as automated and consistent as possible. Therefore, it should be planned to be automated from day one. Modern idea management software can add much value as they have predefined connectors to release management tools such as Jira. It can be configured to ensure your whole process is stable, consistent, and low maintenance.

Developing highly customized applications

In this book, you learned about the importance of the RAD lifecycle and its applicability to Salesforce applications. You practice creating sample Salesforce applications and even a complete end-to-end application. However, there are a few more topics to consider when you develop complex applications that other Salesforce customers will use:

- **Combining specialized software products with your Salesforce application:** You may want to build your application to fit with commonly used third parties or additional Salesforce products. For example, you could build your application to work with **Salesforce CPQ, Conga CPQ, PROS**, and others. Such ready-to-use integrations promote your application further and make it more attractive to potential customers.

- **Careful when dealing with standard objects:** When altering standard objects, try using the existing field settings as much as possible. It is advisable to avoid modifying the standard field features to standard objects, as this could have a negative experience for your customers. For example, making an existing field mandatory can break certain business logic for your customers. Suppose your application is using standard objects like Contacts and Accounts. In that case, you may want to create new record layouts and types to differentiate new types of Contacts and Accounts relevant to your application. You may also need to update existing reports to include filters based on record type.

- **Dependencies:** Avoid dependencies on specific Salesforce products (or third-party products), as this could limit your customer base to only those who already have that product (or are planning to procure it). Make the integration with such Salesforce/third-party products optional via additional packages that can be installed separately.

- **Data quality:** Your application should be designed to ensure high-quality data is captured and used in all processes. Introduce validations (and make them customizable) to ensure that your application is a good citizen within the target customer's landscape.

- **Simple UI/UX:** always thrive for simple and intuitive UI/UX. Your customers are already used to the Salesforce standard experience (for most Salesforce customers, this is the Salesforce Lightning UI). Try to stick to the common behavior of Salesforce applications and their look and feel.

- **Mobile-first design:** Design your application to be mobile-first. Your UI, actions, and user journeys should be targeted for mobile consumption first, with the desktop experience complementing it. Salesforce customers are used to using the standard Salesforce applications on multiple devices; your application should ideally adopt the same principles.

- **Extendable:** If you plan to deploy your application as a managed package, your customers will not have access to the source code. This means that they will not be able to modify any non-customizable logic that you have within your application. Some Salesforce application vendors offer parts of their solution as unmanaged packages. You get the best from both worlds by splitting your code into managed and unmanaged packages. The code of most of your applications will be locked behind the managed package while you ensure a high level of possible customization via the unmanaged packages. To build a smooth class framework that enables you to stitch classes in runtime (rather than in design time), you need to learn more about key **Object-Oriented Programming (OOP)** language principles such as **Polymorphism**, **Abstraction**, **Encapsulation,** and **Inheritance**. There are dozens of excellent resources available online. Keep in mind that Apex is actually an OOP language. For example, you can create a trigger that invokes a different trigger handler depending on runtime parameters.

- **On-platform vs. off-platform:** You learned about the concept of developing applications off the Salesforce platform in *Chapter 1, Introduction to the Salesforce Platform*, under the *On-platform and Off-platform* section. Keep in mind that off-platform applications come with their own set of customization challenges. This is beyond the scope of this book, but you are strongly advised to do complete research before deciding to extend your application with an off-platform element.

Designing highly customized applications is a complex topic that many software companies have not managed to solve entirely. This is a great differentiator to aim for if you decide to develop custom Salesforce applications that will be sold to others.

Creating AI-powered applications

Artificial Intelligence (AI) utilizes computer systems to simulate human intelligence processes such as **Natural Language Processing (NLP)**, **Speech Recognition**, **Machine Vision**, and **Expert Systems**.

AI systems generally work by analyzing large amounts of data (marked as training data) to identify correlations and patterns. These patterns can be used to make predictions about future states. For example, an image recognition program can learn to identify objects in images by reviewing (and learning from) millions of examples. **Generative AI** is relatively new (although rapidly improving) and is used to generate realistic text, images, music, and other media.

AI can revolutionize how we live, work, and play. It has already been successfully implemented in various businesses to smartly automate tasks previously performed by humans, such as lead generation and fraud detection. AI can sometimes perform tasks better than humans, especially when it comes to repetitive and detail-oriented work, such as analyzing large numbers of contracts to ensure accuracy and compliance. AI can also provide valuable insights into business operations that were previously unknown. Furthermore, the growing number of Generative AI tools will play a significant role in fields such as marketing and creative content.

There are many applications for AI across different businesses that are rapidly growing every day. AI-powered applications bring packaged, limitedly configurable AI capabilities into regular business applications, such as Sales, Service, Marketing, Finance, Commerce, Recruitment, Order handling, Pricing, and others.

In today's world, technology users aim for more than a robust application to serve their needs; they are looking for an intelligent application that can predict their needs and serve them. You can augment your Salesforce application with AI capabilities. For example, the recruitment application you created previously in this book can be augmented with AI capabilities to predict the likelihood of a candidate landing depending on the candidate's profile, the recruiter's past engagements, and the hiring manager's history with similar positions. AI can bring even more power by harvesting profiles of potential candidates from internal and external sources. AI can also recognize and parse an uploaded resume and turn it into structural data. AI can even suggest interview questions based on the job description, location, and other parameters.

While designing your application, you might want to consider the Salesforce AI products or use other external third parties. You can even build your own AI module and integrate it with your Salesforce application. Apex is not known to be a language to create AI modules. But you can create AI modules using other languages such as **Python, R, Java**, and **Julia** and host them on **Heroku** or any other **Platform as a Service (PaaS)** provider, such as **AWS** and **Microsoft Azure**.

Salesforce Einstein is a suite of AI products offered by Salesforce. These products can be used with other Salesforce products such as Salesforce Sales Cloud, Salesforce Application Cloud, Salesforce Commerce Cloud, and others. The Salesforce Einstein suite includes several products, such as **Einstein for Sales, Einstein for Service, Einstein for Marketing, Einstein for Commerce, Einstein for Automation**, and the **Salesforce AI Cloud**.

Products such as Einstein for Sales have several sub-products/modules, such as **Einstein Lead Scoring, Einstein Opportunity Scoring, Einstein Opportunity Insights, Einstein Forecasting, Einstein Account Insights, Einstein Activity Capture**, and many more.

Salesforce Einstein can be enabled, configured, and used in the target org with few clicks. A very limited set of the Salesforce Einstein products can be tested in a **Developer Edition** org. You will need at least a **Professional Edition** org for some of them. Others (such as Einstein Lead Scoring) are currently available on **Enterprise, Performance**, and **Unlimited Editions** only.

You can read more about Sales Cloud Einstein and how to set it up from the following link:

https://help.salesforce.com/s/articleView?id=sf.einstein_sales.htm&type=5

You can search for information about the other Salesforce Einstein products from the Salesforce website.

Einstein products are usually bought separately, so you should consider if your target audience would be willing to procure these additional products before creating a dependency on them in your application.

Continue learning

There are endless resources available online for further learning about Salesforce application development, RAD, software application documentation, software design concepts, AI-powered applications, data modeling, business process modeling, wireframing, and product management. You are encouraged to search online and look for further materials about the above topics. No references for paid learning materials will be listed in this book to avoid unintentional advertisement.

Here is a list of free Salesforce training that you can learn more from:

- **Trailhead:** Salesforce's free training site, Trailhead, offers hundreds of modules, quizzes, and hands-on activities. Trailhead provides a gamified experience, making it fun to learn. Trailhead is the number one learning resource for most

Salesforce professionals worldwide. You can learn more about Trailhead from the following link:

https://trailhead.salesforce.com/

- **Salesforce Certifications Days:** Half-day free webinars. The webinars are led by expert Salesforce instructors and cover the main topics of Salesforce professional exams (such as the Salesforce Certified Administrator exam). These webinars are designed to be quick and effective and best suited for individuals who have already completed most of their exam preparation. You can learn more from the following link:

https://trailhead.salesforce.com/en/credentials/cert-days/

- **Salesforce Fundamentals:** Free three-week virtual course to learn about Salesforce, including real-world business challenges and use cases, the Salesforce ecosystem, and potential career opportunities. Salesforce Fundamentals is perfect for those new to the Salesforce ecosystem who want to jumpstart their career journey. Salesforce Fundamentals learning journey is designed for all candidates, such as students, recent graduates, or career switchers. You can learn more from the following link:

https://trailhead.salesforce.com/trailblazerconnect/fundamentals/

- **Salesforce Pathfinder:** This is a 24-week virtual program designed for workforce development. The program provides training and support for all candidates pursuing a Salesforce career. The program includes learning activities such as self-paced Trailhead, live sessions, homework, study groups, practice exams, and more. You can learn more from the following link:

https://www.salesforce.com/company/careers/pathfinders/

- **Clicked:** Clicked has launched a series of hands-on learning experiences in collaboration with Salesforce. These learning experiences are aimed to help you gain practical Salesforce project experience. You can learn more from the following link:

https://www.clicked.com/company/salesforce

There are several other books, online resources, and paid learning courses that you can search and learn more about.

Summary

In this chapter, you learned about the importance of release notes and how to introduce mechanisms and use specific products to ensure your release notes are impactful without investing a lot of effort to produce them. You learned the importance of building an interactive feedback-gathering channel between you and your customers and how to turn their suggestions into valuable sources of backlog items. You then explored the advanced concept of highly customizable applications and were introduced to some foundational topics. You learned about AI-powered applications and the importance of AI in today's and tomorrow's technology landscape. Finally, you were introduced to a set of materials that can be used for further learning and development.

You have learned throughout this book that RAD is a powerful technique that can help you develop applications fast without creating a long trail of technical debt. You learned that Salesforce is a natural fit for RAD and that the flexibility of the Salesforce platform could become a challenge if the introduced configurations and customizations are ungoverned and undocumented. The book walked you not only through general low-code/no-code development concepts on the Salesforce platform but also extended this to give you a full glimpse of the RAD lifecycle for Salesforce applications combined with practical hands-on examples. This knowledge you gained by reading this book is meant to become a solid foundation for your journey in the Salesforce ecosystem and help you further develop in your career regardless of the career path you choose (developer, architect, business analyst, functional expert, and others). You are now set to begin – or continue – your journey into the Salesforce ecosystem. Good luck and best wishes.

Join our book's Discord space

Join the book's Discord Workspace for Latest updates, Offers, Tech happenings around the world, New Release and Sessions with the Authors:

https://discord.bpbonline.com

Index

Printed in Great Britain
by Amazon